OFF TO THE RACES

AGAINST ALL ODDS

GREGORY DIAS

May this memoir of my dear father inspire you to live life to its fullest!

Enjoy,

G. Dias

A DIAS PUBLICATION IN COLLABORATION WITH CARNELIAN MOON PUBLISHING, INC.

This book is based on the author Greg Dias' father's recollections of his experiences over the timeframe depicted within this story. The author has changed some names and characteristics, some events have been compressed, and the author has also recreated most of the dialogue.

Content Editors: Janet Saucier, Naomi Trumper. Editing and publication services:Judith Richardson-Schroeder (Carnelian Moon Publishing). Cover Design by Michael Dias. Interior Design & Layout by 2 Creative Minds.

A Dias Publication in collaboration with Carnelian Moon Publishing, Inc., Ottawa, Ontario, Canada

ISBN eBook: 978-1-7390679-1-5

ISBN Paperback: 978-1-7390679-0-8

CARLOS & BASILIA FAMILY TREE

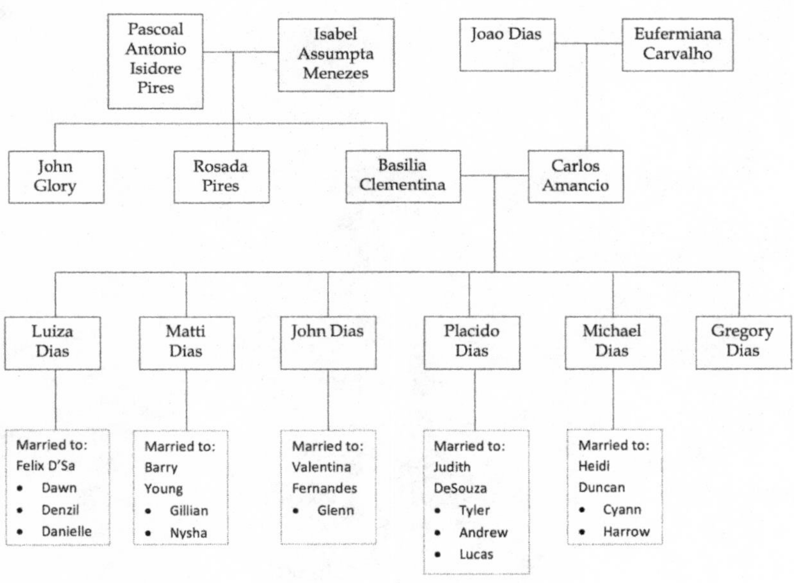

To my parents,
Carlos and Basilia,
My sister, Luiza,
Who were and will always be

ACKNOWLEDGMENTS

I was inspired by my mother to record and share our family history. A year after my father passed away, I felt compelled to put pen to paper and write this book. I am indebted to my parents for sharing their experiences with me. Their invaluable contribution formed the basis of this story.

To Donna Lee Smith, my creative writing teacher, who guided me with my writing skills and for encouraging me to write this story.

Emiliano Joanes led me into the publishing arena. Without his persistence, I would never have considered publishing this book.

Thanks to Regina DeSouza, Helen Fernandes, Eustachio DeSouza and Jerome DeSouza, for further piquing my curiosity of the Goan way. Lino Leitao, Shamrao Madkaiker and his family for their insight on the Portuguese regime in Goa.

I am grateful to Sally Gibbs for providing a venue, where I shared my work with members of our writing group. Valuable feedback from my fellow writers helped greatly in improving this book. Thank you, George Bertin, for insisting that I add more visual content and thus bring this story to life.

I would be remiss if I did not thank Janet Saucier, Naomi Trumper and Judith Richardson Schroeder for patiently editing this book, guiding and encouraging me every step of the way. I would not have been able to complete this book if it was not for their dedication and constant support.

Finally, I would like to thank my brother, Michael for designing the cover of this book and for coming up with the most suitable title. With his creative ability as a Graphic Designer, I can confidently say that you can judge this book by the cover.

CHAPTER 1

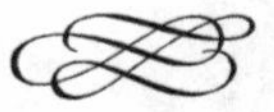

"*TRUQUE*!" I exclaimed as I proudly opened my last hand. The players around the table were speechless. Jacinth's eyes almost popped out of their sockets and his jaw dropped - he had lost nine games.

"*Arrh* Carlit, you won this game too!" a defeated Jacinth said. "Nine out of ten games, this must be your lucky night."

"Another round!" I called out in celebration. The drinks were on me.

I savoured the Johnnie Walker – a perfect way to celebrate my victory. The strategy, suspense and anticipation sent me flying. Things could not be better. I was with my buddies playing cards and drinking at our refuge the Tailors Club[1].

Large, wide stairs rose majestically to the front of the club. Members would pass in between two white rectangular pillars that formed the entrance.

---

1 Formally known as St. Francis Xavier's Club, named after the Patron saint of Goa

St. Francis Xavier's Tailors Society Club members

ON EITHER SIDE of the pillars were concrete railings, complete with a built-in lattice design. Inside was a concrete gallery dotted with windows and an impressive door that led to the dance hall.

The bar was conveniently located at the end of the gallery. It had a dark wood counter and shelves behind it, well stocked with Bell beer and Johnnie Walker whiskey. A warm tropical breeze with a hint of humidity would flow freely throughout the concrete structure, well into the front gallery. There was no need for ceiling fans as the weather was always comfortable in Uganda. Furthermore, the concrete floor that was painted red kept the building cool. Naked incandescent light bulbs shed just enough light on the hard wood table, where we played cards. The smell of warm beer and whiskey permeated throughout.

There was indeed another club: the Goan Institute. Although from Goa, members of the Goan Institute snubbed us since we were mere tailors, whom they considered to be of a lower class. The idea that they, pen-pushers and government clerks would associate with us was wholly inconceivable. We were not allowed to attend any events at the Goan Institute, but then again, I did not care to do so.

"It is closing time!" The bartender hollered.

Those words turned my euphoria into sadness. The night had come to an end. I bid my friends good night. On my way out of the club, I noticed the *askari* on duty was dozing off. I shouted, "*Jambo!*" To my chagrin, he nearly jumped out of his skin. After he managed to regain some composure he uttered, "*Jambo, Jambo Bwana.*"

The barren streets of Kampala were contrasted by the busy, star-studded clear ebony sky. Unlike Goa, Ugandan weather was always pleasant and predictable. There was no need to carry an umbrella, or even wear a jacket. However, some parts of life were unpredictable, so I made sure to keep a solid grip on my wallet as I walked hurriedly toward my Peugeot. I opened the door quickly and slid into my car.

On the drive home, I tallied up my winnings, which totalled about two hundred shillings. I spent almost one hundred on the drinks. That did not leave me with much, but then again, I had a really good time. Isn't that what life is all about? Thoughts of my mother began to seep into my mind. I wondered how she was doing. It had been a while since I last sent her some money. I will go first thing tomorrow morning and have a draft made at Barclays Bank. I am sure that she will be glad when it arrives, she loved to go shopping in Margao, that was always a treat for her.

My reflective journey home was interrupted by pangs of hunger; I realized that I had not eaten since lunch. When I played cards nothing else mattered. I started to think of the piping hot basmati rice and fish curry Basil would have waiting for me at home. I could almost taste it. Although she was a great cook, I could not bring myself to acknowledge her talents. After all, it was her duty to cook for me, since I was the breadwinner and she was my wife. Mother always said that the children and household duties were her responsibility.

I remember Basil trying a stunt during our first Christmas together. She had mixed the dough to make traditional *neuris*. She had the nerve to ask me to help her roll out the dough and cut out the circular shapes. I took the ball of dough and tossed it out of the kitchen window. Basil ran crying to the bedroom putting an end to that episode. She never asked me to help her in the kitchen again. It was simply not acceptable for her to bark orders at her husband.

When I arrived at the front door I fumbled for my keys. I sensed something strange when I walked into the house. My sons were usually making a racket. Placido, the second oldest, was always up to something. He was the ring-leader and the others followed. The house was eerily quiet, almost sombre. I walked into the kitchen and saw Basil sitting at the table with her head bent down, seemingly staring at nothing. My plate of food was not on the table. I glanced at the children's bedroom. They were all huddled up on one bed with a look of apprehension on their little faces.

"Basil, what is it?"

She looked up. I saw tears streaming down her cheeks. Her lips quivered. She opened her mouth to say something, but she choked.

"What happened? Tell me!" I was starting to get anxious.

"Carlit, Carlit," she said in a trembling voice. She pushed a letter towards me. It was from Goa, the four corners of the envelope were coloured black. This was a sign of bad news. I felt a sudden tightness in my chest. When I picked up the letter, Basil looked at me teary-eyed and said "*Mai* is dead."

I felt myself go numb and empty. She was fine, wasn't she? Well, that's what she said in her last letter. This can't be true.

"*Moji Mai, moji Mai!*" I cried out.

I walked slowly into our bedroom and fell on the bed, curled up and cried uncontrollably. I was oblivious to everything and everyone around me. I realized now what it felt like to be an orphan. Alone, very much alone in this big world.

My mind drifted back to my father's house in Colmorod, Goa. It was next to the big house where my grandparents and Uncle Lawrence Santan lived. The palm trees around the house were tall and full of coconuts. I used to watch in amazement when the labourers would climb the trees with such speed and ease. They would place their feet in little wedges cut into the trunk of the palm tree and use them as rungs on a ladder. My mother would tell me that it was the *padkhars* job to harvest the coconuts and the *renderes* job to tap the toddy from the trees. I always wanted to try climbing the palm trees but my mother would not hear of it. She said that it was too dangerous for a little child and besides it was not right for the landlord's son to climb coconut trees. From our backyard, I could see the endless vibrant green paddy fields that were flooded during the monsoons. I liked playing with the frogs that suddenly appeared during the monsoons.

I was about four years old, playing tag with my friends in the backyard. My mother suddenly came out of the back door. I thought that was odd since she would normally be cooking in the kitchen at this time. She looked pale and distraught. I suddenly felt guilty. I thought that she was upset with me for not finishing my breakfast. She picked me up and held me tightly in her arms. I felt the warmth of her body and the pleasant smell of her sari. I wondered why she suddenly decided to hold me in this manner. I was about to ask her to put me down when I felt a warm wetness on my shoulder. Her body shook and her head bobbed gently on my shoulders. I was very confused.

She finally lifted her head from my shoulders. Tears streamed from her eyes.

"*Mai, Mai*, why are you crying?" I asked.

She looked at me and shook her head and continued to cry. I tried to wipe her tears with my shirt, but they just continued to flow like the streams that formed during the monsoons.

"*Mai*, please, please stop crying."

I started to cry not knowing why. My Aunt Florine rushed over and took me from my mother. I asked her what had happened. She looked at me and said, "Your *Pai* has gone, gone far away and is not coming back."

"Yes, he is!" I insisted. "He will come back just like the last time."

She took me into our house. It was full of my uncles, aunts, other relatives and neighbours. Some of them were crying while the others looked very sad. When my aunt carried me through the entrance, they hugged me saying, "You poor unfortunate child, what can the future possibly hold for you?" None of this made sense to me. I did not know why all this fuss. As far as I was concerned my dad was coming home soon just as he had promised.

I went into the bedroom to check on my mother. She was lying almost lifeless on the bed. My Aunt Florine was sitting at her side and stroking her hair. I asked my mother whether she was sick, but she would not answer. All she would do was cry. Oh, *Mai*, I wish you would stop. Aunt Florine took me by the hand to the big house. She bathed me and then gave me some food. When I finished my supper, she made me change into my pyjamas and then tucked me into bed. She kissed me saying, "Sleep well, *Baba*."

Several days later my mother, relatives and neighbours came to the big house. The women were dressed in black saris and the men wore black suits, with white shirts and black ties. My mother emerged from the bedroom wearing a colourful red sari that sparkled in the dim light. Her long slim arms were covered with lots of glass bangles in many different colours - much more than the six-colour pencils that I used to draw with. She had a cluster of bright yellow flowers in her dark hair. I had never seen my mother dressed like this before. I gathered that this must be a very special occasion, something like a feast, but she looked very sad. Her eyes were red and she looked frail and tired. I tried to go to her but Aunt Florine stopped me. I wanted so very much to hug her and make her happy.

Everyone assembled in the main hall at the entrance of the house where the altar stood. Six stern-looking men, with short red capes, walked in carrying a long wooden box and placed it on the table in the center. My mother lunged forward and threw herself on the wooden box and cried out 'Joao, Joao!' She then hit the bangles on the wooden box and they broke into many pieces like tiny bits of shells on the beach. I was afraid that the broken bangles would hurt my mother. I tried to go to her, but Aunt Florine grabbed my arm and took me away. I asked her why my mother was crying and what was in the wooden box. She refused to answer me, instead, she told me that it was lunch time and fed me. After that, she put me to bed. I lay awake thinking about my poor mother and wondering what was in that wooden box.

From that day onwards my mother always wore a black sari and a black band on her head. She would not wear her gold earrings and bangles anymore. I would often ask her about *Pai* and she would tell me that he was in heaven with the angels. I wondered what this place heaven was like. The priest would sometimes talk about it when we went to church, but it eluded me. I hoped that one day I would go there and see my father.

When I was six, I started going to school. On the first day, I was accompanied by my mother. When we arrived, I noticed that all the other children had come with their fathers and mothers. I missed having a father. It was then that I realized my father was never coming back. I felt very sad and lonely all day. When I came home from school I went crying to *Mai* and I asked her what had happened to my father. She told me that my father had died of a terrible disease that had afflicted many people in Europe. Several years later we learned in our history class about the influenza epidemic that struck Europe. It finally made sense to me.

I missed having a father, but most of all I felt sorry for my mother. I had made a vow that I would do everything within my power to make her happy. I felt responsible for her well-being. I was going to earn sufficient money to support her and myself. I wanted her to have everything that her heart desired. Thus, my journey began.

CHAPTER 2

I WOKE up with a throbbing headache. When I gathered my thoughts, I remembered the awful news of last night. Oh! My God, *Mai* is no more! I wished that I was with her during her last days. Did she suffer? Was she lonely? What were her last words? While these questions ran through my mind, Basil came into the bedroom.

"Carlit, how are you?"

"My head feels heavy, and it aches."

"Sorry to hear that. Why don't you take an aspro? It might help if you eat something. I made your favourite, *chapatis*."

I dragged myself out of bed and went into the bathroom. I splashed some water on my face and looked in the mirror, my eyes were puffy and red. I needed to shave, but it was too much of an effort.

I ate the *chapatis* but did not enjoy them. I could not finish my breakfast. I felt the urgent need to get to the bank and send the draft to Goa. Unfortunately, *Mai* would not have the pleasure of spending it. I would have to address it to her neighbour, Cresence Carvalho. After all, she had taken care of *Mai* and all the funeral arrangements. What was going to happen to the house? I hoped that Cresence would look after it. I will ask Basil to write her a letter.

I drove to Barclays Bank in a daze. When I arrived, I asked for my brother-in-law John Glory Pires. Within minutes he came to the counter. I told him that *Mai* had passed away. He was shocked. When he regained his composure, he offered his condolences.

"John, could you prepare a draft for 500 rupees? I need it urgently."

"Carlit, you do not have sufficient funds in your account to cover the draft."

"Oh, don't worry; I will deposit the money tomorrow. Can you cover it for me?"

"Eh...I suppose so."

"Good, when will it be ready?"

"We are quite busy this morning, but I will try to get it done this afternoon."

"Thanks, John, I will come back to pick up the draft later, say around 2:00 p.m."

I had a few hours to kill so I drove to Jaffery's Bar and ordered a coffee and a *samosa*. While sipping my coffee, my thoughts drifted to the time when my mother had decided to move out of the house in Colmorod. I remember her being very unhappy. She told me that Uncle Lawrence Santan did not get along with her. There was more to the story. Aunt Florine had told me in confidence that Lawrence Santan was in love with my mother Eufermiana.

"Yes, I remember that he had tried to win Eufermiana's love on many different occasions," Aunt Florine said.

"At your Uncle Simon's wedding reception the young men were lined up on one side and the young women on the other side of the dance floor. This was in preparation for *Contradance* which traditionally takes place at the beginning of the reception. Lawrence Santan noticed that Eufermiana was about ten women down the row. He would have to dance with the woman directly opposite him as was customary. Just as the *Mestre de sale* had lined up everyone and the music was about to begin, Lawrence Santan slid like a snake behind the row of men and squeezed himself between two other men to face Eufermiana. The band began to play the traditional wedding waltz. When Lawrence Santan approached Eufermiana, she turned away and walked towards her seat. Just before she sat down, he grabbed her by the arm asking her for the pleasure of this dance. Eufermiana huffed, pulled her arm away and sat down. Lawrence Santan stormed off."

After exhausting all his avenues, Lawrence Santan finally decided to ask Eufermiana's parents for her hand in marriage. They were faced with a dilemma since they had already arranged for her to get married to John. However, they thought that Lawrence Santan might be a better choice since he was intelligent and wealthy. When her parents mentioned this, *Mai* was enraged.

"How dare he! He knows that I am to marry John. Why doesn't he leave me alone?"

When Eufermiana's parents notified Lawrence Santan that she would not accept his offer to marry he was very disappointed and despised my mother.

I finally figured out why we lived in a separate house away from my grandfather Rosario's big home. My father did not want to have anything to do with Lawrence Santan. *Mai* had mentioned in one of her conversations that my grandfather had worked hard so that his children could live together. It saddened him when this Goan tradition was broken.

My grandfather, a very strict man, owned a hotel in Margao. He had moved from his home village of Majorda to Navelim to avoid the long commute. He purchased a plot in Colmorod, a district of Navelim, for 90 rupees. That is where he built a large home for my father and uncles. My grandfather expected all of his sons to work at the family-owned hotel. As soon as my father was of age to work, he followed my uncles by going to work on a ship. It was the only form of employment available to young men at that time. My Uncle Baltazar was the only one that stayed behind to work in the hotel. He ended up drinking heavily to cope with his iron-fisted father. He died of alcoholism at a young age leaving behind two daughters and three sons.

As it was his duty, my father would send part of his salary to Lawrence Santan for the family's upkeep. Ironically, Lawrence Santan used this money to set up his furniture shop. After my father passed away, my mother felt that she did not belong to the family anymore. Lawrence Santan and her in-laws harassed her and treated her like an outsider. She could not take it anymore. Feeling like an outcast my mother decided to move to 1st Dando and live with her parents. Gregory, my adopted brother who was six years older than me, moved in with us. He was my cousin who had lost his parents when he was three. Although I missed my friends in Colmorod, I enjoyed being at 1st Dando with my maternal grandparents.

CHAPTER 3

By the time I was 14, both my maternal grandparents had died. A couple of years later, my mother decided to build a large house for us. She told me that her parents' house was too small and that I would need a big house to live in when I got married. She assumed that I would have a lot of children. All the neighbours thought that she was crazy. How could a widow with barely any money fathom such an undertaking?

In May of 1930, my mother embarked on an exhaustive search for construction workers to build the house. Whenever she met a group of workers, they would brush her off because they did not think that she could afford to pay them. After all, she was a poor widow. She decided to dig up all the money that her parents had buried in a pot safely hidden in their small house. She used this money as bait by paying the construction workers in advance. They promised to come the next day to start construction. My mother cooked rice and drained the water called *kanji* which she intended to serve the workers during their break. After waiting for them all day, she went to *Shiroda* where they lived but the construction workers had mysteriously disappeared. Determined to build her house, she decided to sell her gold bangles. This time she gave them only a small part of the money up front. At the end of November 1930 construction of the house finally began. With no form of architectural design in mind she asked the workers to break down the old house and dig the new foundation. Anton, who was the foreman, suggested that she build six rooms, which included a long foyer with an altar, a large living room, two bedrooms, a kitchen and a dining room. The front of the house would have a long balcony that would cover its entire length. Stones and clay were used to build the foundation. When it was completed my maternal great-uncle Sebastao who lived in the neighbourhood decided to tour the site.

He looked at my mother in bewilderment and said "How on earth are you going to build such a large house with no money? Have you gone mad?"

My mother looked him in the eye and said defiantly "I have to build this house so my son will have a place to live in when he gets married."

Then looking up towards the sky she said "The money will come. The good Lord will provide." Sebastao shook his head and left convinced that she had lost her mind.

Tons of clay would be needed to build the walls eighteen inches thick and twenty feet high at the center of the house. *Kunbis* who were of a low caste were hired to dig the clay from a nearby field and carry it in small metal tubs to the construction site. The men did the digging, and the women carried the metal tubs full of clay on their heads. At the site, the clay would be mixed with sufficient water so that it would not slump when forming the wall. Only some of the walls were up when she had run out of money. Construction ground to a halt. My poor mother asked the neighbours for a loan, but none of them had the means. She once again turned to her valuable possessions; her precious and ornate earrings that she had worn only once on her wedding day. With this money, she would be able to pay for the construction of the walls.

Next, she had to decide on the number and type of doors and windows. Anton the foreman came to the rescue once again. He suggested an arched design for the main door and the windows in the façade. The doors leading to the various rooms in the house would be of a similar design. Although the construction would be more complicated it would add character to the house. My mother was a bit nervous about the idea, but Anton convinced her that he would do a good job.

The erection of the walls dragged on because the construction workers were unreliable. There were times when they would not show up for days on end. My mother would send messengers to get them to come to work, but they always had lame excuses. The walls were finally completed in April 1931. Now she needed money to buy the wooden beams and tiles for the roof which had to be built before the imminent monsoons. She had to pawn the last of her valuables, her gold necklace. This broke her heart because it was a wedding present from her dear mother. The roof had to be built by the next month, otherwise, the rains would severely damage the exposed clay walls and the floors. My mother contacted Anton the foreman who managed to recruit a small crew of workers. He ordered the wooden beams made from tall coconut trees. The beams and roof tiles were in short supply since most of the construction workers were rushing to complete other houses before the monsoons. Anton would go to the lumber yard daily to expedite the delivery, but it was to no avail. Finally, after one month of haggling with the suppliers, the lumber and tiles arrived.

Although my mother wanted to have the house built before my 17th birthday, on April 8th, it was finally completed in June of 1931. The very next day the monsoons deluged the entire country. The strong winds which usually accompanied the monsoons blew off some of the tiles at the peak of the house. In the rush to complete the roof, the construction workers had forgotten to secure these tiles properly. We placed pails to collect the water. Every four to five hours they would fill up and I would have to empty them. The rain continued for six days and finally, it stopped for a brief period. My mother had already sent a message to Anton to inform him of the damage. He came by with a couple of workers and they fixed the tiles.

My mother was content since she finally completed what most thought would be an impossible task. Our relatives on my mother's side came by to see our new home. Some of them were genuinely pleased for us. Others would tell my mother that it was not built properly and that she would have problems during the monsoons. My great-uncle refused to come anywhere near the house since my mother had proved him wrong. My uncles from Colmorod never set foot in the new house. As far as they were concerned, my mother was not part of the family.

Although we were happy to be in our new home, there was one major problem, we were penniless. I decided to leave school at the age of 18 and look for a job so that I could support both of us. Gregory decided to go to Bombay and look for work.

CHAPTER 4

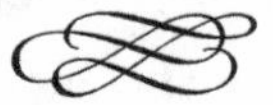

"SOME MORE COFFEE *BWANA*?" the waiter asked.

'Eh...no, no' I said as I emerged from deep thought.

There were leftover crumbs on my plate from the *samosa* I had eaten. Oh, dear! I was still at Jaffrey's Bar. I looked at my watch, it was 11:30 am. What did I have to do next, ah! yes! I had to go back to Barclays bank. It was too early to pick up the bank draft, so I decided to have lunch.

After picking up the newspaper '*Handicap*' I drove to the Speke Hotel for lunch. The front of the hotel comprised a row of white arches with balconies on the second floor. Terra cotta tiles on the roof with the white arches below were typical of colonial buildings in Kampala. At the left of the building was a large jacaranda tree full of purple blooms. When I entered the hotel, I noticed that the left wing was being renovated. The dining room would only be open at noon, so I headed for the bar.

"What can I get you?"

"Scotch with water."

The smell of paint wafted into the bar area. It reminded me of the time when I was eighteen and had left school to find work and support my mother. Uncle Lawrence Santan used to take orders for painting church altars all over Goa. He recognized that I had talent and decided to hire me. The oil-based gold paint gave off noxious fumes as we painted the niche frames and pillars that housed the statues of saints, Our Lady and Jesus Christ. The largest niche on the altar usually housed the saint after whom the church was named.

Lawrence Santan secured a contract to paint St. Rita's church in Aldona. This was about 40 kilometres from Navelim. *Mai* did not want me to go because of my experience of getting sick from painting other churches.

After a four-hour journey on a horse-drawn carriage, we finally made it to St. Rita's.

A damp smell emanated upon entering the church. This was probably due to the residual effects of the monsoons. The clay tiles and high peaked roof kept the church cool as compared with the scorching weather outside. We noticed that it needed some major rework. Father Rodrigues, the parish priest had provided some poles with rope that we used to make the framework of the scaffolding and then placed wood planks for us to work on. We climbed up the scaffolding and started painting the main niche. The fine filigree work around the niche required a lot of patience and precision. I laboured over it for several hours while my co-worker, Dumpidade worked on the pillars.

"Carlit are you alright?"

"I am fine" I replied even though I felt nauseous.

"*Arrh* paint is dripping from your brush and the niche is unevenly painted."

"Is that so? I think that it is fine."

I suddenly felt that I was swimming in a sea of gold paint.

My hands felt limp and the brush fell from my hands. I shook my head and tried to see straight, but everything was a blur.

"Watch out Carlit!" Dumpidade tried to grab my arm, but it was too late. I slipped off the scaffold and dangled.

"God, help him! He is going to fall!"

The parish priest and secretary came out running onto the altar. Fr. Rodrigues climbed up the scaffolding and grabbed me by the waist with his big burly hands. The scaffolding creaked and bent under his weight. I was praying that the scaffolding would not collapse. He managed to haul me down onto the floor. I could barely walk, so they each caught my arms and took me outside the church. They sat me on a bench.

Image of young Carlos

"Have some water," Fr. Rodrigues said as the secretary fanned me.

After drinking the water and breathing some fresh air, I was slowly starting to feel better.

"Come on Dumpidade, let's get back to work."

"No, you are not well, you will have to rest." Fr. Rodrigues insisted.

"You can stay with us tonight. Tomorrow morning you can take the carriage to Margao."

The journey in the carriage was bumpy and I was overcome with nausea. I asked the carriage driver to stop several times so that I could throw up. By the time I arrived at Navelim, I was dehydrated and felt extremely weak.

"Oh! My God Carlit, look at you. What happened?"

"It is nothing *Mai*, I am fine, just a bit tired from the journey."

"You look terribly sick."

"It must be those oil paints. They are making you sick."

"But *Mai* we need the money."

"We do, but you need to find some other work."

Early the next morning my mother went to see Lawrence Santan.

"Carlit cannot do any more painting jobs. It is making him sick."

"Well, I am sorry my dear Eufermiana, I did not force him to take this job. He asked for it."

"Can you find him some other work?"

"You expect me to help you after rejecting my offer to marry you."

"Listen Lawrence Santan, can you help my son or not? I do not need you to lecture me."

"Sorry, Eufermiana there is nothing I can do for you or your son."

Mai came home in tears and told me that Lawrence Santan refused to find me another job.

After a year and a half of severe headaches and fainting spells my career in painting came to an end. It was unfortunate because I liked the artistic aspect of this job. I could appreciate the extraordinary work of the artisans that had created the niches, statues, pillars, and embellishments that tied all these elements of the altar together. Oddly enough I liked the smell of the paint.

I was now close to twenty years of age, time for me to select a profession with some promise for the future. In the evenings I would sit on the balcony and ponder my options. The smell of burning dried palm leaves and firewood used for cooking dinner filled the warm air. I would look up at the ebony skies and gaze at the stars hoping to find some answers. Finally, it clicked. Lawrence Santan whom I respected and was well known in the business community should be able to guide me.

"Uncle, as you know I cannot continue in the painting job. I have to find a new career that is in demand."

"Well, the two jobs that are in demand these days are carpentry and tailoring."

"Which of the two do you think I should choose?"

"I think that you would do well in tailoring."

"Tailoring, I never thought of it. Where do I begin?"

"There is an apprenticeship program in Panjim that is part of a large tailoring shop owned by Portuguese, it is called Rebello's."

When I told *mai* about my decision to go to Panjim tears welled up in her eyes.

Lawrence Santan talked to the owner of Rebello's and made arrangements for me to start my apprenticeship. While I was packing my suitcase, *Mai* shoved in several food items in addition to clothing that I did not need. Although this bothered me, I did not have the heart to say anything to her. She insisted that I eat a huge plate of rice with mackerel fish curry before leaving for Margao. Most of the neighbours came to bid me farewell. *Mai* stayed in the kitchen.

I took the bull cart from the Navelim village square to Margao. The *Caminho* packed with travellers destined for Panjim was my next mode of transport. It made several stops at the villages of Nuvem, Verna, Nagoa and Cortalim picking up more passengers along the way. The rice paddy fields looked barren except for the Palm trees on berms that punctuated the fields. At every stop, a young boy had to crank a handle in the front of the *Caminho* to get it started. By the third stop, I was drenched in sweat due to the extreme heat. Thankfully the breeze as we crossed the Zuari River on the ferry provided some relief. This was the first time I had crossed this wide river, the mouth of which widened significantly before pouring out into the Arabian Sea. We travelled for a while after crossing the river when we saw the magnificent terra cotta churches of Old Goa in the distance, truly a sight to behold. By the time we reached Panjim, my new starched white cotton shirt was creased to the point that the fabric resembled crepe.

I was both afraid and excited when I arrived in Panjim. It was nothing like Navelim, with its church, bar, and convenience store. There were many two-and three-story white buildings with balconies. I had never seen such architecture before. Some of them had guards in the front. There was a large hospital, several shops, restaurants, bars and even a hotel. It was called the *Republic Hotel* and was situated in front of the Mandovi River. I was told that Vincent Salvador Rebello from Navelim worked as the chief waiter in this hotel.

"Are you Carlit Dias?" a pleasant looking stranger said as he put out his hand.

"Yes, that's me," I replied shaking his hand.

"I am Anton Dias. I will be your big brother at Rebello's apprenticeship shop."

"Thank you for coming to pick me up. This is my first time in Panjim."

"I will take you to the tailor's mess where you will be staying."

After walking for about half an hour we arrived at a big two-storey building. He took me upstairs into a large hall with several beds. Some of the men were taking their afternoon nap. He showed me to my bed and told me to meet him at 8:00 a.m. the next day.

I freshened up and changed my clothes. I walked down the street until I came to the Mandovi and then turned left. Within a few minutes, I was standing in front of the Republic Hotel. The entrance was overwhelming with beautiful chandeliers and velvet curtains. I finally gathered enough courage and walked towards the reception. A man dressed in a black suit and a perfectly ironed white shirt and black bow tie looked up and said "Yes, can I help you?"

"I am looking for .... err... a Mister Vincent Salvador Rebello."

"Ah. Yes, our chief waiter. Just a moment. I will send for him."

The lobby had shining marble floors and ornate dark wood furniture. I was admiring the intricate work around the chairs when someone tapped me on the shoulder.

"Hello, I am Vincent Rebello. Are you looking for me?"

"Yes, I am Carlit Dias from Navelim."

"Carlit, I am not sure that we have met before. Who is your father?"

"My father was John, but he passed away several years ago. My mother is Eufermiana."

"Oh yes, John from Colmorod."

"That's correct, but we now live in 1st Dando. My mother asked me to visit you."

"How long have you been in Panjim?"

"I just arrived today."

"Well let's celebrate then. Come on, I will buy you a drink."

We ended up having several drinks while we talked about the people that we knew in common. When we said our goodbyes, I felt quite tipsy and could barely find my way to the tailor's mess.

The next morning, I woke up bright and early, got dressed and went down to the street level. I waited for Anton Dias, but there was no sign of him. I was starting to panic but was relieved when I finally saw Anton walking down the street.

Rebello's Store was much bigger than I had envisaged. Anton Dias introduced me to the owner, Mr. Rebello.

"I hear from Lawrence Santan that you are very talented?"

"I used to do some painting work for him in the churches. It is something I enjoyed."

"Well, tailoring is different. I hope that you will be able to pick it up. We are very busy so you will have to learn quickly."

"I will do my best."

"Anton show him how to hem. Once he gets the hang of it, he can help the tailors."

I ended up hemming for the next six weeks, which was quite boring. Next, I was given the job of button-hole maker, something that required more skill than hemming. It took me a little longer to learn how to make perfect buttonholes. For two months that was all I did. Whenever I had free time, I would go around to learn how the experienced tailors worked. Some of them would cut and sew the entire garment. I looked forward to the day when I would be able to do that. That day finally came when I was asked to sew a full blouse. I worked very hard on doing my best. When I finished, I proudly showed it to Anton. He took one look at it and smacked me on the head.

"Why did you do that? What is wrong?"

"Look at the sleeves. You sewed them the wrong way around."

"Oh! I can't believe I did that."

"You better fix it before Mr. Rebello sees the blouse."

After that, I would tack the all the pieces before sewing them.

I was finally allowed to mark the pattern on the fabric and cut it a year into my apprenticeship. I learnt how to cut and sew various types of dresses. Initially, I was given simple "A-line" dresses to cut. By the end of the second year, I was cutting and sewing sophisticated ball gowns.

"Carlit, you have come a long way. I now consider you a full-fledged tailor."

"Thank you, Mr. Rebello. Is there a chance that I could work for you?"

"I am sorry, but we cannot hire you. We already have our quota of tailors."

I packed my bags and went back to Navelim. *Mai* was pleased to see me.

CHAPTER 5

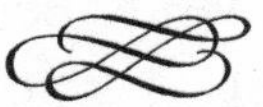

WHILE I SAT at the bar in Speke Hotel, I thought about the time when I was living with *Mai* in Navelim. She seemed so happy that I had finally completed my apprenticeship as a tailor.

"The dining room is open." the barman announced.

I started walking to the dining room but my knees wobbled, and my mind was adrift. Instead of going to the dining room, I made a beeline for the toilets. I splashed cold water over my face hoping to sober up. My cheeks and lips felt numb.

The aroma of roast beef wafted through the air when I walked into the dining room. I knew exactly what I was going to order.

"Here is the menu *bwana*."

"I will come back when you have decided what to order."

"I will have the roast beef."

"Yes, *bwana*."

I noticed a well-dressed young lady walking into the dining room with an older man. He was probably her boss. The dress she wore reminded me of the one I had sewed as an emerging tailor. I was back in Navelim trying to drum up some business after my apprenticeship. Even though the word spread far, and wide orders would only trickle in. Times were tough in Goa, so I decided to look for greener pastures. I thought that I would try my luck in Bombay. I was warned by several people that finding a job would be a challenge. *Mai* was not for it, but she eventually gave in since we had no income.

Mai went into her little storage room and pulled out some of her valuable rupees stashed away in small clay urns and handed them to me. Her parents had generated some income from selling *feni* – a strong alcoholic drink made from coconut. *Mai* had discovered these urns several years after they had died. I used the money she gave me to buy my ticket to go to Bombay.

The entire neighbourhood had come to see me off. I hugged my friends and neighbours. *Mai* reluctantly gave me her blessings. I was sad about leaving my friends and mother but at the same time, I was excited about visiting Bombay – a city I had heard so much about. Most of all I looked forward to finding a good job.

After a twenty-four-hour rocky ride on the ship, the captain announced that we would be arriving in Bombay shortly. Suddenly, a terrible odour permeated through the ship. I decided to go up on the deck to see where it was coming from. I looked down at the brownish water and realized that we were entering the harbour of Bombay. The stench was unbearable.

When I walked down the gangway, I saw throngs of people all around. Some of them were waving frantically with great excitement while others stood and watched the passengers disembarking from the ship. I found the huge crowds quite overwhelming. This, together with the putrid odour made me feel queasy. Fear engulfed me while I pushed my way through the maze of people. Suddenly, I felt someone grab my arm. At that moment I panicked and tried to pull my arm away. I looked at the person and he smiled.

"Gregory is that you?"

"Carlit! Carlit!" Gregory said and hugged me.

"How did you know I was coming to Bombay?"

"Lawrence Santan had written to the president of the tailors club of Navelim in Bombay."

"I am so happy to see you, Gregory. It has been over four years. How are you?"

"Oh, I am not well. I keep getting these severe stomach pains." Gregory replied.

"They must have some good medicines in Bombay." I said trying to encourage him.

"I don't think it will help. This is a severe illness." Gregory said dolefully.

I felt very sorry for him. His parents had passed away when he was a child, and he did not receive the care and attention that most children do.

"By the way, Gregory, where are you working?" I asked trying to change the subject.

"I work as a cook for the parish priests."

"Do you like it?"

"It is okay. At least I have a place to stay, and I don't have to pay for my meals."

We took a bus to the Tailor's Club located in Dhobitalo, located in central Bombay. The wide paved streets were flanked by buildings that had tiny balconies and were several stories high. These buildings had a dull greyish colour from the dirt and grime, complemented with mould because of the monsoons. I found out later that these buildings contained small one-room dwellings that were rented out at exorbitant rates. The Tailors' Club was a cheaper alternative. It consisted of a large hall with suitcases all around belonging to the members. At the far end was an altar with the statue of Our Lady of Rosary, candles, and plastic flowers in a vase. Gregory introduced me as John Dias' son. I was given a place to put my suitcase and then we left to see the city.

Bombay was crowded. Gregory proudly announced that Bombay was the largest city in India. I gathered that people had come from different parts of India from their clothing and the different languages that they spoke. Some men wore translucent white pants and long flimsy shirts with no collars. Sikhs wore brightly coloured turbans with matching baggy clothing. Women wore saris made from a variety of fabrics. The richer ones wore silk saris adorned with intricate gold filigree. The working class dressed in cotton saris with attractive patterns. The poor wore lightweight, maroon-coloured cotton saris. Regardless of their social standing, all the women were decked with bangles, necklaces, earrings, nose rings and anklets. The wealthy wore gold jewelry, and the poorer women wore cheap costume jewelry and glass bangles. Although I found the multitude of different people interesting, I was curious about the languages that they spoke. Gregory told me that they spoke Marathi, Gujarati and Punjabi and that the most common language was Hindi.

"Do you speak Hindi?" I asked.

"The priests speak English and Konkani. I do not need to speak Hindi." Gregory said defensively.

While walking along Marine Drive I saw a group of men in white shirts and pants playing a sport. I could imagine how dirty their white clothing would get with the dust from the red mud. The game was called cricket and was played only by the British. Indians were not allowed to play in white-only sports clubs.

They were only permitted to work as waiters, barmen and maintenance personnel. I thought that this treatment of Indians in their own country was not extremely unfair. When I expressed my discontent, Gregory suggested that the situation might change in the future if Mahatma Gandhi had his way. The British government was struggling with the uproar that this little man was causing. Recently, his movement of civil disobedience paralyzed the Indian economy. His nonviolent resistance strongly appealed to the masses. The British were afraid that they would be losing power soon.

At the end of our political discussion, we found ourselves near the Victoria Train Station. It was a fine example of Victorian Gothic architecture in India, with a large central dome flanked by two wings. The train stations in Goa paled in comparison. Large crowds gathered around the ticket booths inside the station. We managed to squeeze our way through and picked up two tickets. When the train approached, I walked towards the first car. Gregory grabbed me by the arm.

"Not that one, it is a first-class car. We only have a third-class ticket." Gregory said.

"Why is that?"

"We are not allowed to travel first class; it is reserved for the British only."

This infuriated me.

We took the train for several minutes and then got off at Sandhurst Road station. Numerous buildings, shops and restaurants lined the network of streets. Although most of the shops were small, they carried a multitude of different products, from furniture to pots and pans, clothing, books, trinkets, food, jewelry and saris. The products were hung from the ceiling and awnings, packed in shelves and every square inch of the shop except for a tiny area where the store owner would squat. He would shout out in a constant litany of his wares stating that they were good quality yet inexpensive. At almost every corner people were begging for money. Some were young children who barely had any clothing. This disturbed me immensely since it was quite rare to see people begging in Goa. Those who did were usually adults asking for a cup of rice and most of them lived in a house. In contrast, there were rows of makeshift shelters put together with sticks, rags, board, and scrap metal. The number of destitute people and the appalling living conditions saddened me. I wondered if they had originally come to Bombay looking for work and a better life.

In one of the shops on the street, I noticed a glass enclosure with colourful pastries neatly piled. I was tempted to try them, but Gregory warned me that they were expensive. All this walking was making me hungry. We finally stopped near a little box cart. Behind it was a man frying something that smelt sumptuous.

"Here, have some *bhel puri,"* Gregory said as he handed me food wrapped in newspaper.

"What is it?" I inquired suspiciously.

"It's a mixture of deep-fried rice, grains, split peas, onions, spices and tamarind sauce."

Although I devoured the *bhel puri*, thoughts of the pastries lingered on in my mind. I promised myself that I would buy them once I started working.

We took the bus to the heart of Bombay, a place called Colaba. After walking for a few minutes an enormous structure emerged over the horizon. It was honey-coloured and comprised an archway with halls on each side. Gregory informed me that it was built by the British to commemorate the visit of George V and Queen Mary. It stood right in front of the harbour and was appropriately named The Gateway of India.

The sun was setting, and my feet were quite sore. Since we were not too far away from the club we decided to walk. I could barely climb up the stairs to the club. Some of the men were lying down on mats in the main hall.

"What are they doing?" I inquired.

"They are preparing to go to sleep."

"Sleep in this room?" I said, somewhat surprised.

"Yes Carlit, everyone sleeps on their mats next to their suitcase."

"Oh, don't worry you will get used to it."

The mat on the hard floor was very uncomfortable. This together with the symphony of people snoring made it very difficult for me to sleep.

The next morning Gregory took me to several tailoring shops in the area. There were no jobs available. He suggested that I approach Mr. Alfonso who had many contacts since he worked in Bombay for the past fifteen years. I tried to get in touch with Mr. Alfonso for three days to no avail. He woke up at the crack of dawn and went to work. On the fourth day, I decided to wake up early and finally met him. I offered to take him for tea at a restaurant next to the club. While drinking our tea, I told him that I was looking for a job as a tailor. He asked me about my experience, and I told him that I did my apprenticeship at Rebello's and then took sewing orders in Navelim. Mr. Alfonso said that he did not think that he could help me, since there was an influx of unemployed Goan tailors in Bombay. In desperation, I offered ten percent of my salary for the first six months if he would help me. He finally agreed. The following day we took the train from the Victoria Terminus and got off at Bandra Station. We visited several shops. Mr. Alfonso would chat with the owners and then introduce me as a proficient tailor. I was afraid that I might not be able to live up to his expectations. The first five shops had no openings. Finally, the sixth one offered me a job as a junior tailor. I was ecstatic!

I would wake up at 6:00 every morning to take the train to Bandra, where I would work for ten hours a day. I was given a small stool in a corner with very little room to move. By noon it would be stifling in the shop. When the tailors finished sewing the outfits, I would do the hemming, sew the buttons, and do the handwork around the collars and sleeves. I was not allowed to waste any leftover pieces of thread. I had to store them in a little tin for reuse later. I was glad when they asked me to do tacking since it broke the monotony of handwork. At around 10:00 am a young boy, *Chaiwala* would serve us steaming hot tea in glasses. At lunch time the tailors who were mostly Goans would reminisce about Goa and exchange news about their families. Most of the talk revolved around births, marriage proposals, weddings, and funerals.

After working for about six months, I was barely making ends meet. I had hoped to earn sufficient money for my upkeep and to send the left-over money to *Mai*. Furthermore, I did not like the work. I decided to give up my job and go back to Goa, so I booked my ticket. Third Class was all I could afford. I had to borrow some money from Gregory. Needless to say, Gregory was very disappointed that I was going back.

"Carlit, you should stay a little longer, I am sure that you will find a better job."

"I don't think so. There are a lot of people looking for work in Bombay, some of them more experienced than me."

"Carlit it felt good having you around. I do not know when I will see you next."

"Give my regards to *Mai*."

We shook hands and hugged. I boarded the ship and stayed on the deck. Gregory kept waving to me until he disappeared into a tiny dot. Tears welled up in my eyes. He has always been a true friend and brother to me. As for Bombay, I will not miss it. All I can think of are the long hours of hard work and the miserable salary. The sun was setting as we pulled out of the harbour. In the distance, I could see the silhouette of the majestic Gateway of India. "*Salaam* Bombay!" I said to myself.

CHAPTER 6

THE AROMA of Safari coffee made me realize that I had been daydreaming. I looked around and the dining room at the Speke Hotel which was bustling with patrons. The waiters dressed in white Kanzu's and burgundy waist bands and pillar-box hats were serving piping hot coffee. I graciously accepted a cup. For some reason, my mind had been drifting to the past since the news of Mai's death.

After drinking coffee and eating the roast beef I felt much better. I looked at my watch and realized that it was 3:00 p.m. I had better get to the bank before it closes, I thought. I hopped into my car and drove to the bank. I walked up hurriedly to the counter. It was now 3:24 p.m.

"Carlit, where were you? The bank closes at 3:30 p.m." John Glory said.

"I was having lunch at the Speke Hotel."

"That was a long lunch. Basil sent Placido here to look for you."

She always relied on Placido to help her out in times of need, so I wasn't surprised.

"Is the bank draft ready?" I asked.

"Yes, it is, but you have to remember to pay me the difference."

"John, you don't have to worry. I will put the money in a bouquet of roses and present it to you." I replied, somewhat irritated.

"Yes, Carlit. You are good at making promises that you cannot keep."

I dashed out of the bank and rushed to the post office. Luckily it was a short drive. There was a long queue at the post office since it was almost closing time. I managed to send the draft registered mail and felt a little better that *Mai* would have a decent funeral. Poor *Mai,* the last time I remember her being happy was when I had come back from Bombay. Every day she would cook more food than I could ever eat. I was afraid that she was spending all her money just to feed me. I had to start earning my keep, so I decided to visit people in the neighbourhood looking for work. Every morning I would wake up early, hop onto my bike and go around the village asking people if there were any upcoming family events such as christenings, weddings, and birthdays. Fortunately, there was something or the other every week. Weddings were the best. It meant a lot of business for me – from the wedding gown, bridesmaids' dresses, flower girls' dresses and of course the mother of the bride's dress. A wedding was one occasion that even the poorest families would splurge even if it meant borrowing. It was not unusual for the family to save for the wedding and dowry from the day a girl was born in the family.

After working on the last big job, I decided to take a break and have a drink at Elna's bar in the village. One of the neighbour's sons whispered in my ear that *Mai* had sent for me. I thought that she was sick so I jumped onto my bike and cycled as fast as I could to my house. When I arrived, *Mai* was sitting with a gentleman in the living room, patiently awaiting my arrival. She quelled my fears by saying that she was fine, and that Mr. Anton Dias wanted to talk to me. He told me that he was going to Kenya since he got a job with a businessman called Auguste Carvalho. The village folk had informed him through the grape vine that I was a good tailor and so he decided to offer me his clients. I was finally joining the ranks of experienced tailors.

Anton and I met at Elna's bar the next day and toasted to each other's success. Although I was happy for Anton, I was envious that he landed a job in Kenya, something I yearned for. What's more, he would be visiting Africa, an adventurous and exotic place. A week later I bid him farewell and promised to keep his former clients satisfied. Anton's clients kept me quite busy, and my sphere of clients extended beyond Navelim to Benaulim, Majorda, Colva and even as far as Assolna. Thankfully, each village had a bar that I would visit at the end of the day for a shot of *feni* before riding back on my bicycle to Navelim.

Mai would complain that she rarely saw me even though I was living at home. At times like this, I wished that my father was alive to keep her company. Whenever I asked about him, she would have this distant gaze and her eyes would well-up. All she would say was that she could not remember much about him. After all, they were married for only five years, of which he spent most of his time working on the ship. She did mention that he could be quite ill-tempered. Once when *Mai* was spending time with her parents my father had brought a piglet for her to cook. He had gone to the bar for a drink and then returned to have lunch. *Mai* was taking it easy and did not cook it in time for lunch. He grabbed the piglet from the kitchen and buried it in the backyard.. Even though *Mai* had neighbours to talk to, it must have been very lonely without her husband and parents.

What I missed the most while I was in Bombay were the weddings, *ladins*, village feasts, the Carnival and fishing in Goa. *Ladins* were usually held to celebrate christenings, birthdays or when a family member returned from Bombay or overseas. The older men would play their violins and the crowd would sing hymns in the main hall in front of the altar. The head of the family would then recite the litany of all the saints and the rest would reply "pray for us." In the end, drinks would be served with boiled chickpeas and pieces of coconut. *Ladins* were an example of where prayer and social gatherings meshed.

Every village had its feast in honour of the saint of their church. When relatives invited us, we would first go to the mass and then to the fair. Numerous stalls would be set up around the church grounds. People would sell a variety of foods, trinkets, pots, pans, and even furniture. I would buy an assortment of candy and devour it within a matter of minutes. Lunch, an important part of the celebration included *sanas* – steamed rice cakes, *sorpatel* – a dish made from spicy cuts of pork and liver and finally fish curry and rice. The warm afternoon breeze, the tranquillity and overeating were precursors to a great siesta. In the evening there was always an outdoor concert called *theatre*. It was the perfect way to end the day.

Besides weddings, village feasts and the carnival, I used to enjoy fishing with my friends. Our favourite spot was near Orlim on the River Sal where it widens. The pristine blue waters of the meandering river, the palms swaying in the gentle breeze and the low-lying hills on the horizon were relaxing and peaceful. We would fish all day and catch a variety of fish, such as Barramundi and Mangrove Jack. If we netted a large catch before the monsoons, *Mai* would salt the fish and dry them in the sun. That way we would have fish during the monsoons, when fresh fish was in short supply.

Although I was having a great time in Goa, I had this yearning to go overseas–Africa was my dream. I knew that Lawrence Santan would be against the idea; it was too far-fetched even for someone as adventurous as him. I spent a lot of time thinking of how I could make this dream a reality. It finally clicked; I would write to Anton Dias.

CHAPTER 7

SENDING the bank draft to Goa eased my conscience a little, but I surely did not feel like going home. I suspected that condolence visits from the neighbours and relatives awaited me. I was certain that Basil would host them on my behalf. Part of me felt that I should have been there to serve drinks at the very least. Instead, I decided to go to the St. Francis Xavier Club. As soon as I walked into the club, I was overcome with a sense of guilt. I suddenly realized that my friends would offer me their condolences. How was I to react? It was too late to turn back; some of my friends had already spotted me.

"Carlit, we are very sorry to hear about your mother," Jacinth said as he extended his hand. I shook his hand and tried to say something, but I choked. My other friends followed suit and after the third one, I was able to utter a feeble "God bless you," not knowing whether this was the appropriate response. By the time the tenth person offered his condolences, my anguish intensified, and images of *Mai* flashed through my mind. The frame stopped at the time when I was leaving Goa for

Kenya. The image of her frail and disconsolate body sitting on her bed came to mind.

Although I had planned to write to Anton Dias about helping me find a job in Kenya, he had beaten me to it. He had already spoken to Auguste Carvalho about me. Auguste's business was flourishing with the rapid economic development of Kenya by the British. He was in dire need of experienced tailors. Auguste wrote a letter to Lawrence Santan informing him that he had a job for me in Kenya. When Lawrence Santan told me about the letter, I could not believe it. My dream would finally come true. I could just see myself all packed and embarking on the ship destined for Kenya. My excitement quickly turned into utter disappointment.

"Carlit, I cannot send you to Kenya." Lawrence Santan said authoritatively.

"Why not?" I replied in disbelief.

"You have to stay behind to look after the property."

"But, but..., I want to go to Kenya!"

"You can work in Goa. You don't need to go to Africa. My decision is final!"

"Please, Uncle. It has been my dream for all these years."

"Dreams will not protect this property and provide for you. This matter is closed."

I was down in the doldrums for days on end. I avoided some of my clients, especially the difficult ones. I did not bother getting new orders. I did not care about my work in Goa anymore. Kenya was on my mind. I would lie awake at night thinking of how I could convince Lawrence Santan to let me go. After weeks of hopelessness, I finally had an idea. I don't know why I did not think about it before. I decided to reply to Auguste Carvalho's letter pretending to be Lawrence Santan. In the letter, I sang praises about myself and stated that

Lawrence Santan had granted me his permission to go to Kenya.

A month later, Lawrence Santan sent a message asking me to see him immediately.

"Who in God's name gave you permission to write this letter on my behalf?" Lawrence Santan shouted.

"Err... nobody," I replied.

"That was very wrong of you to undermine my authority!"

"I am sorry."

"I am going to write to Auguste telling him that your letter was a hoax and that I do not intend to send you."

"Please, please don't," I begged.

"Auguste will be very disappointed especially since he went through the trouble of applying for my work permit."

"That is true."

"I am going to Kenya, and nobody is going to stop me," I said defiantly.

Lawrence Santan stood there in dismay. This was the first time I ever stood up to him.

My next hurdle was *Mai*. Strangely enough, she offered little resistance to the notion of me going to Kenya. I suppose she knew instinctively that I was determined to go abroad. Besides, she was getting used to me being away from home. I don't think that she realized how far Kenya was. I wasn't sure myself.

The first thing that I did was book my ticket on the ship with McKenzie & Company Shipping Lines. I was told that I had to go to the Portuguese Government offices of Goa, Daman & Diu in Panjim to get my passport. When I arrived at the passport office it was closed for the afternoon siesta. To kill time, I decided to visit Salvador Rebello at the Republic Hotel. He was most happy to see me and treated me to an elaborate lunch at the hotel's expense. After lunch, I walked back to the passport office where I saw a crowd hovering in front of a counter. Three official-looking Portuguese men dressed in uniform were behind the counter. Initially, I waited at the back of the crowd that was funnelling into three apexes at the service counter. After waiting for almost an hour, I realized that I had hardly moved from my spot. I squeezed my way between the crowd in a discrete manner. Within fifteen minutes I was face to face with an officer.

"I, I eh... need to get a passport," I uttered.

"That is why all these people are here," the officer said sarcastically.

"But I am going to Kenya," I replied.

"Everyone here is travelling abroad. What is the purpose of your visit?"

"I have been offered a job and expect to receive my permit soon." I said confidently.

"Do you have any proof?" the officer asked with an air of distrust.

"Yes, yes, I have a letter from Mr. Carvallo, my future employer. Here it is."

The officer scrutinized the letter and then gave me a bunch of application forms.

I got to the *Caminho* station just in time to catch the last one leaving for Margao.

The next morning, I wrote a letter to Auguste Carvalho requesting a copy of my work permit application. As I went through the passport application forms, I was overwhelmed by the amount of information that was required. After receiving my permit application from Auguste, I took my passport application and deposited it at the office in Panjim. Four months later I finally received my Portuguese passport. On November 15th, 1937 – the feast of Our Lady of the Holy

Rosary, I received my work permit from Auguste. I was over the moon.

I was busy completing my orders since I had only a month before my departure. Marriage proposals were coming in more frequently. *Mai* politely turned them down stating that I was going overseas soon. I sewed some new shirts and boxer shorts for myself. I got a gent's tailor to sew several pairs of pants and a new black suit. *Mai* was busy preparing salted fish, pickles, pork sausages and sweets for me to take.

I could not sleep the night of December 14th. Tomorrow, I would be embarking on a journey that would change my life. I was out of bed by 5:00 am, dressed and was ready to leave by 6:00 am. I went to *Mai's* room and stood in the doorway. She was sitting up in bed saying her morning prayers. I waited a while. She sensed my presence, stopped praying and gradually turned her head toward me. As she looked up at me, I saw sadness in her eyes.

"You are really going *Baba*?" she said sadly.

"Yes, *Mai*, Auguste is waiting for me," I replied with a heavy heart.

"Come over here and let me bless you, my son."

I walked towards her and knelt in front of her. She whispered a few prayers and then stopped for a moment. I felt hot tears on my scalp. I dared not look up. I felt her gently making the sign of the cross on my head and heard her controlled sobs.

"May God be with you during this journey and look after you *Baba*."

I stood up and glanced at *Mai*, but she had her head down. I walked out of the door and suddenly felt like every emotion and memory attached to *Mai* and this home was being painfully severed. I quickly picked up my bag and walked out of the house not turning to look back.

I arrived in Panjim at noon and headed for the docks. The stale sulphur smell emanating from the harbour filled my nostrils. As I walked up the gangway I turned around and looked at the city of Panjim. I tried to take in as much of the architecture of the ornate government buildings, the majestic Panjim church of Our Lady of Immaculate Conception on the hillside and the wide streets desperately hoping that it would stay with me, safely stored deep in my mind. While the ship was leaving the harbour, the crowds waved to their relatives on board. Sadly, I had no one to wave goodbye. I went down to the bunks and picked the best one since most of the people were on the deck. I slept soundly all the way to Bombay.

Gregory had come to meet me at Bombay Harbour. We took the bus to the Tailors Club in Dhobitalo where I spent the night. Most of the tailors at the club greeted me with warmth.

"Carlit, you have done well. Just a few years ago you came to Bombay looking for work. Now you are going to Africa. You are lucky." Mr. Alfonso said enviously.

Gregory and I took the bus to the harbour early in the morning. Once again throngs of people were there to see their relatives off to Africa. It was like a sea of brightly coloured turbans, saris, and white *kurtas*. The ship with SS Kenya emblazoned across it was gigantic and made the multitude of people seem quite inconspicuous. I made my way to the gangway and had to drag my heavy trunk to the deck. The ticket master directed me to the lower third-class deck. Once I put my luggage down, I went up to the deck to wave goodbye to Gregory. Trying to spot him among the multitude of people was an exercise in futility. I waved hoping that he could see me while the ship was leaving the harbour.

After one day on the ship, I met up with some other Goans and we played cards for hours on end. I slept the rest of the time since there was nothing else to do. Two days later we arrived in Victoria harbour in Seychelles where we picked up some more passengers. The four-hour stopover gave us a chance to visit Victoria and have a quick drink at the local bar. This tranquil island with sandy beaches and palm trees swaying in the breeze reminded me of Goa. It was a refreshing change from the lower deck of the ship. After seven long and wearisome days on the high seas, we finally arrived in Mombasa on January 1st, 1938.

CHAPTER 8

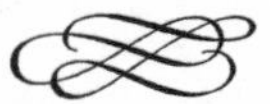

I DID NOT EXPECT the news of *Mai's* death to spread so quickly. After my friends offered their condolences at the club, I decided to get a drink at the bar. While I drank my scotch on the rocks, I thought of Basil at home, accepting condolences from friends and relatives. Some of them would have brought food, as was customary. Basil would make sure that everyone would be well fed. I should have been there.

"Carlit, aren't you going to play cards with us?" Jacinth asked.

"Cards? No, I think I should go home."

"Come on, let's play a few games of *truque*. You will feel better," Jacinth said.

"Well, maybe just a couple."

At the end of each game, I would tell myself that it was the last game, but I would end up playing the next one. This went on right up to the closing time at midnight.

While I was driving home, I recalled my first visit to Africa. A large invincible fort appeared over the horizon as we approached Mombasa. It was built by the Portuguese and was called Fort Jesus. They had conquered several regions around the world. In the 1700's they had been driven out by the British, who had embarked on an aggressive program of colonization. It was odd that the Portuguese still managed to hold onto Goa, even though most of India was ruled by the British. In the harbour, there were myriad boats docked along several quays. The dhows, rigged with large white triangular sails, billowed in the light winds of the sheltered harbour.

Once we landed, I had no idea where to go. I stood at the docks hoping to see a familiar face. After waiting for over an hour, Lawrence Santan's brother-in-law, Peter Fernandes came to meet me. I was pleased and hugged him like I would a long-lost friend. He owned a small hotel in Mombasa where mostly immigrant Goans lived. Flour was in short supply and so he would cut bread into small pieces and distribute it amongst all guests. On Fridays, we would be treated to traditional Goan-style fish cooked in coconut curry and rice. This brought back memories of *Mai* and my friends in Goa whom I missed although it was only twelve days since I left.

The streets in Mombasa were narrow and not as crowded as in Bombay. Mosques, monuments, and whitewashed houses with tiny intricately designed balconies were evidence of Arab influence. The people were a mixture of Africans, Arabs, Swahili and British. I had heard about Africans in Goa but had never seen them before. It was quite a shock seeing so many black people in the streets, markets, and other parts of the city. I was afraid to approach or talk to them. They had black crinkled hair and were dressed in long white gowns called "kanzu". They must have been comfortable in the hot and humid weather since the *kanzu* would allow for free circulation of air around their bodies. They spoke a foreign language called Kiswahili.

The Arabs were similar to the Goans, fairer skinned and with straight dark hair. They wore loose white gowns and a printed piece of cloth on their heads secured with a band. When they spoke, it seemed as if they were fighting or arguing with each other. I thought it best to keep my distance. It was safer for me to stick to the few Goans that I knew.

Peter Fernandes had heard that I was artistically inclined and so he asked if I could redecorate his hotel. He tried to convince me to stay and work with him in the hotel. I told him that I preferred to work as a tailor since that was my forte. He suggested that I stay for at least another month since the trains for Nakuru departed monthly. When I went to book my ticket at the train station, I found out that the next train was leaving in four days. I was happy to hear that since I was anxious to get to Nakuru.

I boarded the train destined for Nakuru. At the entrance of the station was a large sign with Uganda Railway written on it. I thought that it was strange since the entire railway was situated in Kenya. In the eyes of the British, they had built it mainly to protect their interests in Uganda. I hauled my heavy metal trunk and bag and then sat on the uncomfortable wooden seats in third class. I spent most of the time gazing out of the window and seeing miles of grassland and acacia. I spotted some wildlife: gazelles, giraffes, zebras and occasionally lions. It seemed like an artist had painted the patterns on the giraffes and zebras. Although we made several stops along the way, the main stop was in Nairobi, a major city. After a four-hour wait, the train continued its journey to Nakuru. The train entered a wide valley, with sparse vegetation, and red soil. A few miles later a beautiful lake emerged over the horizon and huge imposing mountains loomed in the background. It felt like an artist's paradise. We came upon another lake that was filled with numerous pink birds. I learned that these birds, called flamingoes, were attracted to Lake Nakuru because it had an abundance of algae. An hour after passing this lake we finally arrived in the town of Nakuru.

When we entered the small train station, I anxiously looked out for anyone that looked, Goan. Some British people had come to meet their relatives and friends, there were a few African labourers, and some Asians, but no Goans in sight. I walked to the small waiting room and looked around. By now I was starting to panic as thoughts of me being stuck in the station overnight consumed me. I turned around and suddenly I noticed a couple approaching me. It was Auguste Carvalho and his wife. What a relief!

Their home was divided into two sections. They lived in one half of the house and the other half was converted into a rooming house. The rooms were occupied by tailors who worked for Auguste. It felt good to have a long overdue bath and settle in my room. Auguste's wife prepared a special meal for me. After eating my first decent meal in several days I collapsed on my bed. It seemed like only a few minutes later when I heard Auguste saying, "Wake up! wake up! Carlit!"

"Wha....eh, I just went to sleep a few moments ago."

"You went to bed yesterday. You have been sleeping for almost fourteen hours!" Auguste exclaimed.

"Oh, I still feel very sleepy. What day is it?" I asked hoping that it was Sunday.

"It is Monday, you start work today."

The tailoring shop was in the center of Nakuru. It had two large windows with several mannequins dressed in the latest men's clothing. I could tell from the dust on the mannequins that they had not been changed for some time. At the entrance were two glass counters which contained a variety of buttons on display boards, swatches of different fabrics glued onto boards and reels of thread in a spectrum of colours. Behind the counters were posters of men in well-tailored suits and classy top hats. Auguste took me to the workshop at the back of the store. The tailors were all busy at work. In the centre, were two large cutting tables. Auguste greeted the tailors on his way to the cutting tables. Just before we reached the cutting table, Auguste told me that he was going to introduce me to Mr. Lalani, the owner of the store. Up until this moment, I was under the impression that Auguste owned the store. I suddenly felt uneasy. What if Mr. Lalani did not like me? Would he send me back? When we approached the table, Mr. Lalani, a tall slim man, stopped cutting fabric and looked up.

"Mr. Lalani, this is Carlos Dias, the tailor who did his apprenticeship in Panjim," Auguste said proudly.

"Mr. Carvalho tells me that you are a good tailor," Mr. Lalani said.

"People have been asking for a ladies' tailor. That is why I sent for you. I hope that you are ready to work hard."

"Yes., yes, I am Mr. Lalani," I said nervously.

I spent the morning looking through the stack of Lana Lobelle fashion books. The dresses and recommended fabrics were different from the ones I used to sew in Goa. I would sew mostly loose cotton, ankle-length dresses with Magyar sleeves. For special occasions and evening wear, I would trim the dresses with frills and bows. In contrast, the dresses in the Lana Lobelle books were made from fabrics such as taffeta, georgette, rayon and crêpe de chine. The dresses were shorter (just below the knees) and fitted with puffed sleeves.

I picked out about five different designs and asked Mr. Lalani for taffeta, georgette and crepe de chine. Unfortunately, he only had rayon fabric available in three different prints. I had to go through the pattern books a second time and choose different dresses suited to Rayon. For the next two days, I carefully marked the fabric based on the measurements of the mannequins and cut the dresses. On the third day, I sewed the dresses and finished the handwork. I placed them on the mannequins and showed them to Mr. Lalani. He was pleased and had them placed in the window.

It was not long before female clients started coming to the store. They were mostly British women who were haughty and intimidating. With my limited English, I felt rather inadequate to deal with them. Fortunately, Mr. Lalani had a good command of English and would intervene, when I had difficulty understanding the customers. I was very nervous with the first few dresses that I sewed but it was not long before I started getting the hang of what they wanted. As my confidence grew so did the number of clients.

The first year was very exciting for me. Although the weekends would get lonely, playing cards with the other tailors would fill the void of loneliness. Auguste and his wife were very kind to me and treated me as their son. It was strange that they slept in separate beds and did not spend much time together. I wondered whether it was the large age difference between them.

When the second year rolled around, I started getting very homesick. *Mai's* letters sounded more and more desperate about one ailment or another. I decided that it was time for me to go home. Mr. Lalani agreed to give me a long leave of three months and so I decided to make my travel plans for Goa. I was fortunate to get a booking on the ship that went directly to Marmagoa. I arrived in Goa on a beautiful, sunny day in January of 1941.

CHAPTER 9

I DID NOT FEEL any better after playing cards when I arrived home from the club at around 1:00 am. As usual, Basil had stayed up. She re-heated my supper and brought it to the table.

"Carlit, a lot of people came to offer their condolences," Basil said softly.

"What are condolences going to do anyway? *Mai* is gone."

"Carlit, they were only doing their duty,"

"What purpose does it serve?"

Basil did not say anything. She picked up my plate and took it to the kitchen sink. I washed, changed, and went to the bedroom. By the time I got into bed, Basil was snoring and in deep sleep. I lay awake, my mind sifting through the day's events and then settling on dear *Mai*. She was overjoyed when I had first come back from Kenya. Every time she saw me, she would hug me.

A month later, I started getting restless. I decided to go to Panjim and renew my passport. I was informed that I could not travel overseas since the second world war was in progress. East

Africa was in the thick of it all. The British and Germans were fighting for control over Kenya, Tanganyika, and Uganda. This was disappointing news for me. I had no idea when I would be able to get back to Kenya. Unbeknown to me, *Mai* had other plans for me. She decided that this was a good time for me to get married. News of an eligible bachelor who had worked in Africa spread rapidly through the grapevine. Marriage proposals were being entertained daily. I was never around when the prospective brides and their parents arrived. After several months of accepting proposals, *Mai* finally decided to end this process.

"Carlit, I have chosen a bride for you," *Mai* said seriously.

"*Mai*, I am not sure that I want to get married."

"You are of age, and you have a good job. It is time for you to start a family."

"I don't know if I will still have my job in Kenya after the war."

"Don't worry about that. Now is the best time for you to get married."

"Who have you chosen?"

"Her name is Basil, and she comes from a wealthy family that lives in Fatrade."

"What does she look like?"

"She is from a well-to-do family. You will meet her on your engagement day."

The rest of the conversation focused on Basil's family and wealth. Her father, Isidore Pires, had a respectable job with a large shipping company called P & O Lines." Their house was the only one in the village with a stone wall around it and they owned a lot of property. There were also *sudras*, the same caste as ours. Her mind was made up. I could not possibly think of going against her will. Now and again, I would envisage married life and wondered what it would be like. I would just have to take it in my stride. I was not going to compromise the things that I enjoyed doing.

A month later, a *ladin* was held at our house to celebrate my engagement. It was like a typical *ladin* with the exception that we placed rings on each other's fingers and all the guests applauded. Basil was not what I had envisaged. I thought that she would be fair, with a slim face like her mother. She must have taken up after both her father and mother. Her father had a striking black mustache, wore an imported black suit, and looked very official.

After the engagement, serious arrangements for the wedding were in progress. The date selected for this auspicious occasion was November 4, 1941. I was uncomfortable about getting married but there was not much I could do. Everything had been negotiated right down to the dowry of 5,000 rupees. Basil's father must be well off. I wondered if she had signed off her rights to the family property in lieu of the dowry. *Mai* took me to the goldsmith, Shamrao to have a wedding ring made. After taking the measurements of my finger he showed us the different choices of wedding bands. I was going to choose a simple one, assuming that it would be the least expensive. *Mai,* on the other hand, insisted that we go with a more elaborate design and would not settle for anything but the best.

Three weeks later I went to pick up the ring. Shamrao welcomed me to his shop and offered me a cup of tea. He proceeded to ask me about the political situation in Kenya. I told him that the British controlled the country the same way the Portuguese ruled Goa. We discussed the unfair treatment of Indigenous people by the Imperialists. Shamrao stated in confidence that he belonged to an underground group that was fighting for the liberation of Goa. At the end of our discussion, he told me that my ring wasn't ready. He was busy working on a newsletter to educate the Goans about Portuguese oppression. I admired Shamrao's commitment and determination to the cause for the liberation of Goa.

Mai asked me to sew part of Basil's trousseau and the wedding dress. Basil's father had purchased very expensive lace from Europe during his last voyage. He had come over with the lace and cautioned me not to waste any of it. Two weeks before the wedding, Basil had come with her mother to try on the wedding dress. She was extremely shy and did not say a word. Her mother came out of the bedroom where Basil had tried the dress. She announced that no alterations were necessary. The hem was pinned, and I was asked to complete the dress without any comments on whether they liked it.

It was time for me to get my wedding suit. I went to Alémao's Tailor Shop in Margao. He congratulated me on my upcoming marriage and asked me to choose a fabric. I picked black gabardine. Alémao agreed that it was a good choice. He took my measurements and told me to come for a fitting in two weeks.

On November 4th, 1941, I woke up early, thinking that I was the first one up. *Mai* was already busy cooking for people who might drop by to wish us well. I bathed and had my breakfast. Lawrence DeSouza, my best man walked into the house. He was dressed in a black suit and a bow tie.

"You look very smart Lawrence," *Mai* said excitedly.

"Thank you, today is your son's special day. You must be very happy," Lawrence replied.

"Yes, I am. Would you like to have some rice pancakes?"

"No, I already had my breakfast."

I got dressed and Lawrence helped me put on my bow tie and boutonniere. I walked into *Mai's* bedroom. She was dressed in the snow-white sari and had this glow about her. She looked at me and beamed. Suddenly, the look on her face changed from one of happiness to sadness. Her eyes welled up.

"Why are you sad?"

"*Baba*, I am not. I am happy for you. I just feel like I will be losing you."

"I will always look after you."

"I know, but once you get married, your wife will come first."

"*Mai*, you will always be an important part of my life."

"*Baba*, join your hands and bow your head."

"May God always be with you, my son. May you have a happy marriage and many children."

She hugged me and I felt the warmth of her small and loving body against mine.

A few minutes later, a black car appeared in front of the house. All the neighbours were out on their balconies watching excitedly as we entered the car. *Mai* was in her glory in the front seat, while Lawrence and I sat in the back. We arrived at the church at 8:30 am. It was partially full of guests from Navelim. *Mai* sat in the front pew, while Lawrence and I stood near the altar. Several minutes later, a few more guests trickled in. At about five minutes to nine, hoards of people came in. I guessed that they were from Fatrade. They had come in a bus that Basil's family had chartered. By now, the church was full of people dressed in their Sunday best. Suddenly, there was a hush in the air followed by silence. My heart raced in anticipation. I turned and looked at the entrance of the church and there she was, dressed in her glowing white gown. A piece of sheer linen was draped over her head almost symbolic of Our Lady. While she walked up the aisle with her father, her gold necklace glistened as it caught the rays of sunlight. Basil looked down while her father looked directly at the altar with an air of pride. He glanced at me from time to time, making me feel quite nervous.

After they reached the altar, Isidore left her and walked stiffly to the pew next to his wife. While we stood next to each other, I felt Basil trembling. For a moment I wondered what we were doing there. The next thing I remember was both of us walking down the aisle together and all the guests smiling. As we exited the church, we heard bursts of firecrackers and a group on the bandstand playing festive music.

The reception was in Fatrade at Basil's home. A large outdoor tent was set up and two bands were playing music. Isidore went up to the stage and raised the toast that seemed to go on forever. Isidore had only invited high caste and rich people to the wedding. This upset the poorer and low-caste villagers of Fatrade. The night before the wedding, they collected a whole lot of spiky pods and threw them at the guests from Navelim. This created quite a commotion at the wedding. Isidore and another well-built large man grabbed the troublemakers and took them to a nearby field. They shook them up and threatened to throw them in a deep abandoned well. I was happy when the reception was over. I could not wait to get back to my home in Navelim. When I met my friends the next day their arms were swollen from the allergic reaction to the spiky pods. I comforted them by saying that the people from Fatrade were crazy. While we joked around, one of my friends asked me how was my first night of married life. I was rather embarrassed but made out like it was an earth-shattering experience. The reality of it all was that we did nothing. Basil changed and went to sleep. I did not want to disturb her, so I slept next to her but was afraid to touch her. I did not know where to begin. Once again, I had to turn to my confidante Lawrence Santan – after all, he was married. He must have known what one did to get the ball rolling after marriage. Lawrence Santan briefly outlined how I should go about this. I listened to him intently making sure that I did not miss anything. A week later, I decided that it was time. I had a few drinks too many with my friends and came home around 10:00 p.m. *Mai* was already in bed. Basil sat with me while I had my supper. Instead of changing into my pyjamas, I undressed and kept my boxer shorts on. We both got into bed and fumbled around. Lawrence Santan's instructions were not working out. I decided to change my strategy and do things my way. We finally seemed to lock ourselves into the right position. There was no stopping me until I was finished. I felt good and Basil seemed to be relieved that it was over. We both slept soundly.

Basilia, Carlos and his mother

It was strange having Basil around the house. *Mai,* too, found it uncomfortable. She was used to being the lady of the house. I wondered how the two women in my life would get along. I decided to stay out of it. Strangely enough, it worked out well –

or so I thought. Basil was most comfortable in the kitchen. Cooking was her forte. *Mai,* on the other hand, preferred to lounge around, dress up and go shopping to Margao. Basil ended up taking charge of the kitchen.

A couple of months after the wedding, I received a letter from Auguste informing me that the war was almost over in Kenya and that it would be safe to return. I booked my ticket right away and left for Mombasa in March of 1942.

CHAPTER 10

LEAVING Goa this time around was easier than the last time. I did not have to concern myself with *Mai's* well-being since Basil would take care of her. Although they had their differences, *Mai* always seemed to get her way. They accompanied me to Marmagoa. I was delighted to find out that several other tailors that I knew would be travelling on the same ship – the SS Karanga. Mr. Joanes and other prominent Goan businessmen in Kenya had hired them. The Goan population in Kenya was growing. Some of them were even being hired as civil servants for the British Government because of their loyalty and honesty. They worked as clerks and considered themselves a class higher than tailors.

My journey on the ship from Marmagoa to Mombasa was relaxing and I looked forward to seeing Kenya again. I missed the crisp, cool air, the lush countryside, and the rolling wheat fields around Nakuru. The British settlers had developed wheat and dairy farming in the fertile grounds around Nakuru. Our daily routine on the ship included purchasing a bottle of scotch and congregating around my bunk. We would sit around my trunk, which was used as a makeshift table and play cards for hours on end. During this trip, I learned how to play a new and challenging game called *Sol*. Towards the end of the eight days on the ship, we became wise and would start with *Sol* while we still had our wits about us and ended with *truque* which did not tax our minds as much.

The eight days on the ship flew by and the party ended. I stayed in Mombasa for two days with Peter Fernandes and then took the train to Nairobi. I was pleased to see that some of the passengers that were on the ship were also on the train. They insisted that I stop in Nairobi for a few days and stay with them before heading off to Nakuru. Most of them were going to work for Mr. Joanes. I thought that it would be a good idea to meet this influential and successful businessman that I had heard so much about.

When we arrived in Nairobi, I paid a visit to Mr. Joanes' impressive store. He had thirty tailors working for him and three departments – Ladies, Gents, Hats and Accessories. The windows had several mannequins with a variety of clothes, hats, and accessories to match – some of which I had never seen before. Above the large entrance was a huge sign in green letters with red shading saying: "Joanes Brothers". I first heard of Mr. Joanes while I was doing my apprenticeship program in Panjim. He used to run a tailoring school in Panjim. I envied him and hoped that one day I would own a successful business like his.

I took the train to Nakuru after my brief stay in Nairobi. When we arrived at the Nakuru station, I was overcome with a warm feeling. The quaint station, the slender clock tower and the little restaurant brought back a flood of memories of when I first arrived in Kenya. Auguste Carvalho greeted me at the station. It was a pleasure seeing him again, but I couldn't help feeling sorry for him when he mentioned that his wife had left him and gone back to Goa. The poor fellow had to resort to hiring a Kenyan maid to cook and clean the house. Things were not the same without his wife around.

Mr. Lalani looked relieved when he saw me. He shook my hand vigorously and said, "Hey Carlit, a lot of customers have been asking about you."

"Oh really, but they knew I had gone to Goa on long leave."

"I am not talking about the existing ones. We had to turn down several new customers."

It made me feel important that there was a demand for my services. For the next several weeks I was working twelve-hour days and still could not keep up with the orders. The end of the war certainly created a boom in this great country. Every month, tailors, businessmen, clerks, and labourers were pouring into Kenya from India. White settlers from Britain were coming in droves to occupy and develop this rich agricultural land, especially in the cooler areas of the country. I rejoiced in being part of this era of growth and great prosperity.

The British had introduced one of their favourite and prestigious sports - horse racing into Kenya. The racecourse was in Nairobi since it was the capital. I heard some of the tailors talking about horse racing which piqued my interest since betting was part of this sport. There was a lot of talk about an upcoming race called the East African Grand National. My fellow workers talked with great excitement about their favourite horse and jockey. Most of them were planning to go to Nairobi for the race. I could not help but get drawn in with this enthusiasm and brouhaha. I was thrilled when one of my colleagues asked me to join them two weeks before the race. I asked my friends the names of horses and jockeys and about the betting process. I learned that the race was classified as a handicap when the horses were assigned specific weights based on their race records. Bookmaking is the betting process used in the race in which speculators offer odds against each horse and accept bets against their predictions. Over the two weeks, I had learned quite a bit about horse racing and was now anxiously looking forward to the race.

The day before the race, five of us took the train bound for Nairobi. All we did was discuss the participants of the race. Names such as Black Night, Ambush, Early Mist and Battleship were flying around. I did not know enough about the past race records to choose a contender. When an argument broke out amongst my friends, I suggested that they calm down, and remember that it was only a race. They assured me that I would see the race in a different light once I started betting in earnest.

We arrived in Nairobi, and I suddenly realized that I had no place to stay for the night. One of my friends was going to stay with Mr. Joanes and he invited me to tag along. I agreed since I had met Mr. Joanes and did not think that he would mind.

"Carlit, welcome. Come in," Mr. Joanes said with a smile.

"Hello, Mr. Joanes. How are you?"

"I am fine. Why have you come to Nairobi?"

"To see the East African Grand National."

"The what?" he asked.

"It is the big horse race. Will you be joining us?

"No. No, gambling goes against my religious beliefs. Besides, you should not be squandering your money like that. You are a married man," he said sternly.

"*Arrh*, it is just for fun, we are betting only a few shillings," I said trying to soften him.

"That is how the devil tempts you and then you cannot stop."

I felt rather uncomfortable. Mr. Joanes must have been a

very strict and religious person. I would have to be cautious about what I say to him in the future.

Early next morning, Mr. Joanes' wife gave us some breakfast and after that, we went to the racetrack. We decided to walk since it was only about two miles away from the Joanes residence. As we approached the racetrack I noticed several flags, the largest being the Union Jack. The race track itself was impressive. It was covered with green turf meticulously maintained and bordered by freshly painted white railings forming an oval-shaped center area. A huge crowd had gathered, and the stands were packed. We managed to squeeze our way in and luckily found a spot near the railings giving us a clear view of the racetrack. I turned back to witness the British – mostly men, seated in the sheltered area. They were well dressed, comfortably seated and sipped drinks leisurely, oblivious to the people below. They had the privilege of separate betting wickets. We had to go to the wickets at the lower section, where we placed our bets. I chose Black Night because the name sounded mysterious without any knowledge of his past track record.

The horses were saddled. The jockeys mounted them in the paddock. Anticipation filled the air. The horses were restless while their jockeys tried to restrain them. The gunshot startled me. The horses bolted. They moved swiftly on the turf. My heart started racing. I felt a rush of adrenaline. The jockeys were whipping the horses with a vengeance. For a moment I pitied the poor horses. They were pushed beyond their limits at neck-breaking speeds. I was engulfed by the enthusiasm of the spectators. Unwittingly I started cheering too. The horses were a blur. Names echoed over the loudspeaker. My heart skipped a beat, every time I heard Black Knight's name. The race had ended. I was still reeling from its effects. All my friends looked disappointed. One of them told me that Black Knight had won.

Initially, I was in a state of shock. I had won fifty shillings by betting one. I was overcome with joy. After the game, we headed for the closest bar. My throat was parched from the excitement. I ordered drinks for my friends to celebrate. We guzzled them within minutes. I felt like I was floating on air.

I did not mention anything to Mr. Joanes, lest he ask me to donate my winnings to some worthy cause or the church. I had to suppress my excitement and avoided talking about the race. If only he could have experienced the pleasure of winning at the race tracks, he would see it differently. After supper, he tried to convince me to stay in Nairobi and work for him. As tempting as the offer was, I politely refused, making up some lame excuse. I could not bear to work under someone who was so rigid and strict. The following morning, we took the train back to Nakuru.

I enjoyed working for Mr. Lalani, who was paying me a good salary. The orders were getting more and more interesting, and time seemed to be flying by. Although Basil would write to me regularly, I had not received a letter from her in over two months. When her letter finally arrived, I quickly opened it. She started with the standard opening of blessings and wishes of good health which was a paragraph long. In her second paragraph, she mentioned that she had given birth to a baby girl. I had hoped that my firstborn would be a boy, but nevertheless, I was happy to be a father. *Mai* had chosen the name – it was Luiza, which was my grandmother's name. It gave me a warm and joyful feeling. Grandma was always kind and loving to me. When I was a little boy, she would give me *dosh* – which was like fudge made from coconut. If she did not have anything sweet to offer me, she would secretly give me a scoop of sugar. When I was a little older, I would steal sugar from the pantry and eat it when I craved something sweet. *Mai* could never figure out why we were always running out of sugar.

Auguste Carvalho suggested that I have a *ladin* to celebrate the birth of my daughter. He kindly offered his house. After a week of asking around I managed to find someone who played the violin. I invited some of the tailors that worked for Auguste to the *Ladin*. I purchased some beer and a bottle of whiskey, and I asked the maid to cook chickpeas and cut coconut cubes. One of the tailor's wives took the lead in saying the prayers and afterwards, the violinist started playing. As they sang the concluding song wishing Luiza good health and a long life I was beaming with pride. August the 9th would always be a special day for me.

Over the next three years, Basil would write to me regularly. In each letter, she would update me on Luiza's progress. From what she described, Luiza was always on the move and curious about everything. She would not sit still for a moment, especially in church. Basil would go looking for her and find her in various places. Once she even went up to the pulpit and tried to imitate the priest giving a sermon. She had a little cat as her pet that she carried around like her purse. It was time for me to go back to Goa. I was yearning to see *Mai*, Basil and most of all, my daughter – she was going to be three years old in a few days. I went to Nairobi to book my ticket to Goa. To my disappointment, no ships were available since it was the end of the war. All the ships were fully booked transporting the soldiers from around the world back to their home country. As a result, I had to wait for a year before I could go back to India.

One morning, a British customer, Mrs. Ann Bumpass, asked if she could discuss an important matter with me. She offered to meet me at The Rift Valley Sports Club. I agreed, but I was nervous about the meeting. The club was very posh. I did not think that I would be welcome. I kept wondering what she wanted to talk about. As a result, I found it hard to concentrate on my work.

At 5:00 pm I left the store and walked hurriedly towards the club. I arrived at the gates of the club at 5:20 pm, ten minutes before our scheduled meeting time. I did not dare go into the club by myself. While waiting for Mrs. Bumpass, I peered through the gates and saw the cricket field, which was well-trimmed green grass, with a brown strip at the center. A patio restaurant overlooked the cricket pitch. Mrs. Bumpass arrived at precisely 5:30 pm. We shook hands and walked up to the clubhouse. At the entrance was the doorman, dressed in white with matching gloves and a hat. He looked at me and said,

"You are not allowed in this club."

"Why not, may I ask? This gentleman and I have a business meeting," Mrs. Bumpass said.

"This clubhouse is only for whites," the doorman replied sternly.

I could feel the blood rushing up to my head and the blood vessels in my temples dilate. I opened my mouth to speak my mind, but nothing came out. All I could do was stare.

"In that case, we will go elsewhere, to someplace more pleasant," Mrs. Bumpass said quickly to avert any trouble.

She motioned me to follow her. I swore under my breath. I turned around and strode off. We entered the car, and she ordered the chauffeur to take us to the Nakuru Coffee House. The reception here was more pleasant than the last one. We were shown to our table by the waiter who took our order for two coffees.

"Well, Mr. Dias, I have been your customer for three years and I like your work very much."

"You do? Err... I am glad."

I was taken by surprise. She had always been very fussy and not an easy person to please. I was still trying to get over the unexpected compliment when she said, "I have a business proposition for you."

"Business ...business proposition? What do you mean?"

"My sister and I would like to set up a tailoring business in Kampala and we need your help. Are you interested?"

I could not believe this and could hardly contain my excitement.

"You do not like the offer? We will pay your train fare to Kampala and a salary of 700 shillings a month."

In my mind, I said yes, a hundred times, but all I could do was nod my head. Her proposal left me speechless.

"I take that to mean yes," Mrs. Bumpass said tilting her head slightly.

I could hardly sleep that night thinking about how to break the news to Mr. Lalani. I am sure that he would be upset. I debated when I should inform him and finally decided to let him know as soon as possible. The next day I told Mr. Lalani about the offer and that I was going to resign. He was very disappointed, but he could not match the offer. It would mean doubling my current salary.

I was excited about the prospect of moving to Kampala and setting up a new business. Mrs. Bumpass and I met several times to discuss plans for the business. At our last meeting, she gave me my entry papers for Uganda. A month later, I took the train to Kampala. Although the city was smaller than Nairobi, it had a lot of character. It was surrounded by seven hills and was a very verdant city. The streets were wide and clean flanked with several multi-story buildings. Mrs. Bumpass had already found a location for the business on Market Street. It had two display windows, a front section, and a large sewing room in the back.

We spent several weeks buying sewing machines and supplies for the shop.

After a couple of months, we were all set up and ready for business. The first week was quiet. I took advantage of this time by making sample dresses, blouses, and skirts to dress the mannequins for the windows. I had the liberty to be as creative as I wanted, something I thoroughly enjoyed. Mrs. Bumpass and her sister started spreading the word to their circle of friends and associates about the business. By the end of the first month, we had twenty customers of which five became regulars. We hired a native Ugandan lady to help with the handwork. The following month, we hired a junior Goan tailor whom I trained. As promised, Mrs. Bumpass paid me well and I was content, however, I yearned to go back to Goa. After six months I asked Mrs. Bumpass if I could take a short leave. She was not too happy about me leaving so soon after the start-up but sympathized because I had not seen my daughter yet. She half-heartedly agreed and so I departed for Goa.

CHAPTER 11

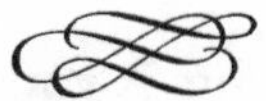

Although I spent only eight days at sea it seemed like a month. My buddies who had travelled with me the last time were still in Kenya and so I hardly knew any of the passengers. The entertainment on the ship was minimal, so I busied myself reading old newspapers and magazines that I had brought from Kenya. I focused mostly on the sports section of the newspaper. This was a good opportunity for me to improve my English and at the same time learn more about horse racing. I had difficulty capturing the gist of some paragraphs because of my limited vocabulary. I could not ask anyone on the ship, since they barely spoke English, except for the officers and the captain who were unapproachable. Over the eight days, I acquired a warehouse of knowledge on horse racing and looked forward to the next race. As I delved more into my reading, the journey on the ship seemed to go faster. I was happy when we finally docked at Marmagoa.

I took the dreadful *caminho* that was packed with passengers to Navelim. When I arrived home, Basil was sitting on the balcony with *Mai* and Luiza was playing with the neighbours' children in the sandy yard in front of the house. *Mai* came running up and hugged me and cried out, "*Baba*! *Baba*!" Basil came up to me with a big smile and asked me how I was. We looked at each other feeling rather awkward and then Basil called out to Luiza, who suddenly stopped playing and looked up at me.

Mai spoke to her, "*Baie*, this is your father, give him a hug."

Luiza looked up coyly, jumped up and wrapped her hands around my legs. I was filled with joy and tried desperately to suppress tears that were welling up. I pulled out my handkerchief and dabbed the tears. I loosened her hands and got down on my knees to get a good look at her. She had sparkling brown eyes, shocking black hair in curls and the most beautiful complexion. I could not believe the similarity between her and my grandmother. I hugged her as she stood with her arms hanging limply in my fold. I was a stranger to her. She must have felt quite awkward.

I was happy to be home with *Mai*, Luiza and Basil. Every morning *Mai* would buy fresh fish from the Margao market which Basil cooked dutifully. I would hold Luiza in my arms and sing to her. In the beginning, she would look confused, and then as she recognized the song she would smile. Her favourite song was "Daddy Catching Butterflies." Her face would light up every time I sang this song to her. I enjoyed seeing the look on her face whenever I gave her candy. Her beautiful brown eyes would twinkle as she ate the candy. I suppose that she acquired her sweet tooth from me.

After spending two weeks with my family, I started getting bored. I decided to get together with my drinking friends. It was different – most had gone to Bombay or overseas. Nevertheless, I enjoyed socializing with those who were still around while making new friends. Most of them envied people like me and others who were working overseas. I could identify with them because I used to feel like them when I felt trapped living in Goa. It was difficult to make ends meet because of the limited job opportunities in Goa. The only way out was to go overseas or work for a shipping company.

I decided to visit my old friend Shamrao. We spent most of the day talking about the political situation in East Africa and Goa. I was astonished to find out how much he knew about the current political situation in East Africa. He informed me that he read about this in the newspaper clippings that I had sent to him while I was in Kenya. He could not fathom how the white settlers managed to displace the black majority, causing them to become squatters on their land. The whites had confiscated the land from the Africans and set up plantations, where they were forced to work. Fortunately, an organization called the Kenya African Union was established to fight for the rights of the unemployed and landless blacks. Although the Portuguese had not done the same thing in Goa, they had taken away all the democratic and civil rights from the Goans, leaving them with little or no say in the political future of Goa. They had also imposed a tax on money remitted by Goans in Bombay to their relatives in Goa. These Goans had made great sacrifices by leaving their families behind to earn a few rupees in Bombay. Taxing their meagre earnings was a grave injustice. Shamrao felt very strongly that it was time for a demonstration. The Portuguese had to be shown that the Goans were strong and progressive and would not stand by and let them run Goa. Shamrao had already rounded up a lot of support by distributing leaflets written in Marathi about the injustices of Portuguese rule. Some Goans from the North were also interested in taking part in the demonstration. I was impressed with his commitment and agreed to help him with the arrangements. We would meet regularly and make plans for the big day - March 1st, 1946.

One day when I was leaving for my meeting with Shamrao, *Mai* called out to me.

"Carlit, where have you been going every day?"

"To play cards with my friends."

"I talked to Jacinth recently and he says that he hasn't seen you for a while."

"Jacinth does not play cards with us anymore."

"He told me that you have been spending a lot of time with Shamrao."

"Oh! Jacinth is a liar. I have seen Shamrao once."

"I don't think that you should associate with Shamrao. He is being watched by the Portuguese officials."

From then on, I was very careful when I met with Shamrao. I would always meet my friends at the bar and later in the evenings tell them that I was heading home. I would go to Shamrao's instead.

To make a statement, we decided to wear special khaki boat-shaped caps that tapered at either end, which was characteristic of the Indian people. White sashes signifying peace would hang from the shoulders to the hips. Shamrao managed to get hold of two old sewing machines. I worked together with another tailor that Shamrao had recruited sewing these special caps and the sashes well into the night.

As time went on, I realized that the demonstration was much grander than Shamrao's description. Dr. Menezes, the Goan MP in the Portuguese parliament was leading the efforts of this demonstration. This was a rare occasion where Goan Catholics joined hands with Goan Hindus in their struggle for freedom. Mr. Lawande, a Hindu freedom fighter, was almost captured by the Portuguese police in a Goan village in Tiswadi. A sympathetic Christian family helped him escape by disguising him as a priest. Dr. Fanchu Loyola, a Goan MP in Portugal who had joined the ranks of freedom fighters, was surrounded in his mansion in Varca by the Portuguese police. He managed to escape by dressing as a labourer and left by the back door, surrounded by Hindu labourers. I thought that Dr. Menezes was taking a major risk. To add fuel to the fire, he had arranged to bring in Dr. Lhoia, a Goan activist exiled in Bombay to participate in this demonstration. This was getting much bigger than I anticipated. I was afraid that *Mai* would be upset when she found out that I had participated in the demonstration. On the other hand, Basil was quite indifferent and never questioned me about my whereabouts. She spent most of her time cooking in the kitchen, looking after Luiza and talking to the neighbours on their balconies.

At 6:00 am, all the demonstrators met secretly at the stadium just outside Margao. We were over five hundred and it took over an hour to get everyone lined up. Dr. Lhoia and Dr. Menezes led the parade. Mr. Lawande and Shamrao were next in line. We left the stadium at 7:00 am and marched towards Margao. By 7:30 am we had entered the city and attempted to block the main street. The *caminhos*, cars, bull carts and bicycles were at a standstill. Many people came to watch the demonstration and cheered. This was a peaceful march. We only waved our placards, "Freedom for Goans". We walked to the *Camara*, where the Portuguese Government offices were and stayed there for a while. Some officers peered out of their windows. The policemen came out and formed a blockade at the entrance of the building. It was a wasted effort since we had no intention of entering the building. We wanted to make a statement. After spending half an hour in the sweltering heat, we decided to march back to the stadium.

From the stadium, Shamrao and I walked to Navelim. We both felt satisfied that the demonstration was a success as no one was hurt. I barely got to the entrance of the house when *Mai* came running out with Basil following closely behind her. She looked pale and worried.

"*Baba*, are you all right? I heard that you were at the demonstration."

"Oh! No fear, I am fine."

"Carlit, we were worried about you," Basil said.

"Worried? About what?

"The Portuguese police could have hurt you," *Mai* said in a distraught voice.

"It was a peaceful demonstration, and nobody got hurt."

"*Baba*, you should not get involved in politics. It can be very dangerous."

"*Mai*, you worry for no reason."

"You are my only son and I do not want to lose you."

I felt a tinge of guilt for getting *Mai* worried. I wondered if I should stop getting involved with this movement for freedom. I could not stand the injustices of Portuguese rule. I hoped that we would get our freedom soon. It was not to be. I heard that Dr. Menezes was arrested by the Portuguese officials, but later released since they had no case against him. Dr. Fanchu Loyola was charged with treason and imprisoned in Portugal.

A few days after the demonstration, I received a letter from Mrs. Bumpass, urging me to come back to Uganda. The junior tailor was finding it very difficult to cope with the customers and we were starting to lose business. I booked my ticket and set sail for Mombasa barely two months after arriving in Goa.

CHAPTER 12

ALL I COULD THINK of while I was on the ship headed for Mombasa was Luiza. I wished I had spent more time with her. She was full of life, always smiling and enjoying the attention. Basil would sew her pretty dresses and she would strut around the house with her little cat. The poor cat must have had a sore neck from being carried around like a bag. I missed her terribly. I spent most of my time reading old newspapers once again. The statistics and results of previous races would whet my appetite for horse racing. By now, I knew the names of the horses, the jockeys, all their race times and the weights assigned for the handicap races.

Upon arriving in Mombasa, I stayed overnight and then took the train to Kampala. I was tempted to spend a day in Nairobi just in case a race was scheduled. However, I knew that Mrs. Bumpass anxiously awaited my arrival in Kampala. The scenery this time around was not as interesting. However, it was still quite fascinating to see the beautiful zebras, the elegant giraffes, and the ferocious lions.

"Carlos, I am so glad to see you. I hope that you are well," Mrs. Bumpass said.

"I am fine, just a little tired from the long journey."

"It must have been quite hard on you. Unfortunately, I cannot let you take any days off to rest. You have a lot of catching up to do at the shop."

"That's okay, I will manage."

I found it extremely difficult to get back to the routine of work. My hands would throb from all the cutting and the drone of the sewing machine was irritating me. I was working fourteen-hour days trying to catch up with the backlog. After one month of this, I finally told Mrs. Bumpass that I needed a weekend off. She reluctantly agreed.

On Friday afternoon, I went to the train station and booked my ticket for Nairobi. I arrived early the next morning and went to my friend, Custodio's house. To my delight, there was a horse race that afternoon. I rushed to buy the newspaper that contained details of the race. It was at 2:00 pm at the main racecourse in Pangani. I needed a quiet place to read the paper, so I headed for the nearest coffee shop. I settled down and ordered coffee and a bun. I flipped through the paper until I came across the Kenyan Grand National. It was a handicap race with twelve top horses and jockeys participating. I studied their weights and track records. The sports editor listed his picks for the race. I chose Early Mist who was the least likely to win according to the editor. I forced myself to read the rest of the newspaper to improve my English. This was a tedious exercise, but I continued since I had three hours to kill before the race. After having a small lunch that consisted of a sandwich and beer, I decided to walk to the racecourse. As I approached the gate, I noticed Auguste Carvalho and the other tailors from Nakuru.

"*Arrh*, Carlit, what are you doing in Nairobi?" Auguste asked.

"I came here to rest only to find out that there was a race. I guess that I was lucky."

"Which horse did you pick?" Auguste inquired.

"Early Mist," I replied.

"Early Mist, why Early Mist? She won't win," Auguste said shaking his head.

"One never knows. We will see. Which one are you betting on?"

"Black Knight, he is sure to win," Auguste said with confidence.

"We better go in and pick our places so that we can get a good view," I said anxiously.

The sound of the trumpets signalled that the race was about to begin. My heartbeat quickened and I craned my neck to get a perfect view. My eyes were fixed on the starting line. The gun was fired. The horses were off. There was a hush all over the stands. Two minutes into the race, Black Knight fell. I looked at Auguste who looked dejected. I felt bad for him. I turned and continued to concentrate on the race. They tensed their muscles while continuously lunging forward with the jockeys crouched low. Early Mist was leading the pack. I tried to contain my excitement and not look at Auguste. Thirty seconds before the end of the race Ambush took over Early Mist and won the race. I was pleased that I had won twenty shillings by betting two.

When I arrived in Kampala, there was a letter from Basil. I was surprised to receive a letter so soon. I glanced through the first paragraph, then the second where she inquired about my well-being. I could not wait to get to the main part of this letter. Did she say pregnant? Oh, my, I could not believe this! I would be blessed with another child. This time I would go back as soon as the child was born. That night I prayed that it would be a boy. As much as I loved Luiza, I wanted a son.

On my first day back at the shop, Mrs. Bumpass greeted me with a formal hello and asked if she could speak to me in private. I agreed, and so we went to the Uganda Coffee House.

"How was your weekend in Nairobi?"

"It was restful."

"Mr. Dias, I am having problems with my sister concerning the business."

"What is the problem if I may ask?"

"She is no longer interested and does not contribute to the business."

"You are right. I hardly see her at the shop." I acknowledged.

"We do not see eye to eye."

"So, what are you going to do?"

"We have decided to sell the merchandise and close the store."

I was dumbfounded. I could hardly believe this. How could she do this to me?

"What am I going to do? I have a family to support." I said in despair.

"Mr. Dias you don't have to worry, we will pay you a lump sum of two thousand shillings."

"Thank you, Mrs. Bumpass. You have been very kind to me." I said almost choking.

I could not sleep worrying about what was going to happen if I didn't find a job soon. Going back to Goa would be a huge blow to my ego. It would be impossible to find any work and I did not want to look for employment in Bombay. Thoughts of not being able to support my family and *Mai* were of great concern to me. I decided to pray and let it go. Suddenly, I was overcome with a sense of calm and was able to fall asleep.

The next day, I went to the shop and tried hard to focus on my work. About an hour later, one of our regular customers, Mrs. Hues walked into the workshop at the back. I was quite surprised since she usually entered from the front of the store as all the customers did.

"Mr. Dias, I hear that Mrs. Bumpass is closing the store. Is that true?"

"Yes, I am afraid so."

"What are you going to do?"

"I don't know."

"Where am I going to get my dresses made? There aren't any good tailoring shops in town." Mrs. Hues left looking downhearted. Although she made me feel needed, I felt hopeless.

Mrs. Bumpass and I spent several weeks winding down the business. We stopped accepting new customers and I tried to complete those orders at hand. We took an inventory of our stock of sewing machines, irons, lamps, rolls of assorted fabrics, numerous spools of thread, zippers, machine oil, buttons, sewing needles, bias binding, lace, rickrack, interfacing, ribbon, cord and five large boxes of remnants. As the days progressed, I couldn't help but feel sad about closing this business.

I visited the tailoring shops in town to solicit work without any luck. After weeks of searching, I was at my lowest point, when Mrs. Hues walked into the store. She had picked up her dress one week ago after making me alter it twice. I hoped that it was not for another alteration.

"Mr. Dias, I have an idea," she said with a big smile.

"An idea? Is it about altering your dress?"

"Oh, no. The dress fits me perfectly. Everyone at the cocktail party was complimenting me."

"So, what is this idea?"

"I have decided to offer you a job as a chief tailor in my own business," Mrs. Hues said.

"Thank you, thank you!"

"As long as I am in Uganda, you will have a job, Mr. Dias. We will meet soon to discuss the details of our arrangement. Have a good day."

"You too, Mrs. Hues."

After liquidating the stock and closing Mrs. Bumpass' shop, I began to order fabric and other materials for the new store. Mrs. Hues played an active role in setting up the business. She appropriately named the shop "Hues Fashions". There were times when she tried to micromanage me. I hoped that she would let me work more independently. As time went on, she gave me more autonomy and began to trust my judgment.

The business was flourishing. Almost all the customers from the old shop became patrons of Hues Fashions. We had to hire two young tailors and three Ugandans to do the handwork and simple sewing tasks. As a chief tailor, I was responsible for cutting and sewing evening gowns. Mrs. Hues paid me an excellent salary of 900 shillings. I needed only 200 shillings for room and board. I would send 200 shillings home to *Mai* and Basil, and I could spend the remaining 500 shillings on whatever I pleased. I would go to Nairobi at least once a month to bet 200 to 300 shillings on the horse races. My friends would advise me to save some money for a rainy day. As long as I was sending some money home, I was enjoying life there wasn't any need to save any money. Saving is for misers and those who do not know how to live life.

Soon after coming back from my last visit to Nairobi, I received a letter from Basil. She had given birth to a baby girl. They named her Matilda, after one of our neighbours, who was a good friend of Basil's and was from a well-to-do family. All those who had come to see baby Matilda would make the same comment: “She is so beautiful that she will not even need a dowry to get married.” As happy as I was to hear the news, I was disappointed that my second child was not a boy. I know that *Mai* felt the same way since I was an only child. A son would be important to carry on the Dias family name.

CHAPTER 13

NOW THAT I was well settled financially, I decided to bring Basil and my two daughters to Uganda. I seized the opportunity to go to the Internal Affairs Office during a quiet time at the shop. I was fortunate that the office had recently been relocated from Entebbe to Kampala – a sign that Kampala was gaining importance as a town. There was talk that it was soon to be named the capital of Uganda. When I entered the Internal Affairs Office, I saw five long queues of mostly Asian people. Next to the five wickets, was a door with a sign that read "British Subjects Only". There was no queue.

"Hello, I am planning to bring my family from India, where should I stand?" I asked one of the Asians standing in the queue.

He did not reply but pointed to the first queue. I stood in the line where the sign above the wicket read "Entry Permits". Everything was very orderly, single file queues and clear instructions were posted on the notice boards. The British certainly had a sense of order and discipline. I kept looking at the large clock and I could have sworn that the arms of the clock were not moving. After two hours, I was finally face-to-face with a British officer.

"How can I be of assistance?" the officer asked, sternly.

"I want to bring my wife and children from Goa, I mean India."

"Are you legally married to her?"

I was dumbfounded by that strange question.

"Mister, I asked you a question."

"Eh... yes, yes, of course."

"You will have to fill this "T" form, adjoin your marriage certificate and your legitimate children's birth certificates."

I left feeling dejected because I was informed that the process could take over a year. Matilda will be almost four years by the time they come to Uganda.

That evening, I wrote a letter to Basil telling her to apply for her passport as soon as possible. I suggested that she speak to Dumpidade to help her with the application. He was an old friend of mine, who was well-connected with government officials. I also asked her to get our original marriage certificate and birth certificates for Luiza and Matilda. I thought about speaking to Mrs. Hues. She probably knew some government official who could help speed up the process. I didn't know if she would be willing to assist me regarding this matter. The last time she checked the books she claimed that the cash flow was not in keeping with her expectations. After that visit, she would ask me for a count of orders and about the quantity of materials like thread, buttons and elastic that were used. Although it bothered me, I convinced myself that she was only trying to manage her business. I finally picked up the courage to speak to her.

"Mrs. Hues, I would like to bring my family to Uganda."

"That is lovely, you must be quite anxious."

"Oh, yes but I need your help."

"My help? What can I do?"

"You must know someone in the government."

"Well...I know a few people who are employed by the government."

"Can you speak to them?"

"I don't think so. That would be unethical."

"Please, Mrs. Hues."

"No, Mr. Dias. That would not be right. You must follow the rules and the process like everyone else."

It was very disheartening that Mrs. Hues refused to help. How could she be so uncaring after all I had done for her? I was the main reason for the success of her business.

After about two months, I received a registered letter from Basil. I was pleased that she managed to get all the certificates and complete her passport application. She mentioned that Luiza and Matilda were both well, but that *Mai* had been under the weather. I gathered that she was not happy about Basil and the children moving to Uganda. I wished that I could bring *Mai* also but that was out of the question. I knew that she would not want to leave Goa. Furthermore, I didn't think that the British government would allow her to enter the country. They were only interested in giving entry permits to those people who could contribute to the Ugandan economy.

Now that I had the certificates, I filled out the "T" form and handed it to the Internal Affairs Office. The officer checked the application and the certificates. He informed me that everything was in order and that I would receive the entry permit in six months. The first officer lied to me. I was elated to know that I would see my family before the end of the year.

I had to find living quarters for my family - something that was in town and close to the shop. In the evenings, I would go flat-hunting. After two months of searching, I decided to look elsewhere. Shimoni, a suburb in the east, seemed like a good neighbourhood and it was reasonably close to the center of town. There was a lot of open green space, a sports club, the National Theatre and even a few shops on De Winton Road. A large greengrocer owned by Mr. Flores, a liquor store called "Wines & Spirits" and several other nondescript shops. On the second storey were flats, so I decided to ask Mr. Flores if he knew of any vacancies. He informed me that all the flats were occupied and that I should try the new flats on Clement Hill Road.

The following week, I visited the flats on Clement Hill Road. After a forty-five-minute walk, I arrived at my destination, perspiring from the afternoon sun. A nice cool lager would do me fine, but there was no bar in sight, only a large field across the road. There were only three single-story buildings on the street. The first one had a large compound in the center surrounded by four flats. I could smell the aroma of fried fish as I approached the flat that was occupied. A curvaceous woman with a curious look on her face appeared at the doorway. I noticed that she was well-endowed.

"Are you Goan?" she inquired with a smile.

"Yes, I am, and you?"

"I am from Bardez and so is my husband," she replied with great pride.

They must be Brahmins, I thought to myself.

"I am from Navelim, which is in Salcette."

"Oh, Salcette," she said in disdain.

"I am in a hurry, I just needed to know if there are any flats available."

She stopped to think. She opened her mouth to say something but hesitated. I was on the verge of saying something unpleasant when she replied, "Yes, there is a two-bedroom flat available, a young family just moved out two weeks ago."

"Who is the owner?"

"It is Mr. D.L. Patel"

"The one who owns D.L. Patel Press?"

"Yes, that's him."

"Thank you, Mrs...."

"It is Mrs. Theo DeSouza. Please come in and have a cup of tea."

"No, it is all right, I would like to secure the flat as soon as possible."

Goan hospitality always surpassed the class system that was deeply entrenched in the people of Goa. As much as I did not want to associate with her, I needed her help, so I tried to be amicable.

I walked to D.L. Patel Press, a large and well-known stationary store in Kampala. The pleasant smell of ink and paper brought back memories of when I first went to school. I met the owner who informed me that the rent was 100 shillings a month and that he required a deposit of 500 shillings. I agreed to give him the money by the end of the week when I got paid. I was relieved that I had found a decent place for my family – it was one thing less that I had to worry about.

At the shop, Mrs. Hues would come in daily, check the sales and watch me like a hawk. She would question me at length about fabric purchases and other supplies. This was getting on my nerves. There were times when I felt like leaving this all behind and going back to Goa, but I knew that was not a practical option. I would lie awake at night thinking of how I could deal with this difficult situation. I began to despise going to the shop. I could not wait to go to the club to cool off with a scotch and settle down to a game of cards.

One morning, as I was walking to work, it suddenly occurred to me that I had sufficient experience to open my own shop. I had successfully set up and operated two shops. Most of the customers from Hues Fashions would come to my new shop. I would not have to work for her anymore, and all the profits from the business would be mine.

I spent several months scouring the streets looking for a shop to rent. All I could find was a hand full of small shops, at exorbitant rents and goodwill. I learnt that goodwill was the value of trade and reputation that a business built over time. Even though it made good business sense to set up on Kampala Road, I couldn't possibly afford it. I happened to meet an acquaintance at Jaffery's bar one afternoon. We got talking and I mentioned that I was looking for a shop to rent. Coincidentally, his brother had a shop to let on Market Street. After negotiating with him for several hours, I managed to secure the place the following day. Although Market Street was just south of Kampala Road, it was in the center of town, so I agreed to pay a goodwill of 6,000 shillings – my entire savings.

It took me over two weeks to get the courage to inform Mrs. Hues that I was leaving. The look on her face was one of shock, disappointment, and sheer haughtiness.

"This is an extremely ungrateful thing to do," she said vehemently.

I wanted very much to explain to her that I was grateful for all that she did for me, but that I could not continue working under her. It was a stifling and unpleasant experience for me. Furthermore, I felt that she did not trust me. I apologized to her, but she was not very receptive. She realized that it would be difficult for her to find another reliable tailor, so she decided to close the shop. I was relieved by her decision since I did not have to worry about finding new customers.

Setting up my shop was much easier for me since Mrs. Hues agreed to sell her inventory, sewing machines and mannequins to me. I guess that she also benefited from this arrangement since she did not have to liquidate it herself. After all these years, it was liberating to own my business. Most of my workers agreed to migrate to my shop. I decided to name my shop "Luiza Gowns", after my first daughter. I painstakingly painted the new sign in black with red shading in an eye-catching script. I hired a few locals to clean up the dusty old shop and paint it pastel blue, which was a pleasant contrast to the original green paint. I was forced to delay the opening of my shop by one month because Mrs. Hues wanted me to complete all the orders before I left. Although I was anxious about opening my shop, I felt that I owed it to Mrs. Hues to help wind down her business appropriately. I did not want to part on bad terms.

On August 9th, 1949 – my daughter's birthday, Luiza Gowns opened its doors to the public. It was a day of great significance, and I was beaming with joy. Not only did the old customers from Hues Fashions patronize my business, but I started getting new and more prestigious customers. I had to hire another tailor and two more assistants. We were six employees in total. I also hired a bookkeeper; since that was something I detested the most about business. I wrote to Basil telling her about the new store and that I had received her entry permit. A couple of weeks later, she wrote back saying that they expected to arrive in two months if everything went as planned.

I realized that I had hardly any furniture for my home. Most of my savings were spent on setting up my shop. I ended up buying mostly second-hand furniture from the thrift shop on Salisbury Road. Discretion was of utmost importance since I didn't want my Goan neighbours to know. In their minds, this would only reaffirm that we were of a lower class. I decided to move the furniture into the flat late at night when the neighbours were asleep.

On October 20th, I received a telegram confirming my family's expected arrival on November 4th. I went to the train station one hour before their arrival time, only to find out that the train had been delayed for another six hours. Instead of waiting, I went to the club where I played cards. After a few hours, I looked at my watch, only to find out that it was an hour later than the scheduled arrival time. I quickly left the club and took a taxi to the train station. When I arrived, I saw Basil with two little girls sitting on their suitcases on the platform, looking lost and exhausted. I hurriedly walked up to them.

"Carlit, Carlit, what happened? We have been waiting here for over an hour," Basil said and burst out crying.

"Basil, I was at the club. I did not realize what time it was."

Both Luiza and Matilda were hanging onto Basil's skirt and looked up at me in a shy manner. Luiza then came up and hugged me. It felt good to see her after four years. She had grown almost a foot. Matilda hung on coyly to Basil.

"Matti *bai*, this is your father."

She left Basil and jumped into my arms and hugged me so tightly that I thought that I was going to choke. I fought back tears of joy. My little Matilda had waltzed into my life. I knew from then on, my life would never be the same. I took them to our new flat in Shimoni where the three of them went to bed soon after dinner. Within a few minutes, they were in deep sleep. I gazed at the peaceful look on their faces, and it felt good. We were finally together as a family. I made a vow that I would do everything I could to keep us together.

CHAPTER 14

UNTIL THE ARRIVAL of my wife and daughters, I'd been free to do what I wanted for the past five years. Now, I felt obligated to go home after work instead of going to the club. However, the benefits were a hot meal and spending time with my daughters. After dinner, I yearned to play cards and be with my friends. Instead, I had to listen to Basil's small talk about the neighbours. I barely knew Mrs. Manu and I wanted to keep it that way. However, Basil had taken to her in a big way.

"Mrs. Manu seems to be a nice lady," she said.

"Basil, I told you to be careful with the neighbours, especially her - she is a Brahmin."

"Yes, I know, but she seems different from the others."

"Different, different, what are you talking about? They are all the same."

"Dias, she listens to me, shares her recipes; she even showed me how to cook beef croquettes."

"Basil don't be fooled by these kind gestures. As I said, be careful and don't tell her anything about our family."

As the weeks went by, I found it more and more difficult to stay at home. I started going to the club after work and then coming home for a late dinner. This did not sit well with Basil. She complained about the girls hardly seeing their father. There were times when she would go on about family matters when I had come home from the club. Most of the time I was too drunk or tired to listen and would end up catching bits and pieces of her conversation. I would let her speak most of the time and would reply with the occasional nod.

One Saturday morning, after waking up at around 11:00 am, Luiza came up to me.

"Daddy, can you help me?" she said with a book under her arm.

"Yes, my dear, with what?"

"My English homework. The teacher punished me for not completing it the last time."

"Punished you?"

"She whacked me with a stick until I started to cry," she replied with tears in her eyes.

"Oh, you poor girl, I will help you with your homework," I said figuring that Primary One English would be easy.

She sheepishly opened her book. The corners of the pages were curled and worn out. The title of the book was "Old Lobb". The illustrations were neat and colourful with large writing. She read the assigned pages with some difficulty, which made me wonder about the quality of the teachers at school. I looked at the sheet of homework where she had to fill in the blanks and for the life of me, I could not figure it out. We tried the dictionary but to no avail. I finally told her that she should ask the teacher for help. She walked away sadly. Basil suggested that we send her to Mrs. Manu for tutoring. Although I was against the idea, I agreed.

A few weeks later, Luiza came up to me smiling. She looked very happy.

"Daddy, Daddy, Mrs. Manu is like a real teacher."

"She is?"

"Yes, she makes it so easy for me to understand. I can finish all my homework."

"Good, I knew that Mrs. Manu could tutor you," I said, relieved that I did not have to help with her homework.

Saturday afternoons were the only times when I would see the neighbours. Besides Mrs. Manu, there was another Goan neighbour – Mrs. Phillip DeSouza who had two children – Clifford and Ruby. Mr. DeSouza used to work at Pedro's Bar on Market Street which I used to frequent when the club was closed on Saturday afternoons. He was a short, stout, and quiet man. Although Mrs. DeSouza was small and skinny, it was obvious that she ran the household. I stayed away from her and cautioned Basil to do the same. Basil would never listen. She loved talking and being with people, even perfect strangers. Clifford and Ruby would stay far away from their mother when she was irate. Their servant and cook, called Gaffa, would escape the reality of his lowly, hard life by drinking whatever potent spirit he could get his hands on. Clifford would find solace in Gaffa's company and on occasion even sleep in his quarters – something I could never understand. There were times when Gaffa in his drunken stupor would claim to be the *Kabaka* – monarch of the Kingdom of Buganda. In reality, the British Government had given Buganda a privileged position compared to the other smaller kingdoms in Uganda, by naming Mutesa as the *Kabaka*. Although poor Gaffa had elevated himself to this position under the influence of alcohol, he would end up vomiting uncontrollably by the end of the evening. At this point, Mrs. DeSouza would rush to Gaffa's quarters and rescue Clifford, who hated leaving the comfort of his dear Gaffa.

Basil was putting on weight and looked more tired than normal. One Sunday, when I was having my breakfast, Basil sat at the table and looked anxious. I was hoping that she would not start talking about the neighbours or the problems that the girls had at school.

"Dias, I have not been feeling well lately. I feel like vomiting every morning."

"Maybe it is something temporary and will go away."

"It seems to be getting worse."

"I suppose that you feel this way because *Mai* is not here to help you."

Basil did not say anything but looked upset. After a long pause, she said, "I was hoping to order food from Mrs. Santos until I feel better."

"Mrs. Santos? What will people think?"

"They will understand that I cannot cook because I am in the family way."

"I don't think so. Besides, I was tired of her cooking when I was a boarder."

From then on Basil didn't bring up the subject and resumed her duties as a housewife.

Although business was going well at the shop, I had to keep abreast of developments in the fashion industry. Unfortunately, British propaganda during the Second World War encouraged women accustomed to discarding worn or outmoded clothing to re-make and update it. During the war, American designers such as Norman Norell and Claire McCardell emerged with sophisticated designs. However, restrictions during the war affected many aspects of women's fashion, such as the width of women's skirts, type of fabrics and heel height. Everything was geared toward minimizing the wastage of fabrics. Some fabrics, such as silk, needed to make parachutes, were banned from use in the clothing industry. Soon after the war, both Britain and the United States hoped to lead world fashion, but neither succeeded. After the Liberation, Paris couturiers abandoned the extravagance of the years of occupation and returned to a simpler look. Balmain, Balenciaga, and Dior emerged as the most eminent of Parisian designers. Dior came up with his first collection, the Corelle line which was immediately nicknamed the New Look. Soft, rounded shoulders emphasized the breasts: waists were heavily corseted; hips were padded, and skirts were billowing, reaching almost to the ankle. This required a lot of fabric, in some cases fifteen yards. I retained this information and would suggest it to my customers who had the appropriate shape and measurements. For the others, I would recommend more conservative classical designs.

By now Basil was starting to get quite big and her dresses were getting snug. I decided to make her several modern maternity dresses. One evening I brought them home to surprise her. I could not believe her reaction. She barely looked at them, put them aside and continued with her housework. I did not think that Basil was going to use them, but ultimately, she had to because she could not get into her other dresses. I had no idea if she liked the dresses or just wore them since she didn't have any options. She was a difficult person to please.

I knew that Basil wouldn't mind, so one sunny September afternoon I decided to go hunting for fowl with my friend, John Fernandes. He inherited a well-known bakery on Burton Street called R.M. Fernandes & Sons. His father started the business by selling small bread rolls to the native Ugandans. After a couple of years, it had grown to a full-fledged bakery that specialized in cakes for special occasions. We had an enjoyable time and managed to shoot several birds. At the end of the day, we split the spoils and then went to Pedro's Bar for a drink. At around 11:00 pm, I finally decided to go home. No one was around when I arrived. I panicked initially, but then I decided to go to Mrs. Manu's to find out if Basil was visiting with her. Basil was not there, however, Luiza and Matilda were at her place. Mr. Manu informed me that Basil had gone into labour and that his wife had taken her to Nsambya Hospital. I was glad that she went since I would not have known how to handle the situation. It was too late for me to visit the hospital.

The following morning, I took a taxi to the hospital. It was about ten miles away, on the outskirts of the city. As we got out of the core of the city the paved roads turned into compacted mud roads. The red dust of the mud filled the air and covered the cars. On the side of the roads were mud huts, and tall acacia trees that hosted large birds. The smell of dust and smoke emanated from firewood burning outside the huts. After a bumpy ride, I finally arrived at the hospital. I was perspiring as I walked through the doors of the hospital. I asked the nurse at the reception where I could find Basil. After checking through several sheets of paper she informed me that she was in room number seven. As I walked down the corridor, I thought to myself, seven is my lucky number. When I arrived in the room, Mrs. Manu stood up and hugged me.

"Congratulations, Mr. Dias, you have a son."

"A son! A son! Thank you, thank God."

Tears of joy streamed down my cheeks. I rushed up to Basil who was breastfeeding the baby. She was embarrassed and quickly covered her breast with the blanket. The baby started crying so Basil tried to console him as I tried to get a good look at him. It did not matter what or who he looked like, as long as he was a boy.

While Basil was recovering in the hospital, I made arrangements for my son's christening party. I invited every friend and relative in Kampala. I arranged for Santos' to cater the food and asked John Fernandes to make a grand four-tiered cake. I sewed my son's christening gown and bonnet with great pride and joy. Basil came home a week later, and we had the christening. We named him John Nicholas after my father. That was one of the happiest days of my life. The Dias family name would live on.

CHAPTER 15

ON SATURDAY MORNINGS, John Fernandes would ask me to help him with special deliveries, such as wedding cakes, birthday pastries and Christening cakes. As a sign of his appreciation, he would allow me to drive the van back to his bakery. He taught me how to manipulate the clutch, change gears, and apply the brakes. Although I struggled a bit in the beginning, especially with the clutch it was not that long before I got the hang of it. On my way to the club, I would pass by the automobile dealers, stopping to observe the cars in the windows. There were British, American, and even French cars on display. The Citroen 2CV, an odd-looking car, was covered in canvas that could be rolled up for an open roof. The dull gray colour was probably chosen so that dirt would not show. The Austin, a British car, although practical, was too small and economical for my liking. My favourite cars were those made by the Americans, which had a luxurious look about them, especially the ones manufactured by Ford. The black Prefect caught my eye. I could just imagine myself sitting in this fine car driving down Kampala Road to the club. I decided that I was going to buy it in honour of my first son, John. At the club, I told my friends about my decision. They all cheered me, so I bought them a round of drinks to celebrate.

"To Carlit and his new car," they toasted as they raised their glasses.

"*Viva, Viva*," I said proudly.

I went to the car dealership on Saturday morning the following week. As I walked in, a dapper-looking man approached me and put out his hand.

"Sir, welcome to our showroom. May I be of assistance to you?"

I was a bit taken aback by this warm welcome. For a moment, I did not know what to say.

"Err.... yes. I am interested in buying a car, the Ford Prefect."

"The Prefect? May I suggest the Austin, it is very popular."

"It is?"

"Yes, sir...sorry I did not get your name."

"It is Carlos Dias"

"Mr. Dias, we have sold five Austins in the past month. They are much more economical than the American cars."

For a moment, I considered the Austin but did not like the idea of buying a frugal-looking car. Owning my first car was a luxury for me so I had to buy what made me feel grand.

"I prefer the Ford Prefect. How much does it cost?"

"It is rather expensive – 12,000 shillings."

I almost choked. I had only two thousand shillings in the bank.

"Can I pay for it in installments with an initial payment of two thousand shillings?"

"Sorry, Mr. Dias that is against our company rules. We are

not a financial institution. However, you could borrow the money from the bank."

"Would they lend me the money for a car?"

"Of course, Mr. Dias, we will give you a letter that you could present to the bank. They will loan you fifty percent of the value of the car."

Fifty percent would be 6,000 shillings, I still needed another 4,000 shillings. Where could I find this amount of money? I thought for a moment and then it occurred to me, John Fernandes could lend me some money. His bakery business was very prosperous so he could easily afford it.

"When can you give me the letter?"

"I need to take down certain details and we will have the letter done by Monday."

I shook hands with the man and headed directly for R.M. Fernandes and Sons whistling all the way.

I passed by Lada Kassam, the largest grocery store in Kampala. They carried every possible fruit imaginable – mangoes, jackfruit, passion fruit, bananas and even imported fruit such as apples and grapes. The local fruits were affordable, but the imports were outrageously expensive. There were times when I would indulge and buy a couple of delicious apples. The shop was always full of customers, both English and Asian. Mr. Kassam must have been making buckets of money.

Mr. Fernandes greeted me with a smile and a firm handshake. His son Julius was running around the store pretending to help his father. Upon seeing me he ran to the back room of the bakery. I offered to take Mr. Fernandes for a drink but he refused since his wife was not around to take care of the bakery.

"John, I am thinking of buying a car."

"You are? That will cost you a lot of money."

"Yes, that is why I need your help, John. Can you lend me 4,000 shillings?"

"Four thousand ...."

"Think about it. We can go on our hunting trips and even to Nairobi for horse races."

"The children are young, and I need money to run the business."

"John, it is only four thousand. We will have the freedom to travel anywhere in East Africa."

"I don't know if we have that kind of money. I will have to speak to my wife."

"Come on John, it is your money. You don't need to ask her."

"I don't know, Carlit. Will you be able to pay me back soon?"

"Ay, John my business is doing well, it will be easy to pay you back."

"Okay Carlit, come to the shop tomorrow afternoon. I will have the money for you."

"Thank you, John. Why don't we have a drink?"

"Sorry, Carlit, I cannot. We are very busy today."

"Another time then."

I went to the licensing office on Kampala Road and made an appointment for my driving test. At the same time, I picked up a driver's manual. I studied the rules diligently and when I was confident that I knew them well I went for the test. We barely drove for about ten minutes when the examiner asked me to drive back to the licensing office. I couldn't figure out why he terminated the test so soon. I thought that I had failed the test. When we got back to the office, he asked me to sit down in the waiting room. After twenty minutes, my name was called out, so I went to the counter. To my surprise, the lady behind the counter handed me a temporary license. I was extremely pleased.

During the week, I managed to get all the money together and on Saturday, I walked to the car dealership. I spent almost an hour completing the paperwork and the salesman finally gave me the keys. I slid into the car and savoured the moment. Just the smell gave me tremendous pleasure. I could not stop smiling. I turned on the engine and quickly put the car into first gear. I forgot to press the clutch, so the car lunged forward and stalled. I could have kicked myself, how could I have forgotten about the clutch? I re-started the car, carefully released the clutch, gently pressed the accelerator and then drove off to the club feeling like a million shillings. I parked the car right in front of the club's main entrance. My friends came to the car and greeted me with great excitement. I took them for a drive around the club and felt elated.

I got home quite late and ate supper that Basil had reheated for me. I did not tell her about the car. The next morning, I told her to look out of the kitchen window.

"That is the car that I bought for *Baba* John."

"Dias, you bought a car - a car? How could you afford it?"

"Oh, Basil, why can't you be happy for me for once?"

"I am happy, but you could have told me."

"You always know how to put a damper on things. I am going to the shop."

"Aren't you going to eat breakfast? I made some *chapatis*."

"No, I will have my breakfast at the Uganda Coffee House."

As I drove off, our conversation kept ringing in my head. I could not understand why Basil was always so worried. She should enjoy life like me. When I arrived at the shop, all the workers came out to observe the car. The workers blocked the car since they were gawking at it. As for Georgie, our *toto*, he was awestruck.

I had a lot of cutting to do at the store; I could not

concentrate on my work. My mind kept wandering off to places that I wanted to visit with my new car. I could go hunting in the Mabira forest, or fishing at Port Bell or Entebbe. Why, I could even go to Nairobi for the weekend! I was told that it was a long twenty-hour drive but what the hell, we only live once. I made up my mind to go to Nairobi for a horse race as soon as I got a chance.

At lunchtime, I headed to R.M. Fernandes' bakery. Fortunately, John was behind the counter.

"*Arrh,* John, how are you?"

"*Aih*, Carlit, what are you doing here?"

"I bought the car."

"You didn't waste any time."

"I had to buy it. John, I am taking you to Nairobi to celebrate."

"But I cannot leave the bakery."

"It is only for the weekend. We will leave on Friday night when you close."

"I need to ask my wife Helen."

"No fear, just tell her you are going with me. She won't mind."

"Well, I must say that it sounds tempting."

"John don't think about it. We will have a good time. I will pick you up on Friday night."

CHAPTER 16

I LEFT the club earlier than usual to pack for my trip to Nairobi. On my way home, scenes of the Maasai plains with exotic wildlife flashed through my mind. The rolling plains of the savannah seemed to go on forever. Marabou and vultures rested on majestic baobab trees that punctuated the golden grassland. It all seemed like a dream, and what was most exciting, is that it was about to come true. This would be my first long-distance trip with me in the driver's seat. I could not wait to embark on this great adventure.

I woke up early the next morning. As I walked in the kitchen, I noticed that Basil had put on some weight.

"Dias, I would make you your breakfast, but I feel very tired. I suspect that I am in the family way," Basil said nervously.

"You are, but John was only born a few months ago," I replied, somewhat surprised.

Although I was hungry, I decided to skip breakfast to allow Basil to rest. I wore my favourite tan safari suit. I threw my suitcase into my new Prefect and drove to Jaffrey's for a coffee and a bun.

I opened the shop at 7:00 a.m. and my employees, Andrew, Margaret, and Georgie, sauntered in at different intervals. Georgie arrived at 8:30 a.m., late as usual. My efforts to instill discipline were in vain.

"*Jambo* Margaret, *Habari gani*?" I said joyfully.

"*Jumbo Bwana*," Margaret replied.

"Margaret, I am going to Nairobi in my brand-new car."

"*Bwana*, Nairobi? But that is very far away."

"It is not that far; we will be there by tomorrow."

Margaret looked at me, rolled her eyes and sighed.

"Are you not afraid of the *Mau Mau* rebels?" Andrew queried.

"Oh no, they hide in the forests waiting to attack the British. They consider Asians to be their friends."

I could understand why Andrew, who belonged to the Kalenjin tribe, feared Kenya. He had escaped persecution by the Kikuyu. This rift between the tribes was created by the British, who used the strategy of "divide and conquer", not only in Kenya but in all their colonies. Most of the Mau Mau rebels were Kikuyu. They fought fiercely for the independence of Kenya and eventually became the ruling tribe.

I worked enthusiastically, knowing that I had an exciting weekend ahead of me. By noon, I could not focus anymore, so I closed the shop early. I gave Andrew and Margaret a five shillings bonus each and Georgie one shilling and let them go.

"*A cente sana, bwana*," they all said in unison bowing their heads.

I quickly drove over to John Fernandes' bakery, only to find him busy at work.

"*Arrh* John, are you ready?"

"Yes Carlit, I just have to say goodbye to Helen."

"Hurry, John we have to leave before it gets dark."

Just then Helen came from the back room of the bakery.

"Oh Helen, how are you?" I asked.

"I am fine. Mr. Dias, make sure that John does not gamble away all his money."

"No fear, Helen, we are just going to have some fun and watch the horse race."

She had this look of disbelief. I could not understand why women were always so cautious and economical. I always believed that there was more to life than just hard work and pinching pennies.

We left the bakery and drove to Kampala Road, which turned into Jinja Road. As we left town, I was overcome with a feeling of elation, free as a bird flying through the lush countryside. We came across large coffee and tea plantations which were owned by the British. They extended as far as the eye could see. The Africans were only allowed to grow their produce in small patches of land around their huts. This injustice was already causing social unrest in Kenya, hence the dawning of the *Mau Mau* rebellion.

The sky turned crimson and within a few minutes, and shortly after the sun disappeared over the horizon. We were enveloped in darkness. All I could see were the beams from the headlights of my car. From time to time, I would spot wild animals darting across the road startling me. I could not afford to hit any of them and damage my new car. Occasionally, blinding headlights from oncoming cars caused dangerous driving conditions on the narrow and bumpy road. John was sleeping and snoring quite loudly. I kept nudging him, but he was deep in slumber. I nudged him harder and finally managed to wake him up.

"*Aye*, have we reached Nairobi?" he croaked.

"No, we are not even halfway, and I almost fell asleep. Your dozing off like that did not help either."

"Well, let's sing some Konkani songs then," John suggested.

We sang for most of the night until we were greeted by a glorious sunrise that flooded the Maasai plains with a golden hue. Gazelles and long-necked gerenuks were dashing off in different directions. We saw a few of the Maasai people adorned with heavily beaded jewelry around their necks and head. They would give furtive glances and run off as soon as we spotted them. Once again John fell asleep, but thankfully the magnificent landscape kept me awake until we reached the city of Nairobi.

We were greeted warmly by Custodio and his wife Carmelina.

"You look hungry and tired. Have some coffee while I prepare eggs and sausages for you," Carmelina said as she led us through a hall into the kitchen.

I drank the aromatic Safari coffee and scoffed the eggs. The upland sausages were delectable. Feeling satisfied with the wholesome breakfast, I went to the bedroom that Carmelina had prepared for us. I flopped into bed dressed in my sweaty safari suit. I was hoping to change into my pyjamas but the next thing I knew Custodio's wife was waking me up for dinner. I ate the sumptuous fish curry and rice that was almost as delicious as Basil's. After dinner, John and I took Custodio to the Tailors' Club for a drink and a game of cards.

We slept in the next day and then went into town to pick up the "Handicap" newspaper to find out the timing and participants of the horse race. I could not believe my luck - most of my favourite horses were participating. I studied their weights and statistics intently and finally chose "Emerald". It was now around noon and the race was scheduled to begin at 3:00 p.m.

The three-hour wait seemed like twelve hours. I kept re-reading "Handicap" which made me feel more than ever that "Emerald" was a sure winner.

We arrived at the racetrack at 2:30 p.m. to get ideal seating. There were only a few spectators. Within minutes, people started filling the stands. The hustle and bustle of people placing their bets was exciting. John and I rushed to the wickets and placed our bets too. John bet 100 shillings on "Black Knight". I thought that certainly was a wasted bet. I bet 500 shillings on "Emerald". With the horse's remarkable track record, this was a sure bet, I could feel it in my bones.

The race began at 3:00 p.m. on the dot. All the horses were lined up at the start gate. My heart started racing and I felt a surge of energy. At the signal of the gunshot, the horses plunged from the gates and were off. Emerald was galloping like the wind. He was in the lead. I had made the right decision. It was now the last round, and Emerald was still in the lead. Black Knight trailing in the fifth position. Mid-way through the track, Black Knight started passing the fourth horse and within seconds caught up with Emerald. They were neck to neck when Emerald's jockey started whipping him harder and yelling at him. Instead of moving faster Emerald slowed down and neighed mournfully. In the last ten yards, Black Knight passed the illustrious Emerald and to my dismay won the race. John was shocked. He froze for a moment and then started jumping up and down.

"I won! I won! I can't believe it. I won!"

I felt the wind go out of my sails. John immediately ran up to the wicket to collect his winnings. I stood still feeling dejected and thwarted. It had taken me months to save the 500 shillings and I lost it all in a few minutes. At that moment, I made up my mind never to bet on horses again. My luck had run out.

"Carlit, look! I won a thousand shillings!"

"Yes, John, good for you," I said acrimoniously.

"Let us celebrate. It will be my treat."

I had nothing to celebrate.

"Sure John, why don't we have a couple of beers," I said trying very hard to sound happy.

At the club, John was boisterous, telling everyone, even strangers, about his winnings. I could not believe how insensitive he could be. Yes, he paid for one round of beers, but I thought that he might calm down. He was on a high. There was a group that started playing cards, and they invited me to join them. I refused. I stayed at the bar and drank several beers. Time seemed to have passed slowly and I vaguely remember John dragging me to the car. I woke up the next morning at Custudio's with a terrible headache. Once again, I vowed that I would never again bet on horse races.

We packed our bags and loaded the car. Sitting in my new car made me feel a little better. We drove back to Kampala. The journey seemed to be even longer on the way back than when we drove to Nairobi.

"Hey, Carlit, when will we be coming back for another race?" John inquired happily.

"Oh, John, not for a while."

"I am looking forward to the next race already."

"I am thinking of giving up betting on horse races and focusing on my family and work."

"Carlit, I am surprised. You delight in the sport."

"Not anymore. My luck has run out."

We drove out of the city and then entered the Rift Valley. It began raining. The normally breath-taking red expanse of the valley now looked grey and barren. The exotic wildlife was nowhere to be seen. After driving for over 100 miles, we finally entered the savannah grasslands, but it was engulfed by nightfall. John was asleep. I was alone with my thoughts. Maybe, I should give up working in Africa and move back to Goa. At least I would be close to *Mai* and she would have the pleasure of seeing her grandchildren growing up. I could see her pale sad face in the pitch black that lay ahead. She looked lonely and sad. Tears stung my eyes and then started streaming down my cheeks. I yearned to feel her warmth.

The crimson-orange sun struggled to break through the horizon. The clouds took on a pale shade of red and seemed to be on fire. As daylight was breaking, we passed a sign saying, "British Protectorate of Uganda." It was a joy to know that we were in Uganda. I looked forward to seeing my children, especially my son John.

When I arrived home, Basil was nowhere to be seen. I went into the children's bedroom to find Luiza taking care of John. She told me that Mrs. Manu called a taxi and rushed Basil to the hospital. A few hours later, we received a telephone call from Mrs. Manu, saying that Basil had delivered a baby boy. I was now a father of a fourth child, truly I was blessed.

CHAPTER 17

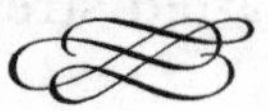

My shop on Market Street was getting too cramped. Bolts of fabric were almost falling off the shelves and dresses were packed so tightly that they were getting creased. I had just paid goodwill of 6,000 shillings, mainly due to the location of the shop. I would lose it if I moved to another location. My customers were multiplying, and the calibre was on the upswing. I could barely keep up with the orders and Andrew complained that his workspace was limiting his ability to sew efficiently. This was no way to continue doing business. It was time to move to a bigger shop in a better location.

The weekday evenings did not leave much time for shop hunting. On a Saturday afternoon, I looked around on Kampala Road and I could not believe the rents that they were charging. I desperately wanted a place on Kampala Road, since it was the main street with well-known stores such as Deacons, Drapers, and Bata. I was sure that my customers would prefer that location and I would certainly be able to attract new customers. I had to give up hope for a shop on Kampala Road, since goodwill was outrageously expensive, from 20,000 to 40,000 shillings. I temporarily abandoned my search for a new store, but very soon one thing led to another.

I loved eating *samosas* from Tapuby's, a popular restaurant in town. At around 9:30 a.m., I drove to the restaurant, ordered a dozen samosas and just before leaving I decided to speak to the owner.

"Hey, Tapuby, do you know of any vacant shops around Kampala Road?"

"I know of a shop near Deacon's that is vacant."

"No, I am not looking for a shop on Kampala Road, they are too expensive."

"My cousin owns a shop on Salisbury Road. He mentioned that the store next to his was vacant."

"Salisbury Road? Where is that?

"It is just below Kampala Road, near the railway station."

"That sounds like a good location. What is your cousin's name?"

"His name is Dilip Patel. He will put in a good word for you if you give him my name."

"Thank you, Mr. Tapuby."

I went back to the shop and distributed the samosas. Georgie took one bite and started breathing like a donkey in heat. He ran to the sink for a drink of water to soothe his burning mouth. Margaret and Andrew had eaten samosas before and seemed to have cultivated a taste for them.

I kept thinking about the shop on Salisbury Road but could not get to it during the week. Finally, on Saturday I walked to Kenya Shoe Store.

"Good afternoon, Mr. Patel?"

He was busy repairing a pair of shoes and looked up, somewhat startled.

"Yes, what do you want, mister?"

"My name is Carlos Dias. Your cousin Tapuby informed me that the store next to yours is vacant."

"Yes, it is."

"Do you know the landlord? The rent?"

"He is Kiren Patel. I think that he is asking for 500 shillings."

"Good, can you speak to him?"

"He will be coming to collect the rent on Wednesday, I will speak to him then."

"That is very kind of you, Mr. Patel."

"Mention not," he replied.

I walked onto the street and looked at the vacant shop. It had two large windows which would be perfect to display the dresses and accessories. I peeped through the door, and it seemed to be quite large. There were several shops on the street, with a reasonable amount of traffic. It was a better location compared to Market Street.

On Wednesday afternoon, Mr. Kiren Patel informed me that he was willing to rent the shop for 450 shillings and goodwill payment of only 2,000 shillings. I was pleased with his offer, so I went to his office in the evening and signed the contract. We spent the next month packing all the merchandise and moving it into the new shop. The shop was twice the size of the old one on Market Street, so I had the luxury of arranging the furniture and sewing machines more efficiently. Andrew was pleased that his workspace had doubled, and as a result, worked with an air of pride.

We opened the shop at the beginning of the month. Five new customers came to the store on that day, the most that I ever had on a single day. As the week progressed, I decided to hire Andrew's friend to help with the finishing, since poor Georgie could not cope with the volume of work.

One afternoon a sleek white car with a small Union Jack on the bonnet pulled up in front of the shop. People from the neighbouring stores came out to look at the elegant lady that gracefully stepped out from this posh car. Her hat was adorned with feathers and her ankle-length dress caressed her slender body. I could not believe it when she strutted into my shop, escorted by an aide who was dressed in a smart white uniform and hat. Although I was nervous, I did my best to look calm.

"Mr. Dias, my friends say that you are an excellent tailor."

"They do? Who?"

"Mrs. Hues, for example, sings your praises."

"Oh, yes, I used to work for her. That is very kind of her."

"I will be attending the governor's ball and would like you to sew an evening gown for me."

"It will be a pleasure for me, Mrs....."

"Lady Catherine, I am Sir Andrew Cohen's wife."

"Governor Andrew Cohen?"

"Yes. That is him."

I was awestruck. The governor's wife was in my store. She chose a beautiful scarlet gown from the *Lana Lobel* fashion book. It was corseted, full skirted with a low V-neck and three-quarter sleeves with a slight puff at the shoulders. The long gloves and matching feathered hat gave the ensemble a sophisticated look. I measured her slim figure and knew that the gown was going to be exquisite. I suggested moiré taffeta fabric.

I spent long hours carefully crafting this special gown. I put all the other orders on hold. On the third day, Lady Cohen came for her fitting. My heart rate quickened, and I was sweating as I anxiously waited for her to come out of the dressing room. When she did, it was as though she had stepped off the runway.

Even though the handwork was not complete, she looked stunning.

"Mr. Dias, it fits me perfectly!"

"Lady Cohen, you have the ideal body type for this gown."

"Thank you. It feels like I have been your customer for a long time."

"Let me tack the hem while you are still in the gown."

I worked on the gloves and hat and got Georgie to do the handwork, which I made him redo until it was perfect. I always believed that finishing was very important since sloppy handwork takes away from the beauty of the gown. She picked up the gown and accessories the next day. She paid me 120 shillings.

"Lady Cohen, you have overpaid me, it should be 100 shillings."

"I am aware of that; the 20 shillings is for a job done well."

"Thank you very much. By the way, when is the ball?"

"Oh, unfortunately, the ball has been delayed due to the Buganda crises."

I knew what she was talking about but decided not to pursue the conversation. Her husband must have been in the thick of it. The Kabaka Mutesa II was demanding separate status for Buganda. Andrew Cohen had frequent meetings to dissuade the Kabaka from taking this position but instead consider self-government for all of Uganda. Their meetings ended in a deadlock and the British finally deported the Kabaka to London.

The news about me sewing for the governor's wife spread like wildfire. This brought in more high-calibre customers. I was able to pay John Fernandes the money I owed him. Almost overnight, I became one of the most successful tailors in Uganda, making between 1,200 to 1,500 shillings a month. This exciting development was well-timed, coming right after the birth of my second son. I decided to name him Placido, after my good friend Custudio Placido from Nairobi. I believed that my son Placido had brought me luck. It was time to reward myself, so I arranged another trip with John Fernandes. He was shocked when I told him that I was planning to go to the horse races.

"Carlit, I thought that you had given up on horse races."

"Oh, John that was months ago. I am doing well now; I can afford to bet a little money on horses."

"I am willing to go with you. I just need to inform Helen."

"Do that. I will pick you up tomorrow."

I bet a small amount on the first race, and I won. I bet much more on the second race, I lost. I bet the third and fourth time, I lost again. John lost all the races, but he only bet 100 shillings in total. I had lost 1,000 shillings in total. I was disappointed with losing but I convinced myself that it was just a phase of bad luck. I was certain that I would be lucky the next time around.

When I got back from Nairobi, orders were starting to pile up. My workers could not handle the volume of work. I was afraid that I would start losing customers since they were starting to complain about the delays. I had to hire an experienced tailor, which was hard to find in Uganda. The economy was growing in leaps and bounds so all the Asians were employed. At the club, one of my friends mentioned that a Chrispin Furtado from Goa was looking for work. I decided to write to him. I received a reply within a month saying that he was most willing to accept the job. I embarked on the process of getting him a permit.

I informed Basil that I was planning to get a tailor from Goa. She did not look too happy about it.

"Dias, do you think we can afford to bring him to Uganda?"

"My business is growing, and we need to hire another tailor."

"We already have four children to feed and now another one is on the way."

"Another one?"

"Yes, I went to the doctor today, and he told me that I am in the family way again."

I was overwhelmed that I was going to have a fifth child. If anything, I hoped that it was a boy once more, since dowries for girls were too costly. I knew that *Mai* would be thrilled to hear that I was going to be blessed with another child. Unlike myself, my children would have the pleasure of having many siblings. They would be spared the experience of being an only child.

CHAPTER 18

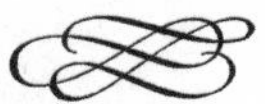

THE NEXT SEVERAL months passed quickly. I recall that Placido's birth went calmly, but this pregnancy was different.

Mrs. Manu would drop in quite frequently and was becoming very friendly with Basil. She would visit during the day while I was away. I did not like that, but I could not prevent their friendship from growing.

"Daddy, Daddy! Hurry up. We must go to the hospital!" Luiza cried as she burst into the shop.

"What is it Luiza?"

"It is Mummy. She is having a baby."

"Baby! Who told you?"

"Mrs. Manu told Clifford to tell me when I came back from school."

"Okay, let's go, but what hospital?"

"I... er don't know."

I assumed that it must be the Asian Hospital in Nakesero. We sped to the hospital, experiencing several near misses on the way. Luiza looked pale. I wasn't sure whether it was my driving or her concern for her mother. She was a worrier, just like Basil.

When we arrived at the hospital, Mrs. Manu was waiting at the entrance.

"Hello Carlit, God has blessed you with another son," she announced with a big smile.

"That is wonderful news."

Basil told me later that Mrs. Manu insisted that she stop cooking and go to the hospital. Mrs. Manu hailed a taxi while Basil was frantically trying to get dressed. In the rush, she ended up with one black and one blue shoe. They had barely arrived at the hospital when Basil could feel the baby's head. They just about made it to the delivery room when the baby was born. I was grateful to Mrs. Manu, but I was not going to express my appreciation. She would misinterpret it as encouraging her friendship with Basil.

I could not believe it. Another son, *Mai* would be overjoyed. I rushed into the room to see Basil holding a tiny child in her arms.

"Carlit, here is your son," Basil said with tears in her eyes.

She smiled even though she was exhausted. The baby had a shock of black hair, was fair skinned and had plump cheeks. I had to fight back tears of joy. At that very moment, the name Michael popped into my mind. Strangely enough, my good friend and neighbour in Goa was Michael too. I decided that he would be my son's godfather. I knew then that he would always be the apple of my eye. I wanted to pick him up, but he was busy sucking on Basil's breast and would not let go.

When Basil came home with Michael, I promised to spend more time with him and my other children. As much as I wanted to, I could not keep this promise, since my business continued to prosper and took up most of my time. Thankfully, the permit application for Chrispin Furtado came through. I sent it to him right away so that he could make arrangements to come to Uganda. He was well prepared and anxious to come to Uganda because he arrived a month later. I did not have to spend too much time training him since he was an experienced tailor.

Chrispin made me feel nostalgic about Goa and I realized how much I missed *Mai*. She would write, asking to see her grandsons. I wanted *Mai* and our neighbours to see my sons but leaving at this time would spell disaster for my business. I was torn between going to Goa and staying back to keep my business going.

I had to come up with a plan for running the business in my absence. I would need to spend at least six months with *Mai* to allow my children to get acquainted with her. My sons only spoke English and some Swahili. It was important for them to find their roots and learn their mother tongue.

After weeks of pondering, I finally came up with a plan. I would train Chrispin Furtado in all aspects of the business except finance. This would include handling customers, taking measurements, ordering materials, distributing the work among the employees, and doing the fitting. The collection was also important, but this wasn't a major problem because most of the customers paid cash when they picked up their orders. My main concern was the financial part of the business since I had trouble keeping track of money. Even though business was booming I was never able to cover my expenses. There were times when I had to borrow money to make ends meet. It suddenly dawned on me that the perfect person to handle the finances of the business would be my brother-in-law, John Pires. He was an accountant and very good when it came to money. This would be a good time to get him involved, so I decided to discuss this with Basil.

"Basil, I have been thinking about going back to Goa."

"*Mai* will be happy to see you and the children, but what about the shop?"

"I have decided to train Chrispin to handle the shop and your brother, John Pires to handle the finances."

Basil looked down and did not say anything. I found this quite unusual. Something told me that she did not like my idea.

"What is it, Basil? I thought you would be happy that I am involving your brother in the business."

"I don't think that it is such a good idea."

"Why, what is the problem?"

"When you mix business and family it creates problems."

"What problems? He is a qualified accountant. Besides, what do you know about business?"

"You are right, I don't know anything about business, but I do know of some families that have grown apart because of it."

"You should take care of the kitchen and look after the children. I will handle my business."

I thought that Basil would have liked this idea, but I was wrong.

I went to the shop the next day and informed Chrispin that I would like him to manage the business while I was away in Goa. He was thrilled with the idea. I cautioned him that while I trained him, he would have to demonstrate that he could handle the business before I left for Goa. I decided to wait before I informed my brother-in-law about handling the finances of the company. There wasn't any need for training since he was an experienced accountant.

I could now put this problem at rest and focus on my family. *Baba* Michael was growing into an adorable and charming child. His piercing black eyes were full of mischief. There were some nights when I would skip going to the club so that I could spend time with him. Not surprisingly, he loved the attention. He was truly a joy to have around and certainly my favourite.

A celebration was in order. I decided to purchase a car to mark the birth of Michael. Besides, I was getting tired of my old Prefect. The new Fiats looked great. I had seen only a few in town. I gathered that they were a prized item. I expected that the waiting time for this car would be quite long. Another hurdle became evident when I visited the only Fiat dealership in town. The cost of 7,500 shillings was a lot more than I had in my bank account.

The next day, after closing the shop, I decided to go to Pedro's Bar instead of the Tailors' Club for a change. The only drawback would be the absence of a good game of cards. I had been on a losing streak for the past couple of months. I thought it best to take a break from playing cards.

As I drove to the bar, the sun had just set, and I could feel the cool air as it flowed through the window. When I turned the corner to get onto Market Street, some Ugandans hovered around a streetlamp holding large white fabric sheets and swirling them around. When I looked up at the lamp, I saw hordes of green locusts. It dawned on me that they were using the sheets to trap the insects. They are delicious snacks especially when they are fried in butter.

The smell of whiskey emanated from Pedro's Bar which made me thirst for a drink.

"Hello, Carlit. We haven't seen you for a while," Bernard Paes said with a smile.

I knew that he would be happy to see me since he was one of the owners of the bar.

"How is business, Bernard?"

"It is going well."

"Get me some scotch and soda."

"Johnny Walker, I presume?"

He mixed my drink in a scotch glass and handed it to me.

"Hey, Bernard, I am thinking of buying a new car."

"You already have a Prefect. What are you thinking of buying?"

"A Fiat"

"That is a nice car. They have just come on the market."

"I can wait to own it; the only problem is that I do not have sufficient money."

"That is too bad."

He poured me another drink and topped it with soda. I had a few more sips.

"Hey, Bernard, can you lend me 2,000 shillings? I will pay you back."

"That is a lot of money. I cannot possibly afford to loan you that sum."

"I need to buy the car. I promise to pay you back in a couple of months. I will even give you interest of 200 shillings."

The wheels in his head were turning. This tidy sum of interest must have whet his appetite.

"Well, if you promise to pay it back in two months, I will lend you the money."

"Thank you very much, Bernard. You have made me a very happy man."

I had a couple of drinks and then left the bar whistling away. The following day I went to Barclays Bank to get a loan for the remaining amount. I spoke to my brother-in-law who sighed when I asked him for help. I found that annoying but decided to be polite. After much haggling with his manager, he was able to arrange a loan for 4,000 shillings. I finally had all the money that

I needed to purchase the car. I went to the dealer and signed the contract. I was now a proud father and soon to be the owner of a new Fiat. Sadly, *Mai* could not be here to share my joy. If it wasn't for the lack of work in Goa, I would never have left.

CHAPTER 19

I WAS busy working on a ball gown that was due that day when Bernard Paes walked into the shop. I was a bit surprised since he had never come to the shop before. It could not have been to pick out a dress for his wife since she did her own sewing. She had set up a sewing school in their home.

"Carlit, you promised to pay me, but I have not received a cent from you."

"I told you that I would pay you back in six months."

"No, you said a couple of months. You even promised to pay interest," he retorted, angrily.

"No fear, Bernard. I promised to pay you and I will do so."

"My wife keeps asking about the money. You better pay up soon."

"I will, I will. You have my word."

He walked out of the store in a huff threatening to send his wife the next time. I was glad that there were no customers around. If his wife came to the shop, she would not leave until I paid the full amount. I checked my bankbook only to find out that I had 500 shillings, most of which was accounted for. How was I going to raise 4000 shillings within two weeks? My only option was to bet on a horse race.

According to the "Handicap", a big race was on this weekend in Nairobi. Jacinth was planning to go to Nairobi with the gang. I could send in my bet with him. It was Thursday. I had only one day to select the winning horse. I decided to skip the club tonight. I went home to study statistics and predict which horse would overcome his handicap.

"Dias, you are home so early!" Basil remarked nervously.

At that moment, I heard the back door shut.

"Basil, how many times did I tell you to stay away from Mrs. Manu?"

"It...it was only for a few moments. She was helping me make cutlets for tonight's supper."

"Can't you make them on your own?"

"Yes, I can but I like to have some help and company when I cook."

I went into the bedroom and started reading the "Handicap". The front page had a listing of the top ten favourite horses and jockeys. I scanned the list and noted that *War Admiral* was ninth on the list. He was a thoroughbred descendant of the Darley Arabian Stallion. I had a good feeling about this horse. I read his statistics in detail on page seven. His jockey, Sir Barton, was 5 feet tall and weighed 106 pounds – a perfect match. War Admiral was in excellent physical condition, so I was surprised that he was placed ninth. My daughter, Luiza was born on the 9th. It must be a sign that War Admiral would bring me luck.

It was Friday evening, time to go to the club. We played several rounds of *truque* that I enjoyed very much. I was feeling thirsty, so I decided to get a drink from the bar. I invited Jacinth to join me. I gave him two hundred shillings to bet on my behalf.

He was shocked by the amount I was betting and cautioned me that I was risking a lot of money.

It always surprised me why people bother betting small amounts. Risking a large sum of money on a bet is what makes it exciting.

As I drove home, I could smell the dry earth in the air. It hadn't rained for the past two months. December is a nice time to drive to Nairobi. The temperature is mild and most of the trees and bushes are in full bloom. Poinsettias with large red bracts are at their peak. How I wished that I could go to the race. The frequent travelling was starting to wear me out. I decided to stay in Kampala.

The next morning, I decided to take the "Handicap" with me to the shop. While driving on Kampala Road, I noticed Bernard Paes walking to work. I panicked when I thought about the money that I owed him. I could always convince him that I had not received payment from my customers. However, I was afraid of his wife. She was exacting. I quickly put the thought of her out of my mind. After I entered the shop, the first thing I did was to open the "Handicap." I checked the top contenders. I was convinced that I should stick to War Admiral. Page three stated that the BBC would be airing the game on Radio Kenya at 11:00 a.m. on Sunday.

When Sunday rolled around, I was glad that Basil had gone to church with the children. I would have some peace. The only way I could decipher who was winning the race was if the reception was good. The radio in the living room would pick up Radio Kenya sometimes. I adjusted the antenna several times and was getting a decent reception for Radio Uganda. It was now close to 11:00 a.m., so I tuned into Radio Kenya. It sounded like heavy rain. I played around with the radio without much success. I was about to give up after twenty minutes when I started picking up the station. I could actually hear what the broadcaster was saying. At that moment, the front door opened, and the children came running into the living room chasing each other.

"Basil, get them out of here. Can't you see that I am listening to the radio?" I yelled.

"*Baya, Baba* come let's go to the kitchen," Basil said.

John was still chasing Placido around the living room. I had to push them out and lock the door. I finally settled down to listen to the radio, only to get a poor reception. I had no idea of the outcome. I would have to wait until the following evening to find out if I had won.

On Monday, I locked up the store at 5:00 p.m. and drove to the club, only to find out that Jacinth hadn't arrived. I ordered a scotch and made small talk with my friends while I looked over their shoulders. About half an hour later, I saw Jacinth coming towards the bar. I jumped off my barstool and I walked hastily to meet him.

"Tell me Jacinth, who won the race?"

He looked serious, so I thought for sure that I had lost my bet.

"Carlit.....Carlit...I..." he stammered.

I sighed and was starting to get irritated.

"Jacinth, it is okay to say that I lost.

"Carlit, War Admiral was the winner."

"Great! A lucky break after a losing streak!"

"Yes, you won 6,000 shillings."

"6,000 shillings! I can pay Bernard and still have over 1,000 shillings to bet on the next race."

"You are going to bet 1,000 shillings?"

"Of course."

Jacinth shook his head in disbelief.

The next day, I went to Pedro's Bar. I asked for Bernard Paes. Principe, his partner, fetched him from the back. He must have been working on the books.

"Here you go Bernard – 4,000 shillings plus 400 shillings of interest."

"Carlit, I am surprised, where did you get all this money from?"

"That is not your concern.

I came home from Pedro's Bar feeling good. I was not going to utter a single word about my winnings to Basil. She was already in bed but stirred when I entered the bedroom. I was pleased that she was awake. We talked for a little bit and then I decided to celebrate by making love to her.

CHAPTER 20

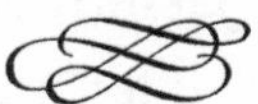

THINKING BACK about the past several years, I realized that I had a lot to be grateful for. Many events gave me a great sense of satisfaction which I took for granted. Our Goan Carnival was celebrated in the middle of February. It seemed like we had just finished Christmas and it was time for another major celebration. I had been elected social secretary of The Tailors Club Social Committee last year. It was my duty to attend the meeting to plan for the upcoming festivities on the following Sunday. Usually, I would sleep in, have a late breakfast, and spend the afternoon reading my favourite newspaper, the Handicap. I would have to sacrifice a leisurely Sunday morning to attend the meeting.

The meeting began with the usual formalities – taking attendance, ensuring that we had a quorum and other trivialities. Lino Fernandes was president, and he would monopolize the meeting – he loved hearing his voice. His wife probably did not give him the time of day. The discussion dragged on and I was almost falling asleep when I heard my name.

"Carlit, why don't we organize a concert this year?" Jacinth asked.

"We will be having the fancy dress competition. Isn't that enough?" I replied hoping that I did not have to take on additional responsibilities.

"But you have had a lot of experience participating in concerts, especially in Goa," Jacinth said.

It seemed like such a long time ago when I used to participate in the Goan *theatres*. I remember the time when Santan Fernandes wrote the script for our plays in Goa. He was an excellent playwright. Our village chapel would celebrate the feast of St. Sebastian on the 29th of July. It would commence with a special mass and in the evening, the celebration would conclude with a *theatre.* A makeshift stage built with wood from palm trees, bamboo and white cotton saris would be set up in front of the chapel. The ladies kindly donated their old saris for this purpose. The villagers of Navelim would congregate in front of the chapel for the evening's entertainment. Grandparents, parents, children and at times even the cows would attend. Quite often, I was asked to act. I would invariably end up playing the female role since most of the women were too shy to participate. I must admit I did have fun acting and would get quite the laugh and applause from the audience.

"Why don't we have a variety show instead of only a *theatre*?" I suggested.

"That's a good idea. Our children could participate too," Lino said enthusiastically.

"I will work on the *theatre,* but I would like someone else to handle the other activities."

"I can take care of that." Mrs. Fernandes volunteered.

I thought hard and long about a *theatre* that people would find interesting. This would be the highlight of the variety show.

Mrs. Fernandes worked well with the children. She would organize traditional Goan dances for the rest of the show. The *theatres* that I had participated in while I was in Goa would not be appreciated here in Kampala. I finally based it on a Goan movie called *Nirmon*. The play was about a working-class married man with three young children. He worked for the P&O shipping line. He was lost at sea when his ship sank off the coast of Goa. With no sign of her husband returning, and on the brink of poverty, his wife finally decided to marry a rich man. He had been pestering her for years to marry him. She did not love this man but thought it would be best for her children. Things started looking up for the family, and the children were enjoying a good life. The play ends with her former husband coming back and shocking the family. He told them how he had survived at sea by hanging on to a log. He went on to live in a remote village. His family welcomed him back. The rich man was forced to leave his home.

My first task was to cast the actors. This time, I was determined not to play the female role. Fortunately, Maggie Martins was only too glad to oblige. I cast myself in the lead male role and Jacinth agreed to play the role of the supporting actor. I included three of Lino's children in the play. He was ecstatic. We practiced frequently before the show. Maggie was working out quite well, but I had a difficult time with the children. They had never acted before. I had to train them to put in more feeling when reciting their lines. I was beginning to wonder if I had made the right decision, but it was too late to find other actors.

The other important task was to design and sew the costumes. In addition to the leftover fabrics from my store, I had to buy additional fabrics. "Kachra's" was a little Indian *duka* located on Vikram Street. He carried a variety of reasonably priced fabrics and bargaining was an acceptable practice. It was a dimly lit shop that had a characteristic smell of fabric dye. I was overcome with a warm and comfortable feeling when I entered the *duka*.

"*Jambo* Kachra, how is business?"

"*Jumbo,* Dias. Business has been slow."

"Well, I have come to give you some business. I require five yards of Jinja fabric in black, green and red."

Mr. Kachra's face lit up. I could almost see the shillings in his eyes.

"Yes, I have all those colours at a special price of three shillings a yard."

"Three shillings is too much. I will pay you two shillings."

"Do you want to put me out of business? Two seventy-five." Mr. Kachra said adamantly.

"Two twenty-five," I replied.

"That is how much I pay the mill. Two fifty is my lowest price."

I sketched out the costumes and cut them at the end of the day. In the mornings, I got Margaret to sew the costumes. Since we were very busy at the shop, I would take the costumes home for Basil to complete the handwork.

"Dias, I am very tired these days. I cannot do all this handwork, look after the children, and cook."

"Basil, we are very busy at the shop, and we need the costumes for the carnival."

"I suppose that I have no choice then," she said with a sigh.

It was only when she got up from the dining table that I noticed how big she had become.

The following week, we had our last practice. Basil was still working frantically the night before the concert to complete the costumes. On Saturday morning, we had the dress rehearsal, and it was a disaster. Right in the middle of the play, Maggie's dress split. She must have gained weight since I had taken her measurements. The children kept forgetting their lines and I could not stay focused. Jacinth was the only one who acted well. I reprimanded the children and told them to study their lines. I reminded Lino to ensure that they would practice their lines.

It was 6:00 p.m. and everyone was on time except for Maggie. The children were cramming their lines backstage. Ten minutes before the show began, Maggie came in panting. Her taxi had broken down halfway and she had to walk the rest of the way. I was surprised to see the number of people that showed up, including members of the Goan Institute. There was a lot of banter until the lights in the hall went out. There was a sense of anticipation and excitement in the air. My heart was racing, and my mouth was dry. The band played the *Alvarod*, which is typically played at the beginning of festivals in Goa. The drummer struck the cymbals to simulate the ringing of the church bells. At the end of the *Alvarod*, the curtains were drawn, and the *theatre* began. Maggie played her role beautifully and with great emotion. The children remembered their lines and acted much better than I had expected. The audience was in tears during the poignant part of the play. When the entire cast was taking their final bow, I heard the stage creaking and thought that it was going to cave in. I could not believe it; we received a standing ovation.

CHAPTER 21

I WAS glad that the Carnival celebrations went well. It was especially gratifying when people congratulated me on the success of the *theatre*. The members of the club, including Basil, were surprised that I could act. Luiza told me how much she liked the play and the costumes. Rock Santan, my cousin, had taken photographs of the cast at the end of the performance and Luiza would proudly show them to anyone that visited. I found it a bit embarrassing.

It was a Monday morning, the week after the carnival. Everything was getting back to normal when a well-dressed lady entered the shop.

"Are you Carlos Dias?" she inquired.

"Yes, that is me," I replied, wondering who this familiar fair-skinned lady was.

"I am Barbara Kimenye from......"

"The Uganda Nation," I continued.

It took a few seconds for me to realize that she wrote the weekly fashion column for the newspaper.

"Mr. Dias, I have heard a lot about your work."

"You have?" I asked.

"I have seen your customers at state events and the Governor's Ball. Your work speaks for itself."

I was dumbfounded. This was quite the compliment, coming from a fashion authority. I wished that I had known earlier that she was coming. I would have tidied up the shop, improved the lighting and changed the décor.

"Are you interested in a ball gown?" I inquired nervously.

"No, I would like to write a column on you."

"You mean in the Uganda Nation?"

"Yes, the interview would only take about thirty minutes."

"I would be happy to oblige."

I spent more than half an hour answering her questions and taking her around the shop. We had just ended the interview when I noticed Basil coming in from the back door with coffee and buns. She was wearing her housedress and sandals. I froze for a moment. I quickly made eyes at her signalling her to leave. Thankfully, she got the message and left. All I needed was for Barbara to see my wife in a casual dress. As soon as she left the shop, Basil walked in with the coffee. I scolded Basil for not being properly dressed. She put her head down and left the shop. The dress was tight around her belly. I realized that she needed some new maternity dresses. I felt bad for scolding her.

On my way to the shop the following morning, I stopped at "Flores's Green Grocery". The scent of ripe fruit permeated the store. There were crates of mangoes and jackfruit at the entrance of the shop. I had to weave through the shop before I reached the main counter. I picked up the Uganda Nation and gave Mr. Flores twenty-five cents. It was surprising that he would sell newspapers in his shop, just to make a few cents of profit. As I walked out of the shop, I was tempted to pick up a dozen mangoes, but quickly changed my mind when I saw the price.

8 UGANDA NATION, Wednesday, July 31, 1963

UGANDA HAS HER TOP DESIGNER

BARBARA KIMENYE

(... and we wouldn't swap him for a Bohan or a Hartnell)

PARIS may have its Mark Bohan, London has Norman Hartnell, but I doubt very much if Uganda's fashion-conscious women would be prepared to swap their own Carlos Dias for either of these famous figures.

Carlos Dias is a quiet little Goan whom one never meets at parties — in fact few women can ever remember seeing him outside his dim, pokey shop — and yet he is usually the first man we think of when we are invited to that very special occasion.

He came to Uganda eighteen years ago, and one of his first customers was Lady Hutton-Hall, wife of the Governor of the time. Since then, he has never looked back.

Abreast of fashion

Under the somewhat formidable name of "Luiza Gowns," Carlos now operates two shops in the same street, with several assistants to help him, but he himself still does such delicate jobs as styling, cutting and fitting.

Perhaps more than any other man, Carlos is responsible for the way Uganda's women always manage to keep abreast of current fashion trends, because, using gentle persuasion, he weans them away from lines which are definitely on the way out.

The most gregarious females wouldn't dream of arguing with what he considers suits them best, and for a favoured few he even takes the trouble to make original designs.

Regarding the prescribed 4" drop in hemlines, he thinks it will be slow to catch on in Uganda, but when it eventually does he hopes it will be accompanied by the return of floor-length evening dresses.

Favourite customer

"There is nothing like a ball gown," Carlos maintains, "it can make the most ordinary woman look romantic."

His customers come from all parts of Uganda, especially when there is a wedding in the offing, for he is famous for his ethereal wedding dresses, and high on the list is Her Highness the Nabagareka of Buganda. Of her, Carlos says, "It's a pleasure to make her things, because her slenderness and height transform the simplest dress into something fabulous."

News Article by Barbara Kimenye - Luiza Gowns

I got into my car. I felt my heart beating rapidly. I anxiously flipped over the pages but did not see any article on Luiza Gowns. Maybe Barbara changed her mind and printed another article. I went through the newspaper a second time. This time slowly and focused on more than just the headlines. There it was, on page 8. The headline in bold and large font, "**UGANDA HAS HER TOP DESIGNER**". The first sentence mentioned Mark Bohan of Paris and Norman Hartnell of London and then I saw my name. I could not believe it. She compared me with these world-class designers. She even mentioned Lady Hutton-Hall, wife of the governor as being one of my first customers. She credited me with the way Uganda's top women dressed. I was overwhelmed with the accolades. While driving to the shop, I heard a knocking sound coming from the car. It irritated me that something was wrong after paying a fortune for it.

After closing the shop, I decided to go home to show Basil the newspaper, only to find out that she was not there. Matti was at the front door crying.

"*Matul, Matul* what happened?"

"Mummy was crying and was in a lot of pain – she said that the baby was coming."

"Baby...so where is she?"

"Mrs. Manu took her to the hospital."

I got in the car and dashed to the Asian hospital. When I arrived at the hospital a couple of doctors were rushing into the delivery room. The receptionist informed me that Basil was in the delivery room. I waited outside the delivery room. A stream of sweat was flowing down the center of my back. My heart was pounding. I was overcome with guilt. I hadn't sewed her maternity dresses. After waiting for what seemed like hours, Mrs. Manu came out of the operating room. She happily announced that Basil delivered a baby boy. Tears of joy welled in my eyes. What a blessing to have a fourth son.

"How is Basil?"

"She is stable, but she had a few complications."

"What kind of complications?"

"I don't know the details, but the doctor told me that she had to be operated on soon after the delivery."

"How is the baby?"

"He is fine but has jaundice which is common in newborn babies."

"Thank you, Mrs. Manu. You have been a great help."

"It is okay. You better go home now; Basil will need to rest."

On my way home I thought of how I had neglected Basil. I decided to make it up to her by sewing some petticoats and a housecoat. She could use them in the hospital. I had to think of a special name as this would probably be my last child. I wished that *Mai* was here to witness this joyous moment and to help me pick a name. Just then it struck me. She loved my adopted brother and cousin Gregory. My last son would carry his name.

CHAPTER 22

I WAS DRIVING HOME from the club when I heard a clanking sound and then a thud. The car sputtered to a gradual halt on Kampala Road. I got out and opened the bonnet hoping that it was safe for me to do so. It was hard to tell if anything was damaged since the engine was covered in soot and mud. I got down on my knees and looked under the car. I was shocked when I realized that the axle had fallen onto the road. I could feel the blood rise to my head. Coincidentally, I was about fifty yards from Cooper Motors – the place where I purchased the car. No breakdown truck would be available at this time of the night. Getting a taxi would be a problem, so I locked the car and walked home.

It was a foggy and cool night. The scent of frangipanis filled the air. I shivered as I walked along Kampala Road. I wished I had worn a cardigan. I passed the grand Barclays Bank building and turned left onto Colville Street. From a distance, I could see the steeple of Christ the King Church rising above the palm trees. It was like an oasis in the middle of the city. I uttered a prayer of thanks for my children, especially my newborn Gregory. I thought it would be appropriate to mark his birth with the purchase of a new car. I was tired of the old car, and I did not think that it would be worth fixing. A station wagon with room for six children would be ideal. About thirty minutes later I was in Shimoni, close to home. I passed by Flores' big house with an opulent wrought Iron Gate and a stone wall partly covered with purple bougainvillea. There were several mango and guava trees in the compound. I noticed a brand-new Morris station wagon, as I peered through the gate.

I called Cooper Motors and asked them to tow my car to their garage the following day. The manager told me to call the Breakdown Company since they did not provide a towing service.

"What do you mean you cannot tow my car? You sold it to me."

"Mr. Dias, your Fiat is a very reliable car according to the Royal Automobile Association."

"So why did it break down?"

"Have you been following the maintenance program recommended by Fiat?"

"The car has been serviced whenever there was a major problem."

"I meant the regular maintenance that includes lubrication, oil changes and so on."

"I am not happy with this worthless car."

"We can help you select another car."

"I was thinking of buying a Morris station wagon."

"That is an excellent car for a family. Can you come in tomorrow afternoon?"

"Yes, I believe I can."

"Right, then. I will see you at 4:00 p.m."

I kept picturing the Morris station wagon several times during the day. It would be practical for travelling to Nairobi. The only problem was that I did not have the money to purchase the car. Barclays Bank may lend me the money since I have an account with them. Even though the manager was reluctant to give me a loan, he finally agreed. He had heard about the reputation of Luiza Gowns. The newspaper article in the Uganda Nation must have helped. I took the loan guarantee from the bank and went to Cooper Motors. We filled out the necessary papers and I signed the purchase order. They gave me a measly credit of 500 shillings for the Fiat.

"Basil, look out the window."

"Why Dias? I am busy cooking."

"Just take a look. There is a beautiful bird on the tree."

"I don't see any bird except for a few crows."

"Look at the green car – it's ours."

"New car? But...but you just bought the last one two years ago."

"I know but it broke down."

"We cannot afford another car, now that we have six children."

"Don't worry Basil, it is all paid for."

I could tell from the look on her face that she did not believe me.

I was glad when Saturday rolled around, after a hectic week. I was getting ready to close the shop when I saw Margaret walking out. She had changed from her work clothes into a bright yellow and brown *Gomesi* – something that was becoming very popular among Ugandan women. Mr. Gomes, a Goan tailor had cleverly converted the simple wrap that the native Ugandans wore into an elegant robe. The small yoke had a rectangular neck with buttons to the right. It had puff sleeves, and the bottom part was a wrap that was buttoned to the side above the waist. A wide band was tied below the waist.

"*Kwa heri bwana,*" she said as she walked out the door. Her buttocks swayed from side to side. I assumed that she going to spend some time in town before going to her village.

I drove home after closing the shop. I was looking forward to a quiet lunch and an afternoon nap. That was not to be. Basil talked at length about visiting the doctor because of her rheumatism which made her knees swell to double their normal size. I was quite shocked to see that when she lifted her night dress. Dr. Ahmed had recommended that she bathe in the ocean as salt water had healing properties.

The next morning, I was enjoying driving my new car to work when it occurred to me that we could drive to Malindi, an idyllic coastal town in Kenya. We could stop in Nairobi for a break and then continue our journey. Basil could rest and bathe her knees peacefully in the ocean. It would also be a good opportunity to test the durability of my new Morris. Chrispin Furtado could take care of the shop.

Chrispin was already sewing when I arrived at the shop at 8:00 a.m. He was diligent and very hard-working. I felt confident leaving the shop in his hands.

"Chrispin, I have decided to go to Malindi."

"Malindi! It will take several days to get there. Are you going to take the train?"

"No, I will be taking my new car."

"New car? When did you buy it?"

"Yesterday. It is a Morris station wagon."

"How long will you be away?"

"About two weeks. Can you do me a favour and look after the shop?"

"Me...me. I have never managed workers before."

"This will be a good opportunity. I will pay you an extra hundred shillings."

"Hun...hundred shillings. Oh Carlit, I don't know how to thank you."

That evening I announced my plans to Basil. Surprisingly, she agreed. Her knees must have been the source of a lot of pain. Basil spent several days cooking and packing for the trip. Every evening when I got home there was another bag in the living room. By the end of the week, she had about twenty bags and packages.

"Basil, we will not have space for all these bags in the car."

"But we need to take food and clothes for eight of us."

"I know, but you will just have to reduce the number of bags. Take fewer clothes. We can buy some more food in Nairobi and possibly in Mombasa."

"Nairobi? Are we going to stop there?"

"Yes of course. It is on the way. Besides I will need to rest for a couple of days. It is a long drive to Malindi."

I could tell from her expression that she did not like the idea of staying in Nairobi. She must have suspected that I was planning to go for a horse race.

CHAPTER 23

"Michael refuses to wake up. I have called out to him several times, but he won't get up." Basil said in a panic.

"What do you mean, won't wake up? We must leave soon."

"He will never be ready. He doesn't move fast in the mornings."

"I know what will get him up."

I started tapping the inside of the cup with a spoon next to his bed.

Michael opened his eyes and sat up. He loved beaten egg yolk with sugar. That was one of Basil's cold remedies. Michael was disappointed to see just an empty cup. The trick worked and we were out of the house in twenty minutes.

Basil managed to get the entire brood into the car while I loaded the baggage. As I walked towards the car, I noticed that it was quite low. I would have to watch out for any big bumps on the road. It was around 6:30 a.m. and the sun was barely visible over the horizon. The clouds were ablaze. I drove down Shimoni Road to Colville Street and turned right onto Kampala Road.

The Caltex station was right around the corner. It was the only petrol station in this part of town. The Aga Khan Foundation probably funded his business, as they did for most Ismailis.

Within half an hour, the sun had risen, and we were out of the city. We drove past tall grass and scattered forest. In contrast, the western part of Uganda was almost desert-like, with acacia trees and thorn bushes. Now and again, we would spot antelope, impala and dik-dik. It was around 10:00 a.m. when Basil started serving meat patties. She had the uncanny ability to know when I was hungry. From a distance, we could see the astounding Owen Falls dam. We were entering the charming city of Jinja, the source of the Nile.

I pointed to the dam and told the children that it was the source of our electricity. They all turned and looked in awe at this engineering feat.

Although Jinja was smaller than Kampala, it was becoming a major commercial center. We drove on Clive Road and stopped at the Caltex station located on Main Street. We topped the tank with petrol. I was tempted to go to the Jinja Goan Institute for a couple of Club Pilseners. I dropped the idea since I would have to drag the whole family there. We left Jinja and continued along the road to Tororo. The tea plantations on both sides of the road extended as far as the eye could see. The plantations were dotted with labourers picking tea leaves, an indication that it was harvest time. We arrived in Tororo two hours later. Although it was a small town, it had two large Hindu temples. A forest-covered volcanic plug rose abruptly from an otherwise flat plain just outside the town. We stopped at the Crystal Hotel for lunch. The corned beef sandwiches cost 15 shillings, three times what we would pay in Kampala. The children wolfed the sandwiches.

As we journeyed on the landscape changed from woodlands

into vast grasslands with trees and clusters of bushes. We came across hordes of wildebeest and zebras grazing these grasslands. I looked in the rear-view mirror only to see all the children fast asleep. Basil kept giving me coffee at regular intervals. We drove through Eldoret, the main town in the Rift Valley. It had attracted many British settlers because of the mild climate. A couple of hours later the sun was low on the horizon. We stopped to have dinner while it was still bright. As we got out of the car, I observed the Mau Forest a few hundred feet away. Basil laid down some mats and started putting out the food. Suddenly, I heard shrill sounds coming from the direction of the forest. From a distance, I saw a group of blacks coming out of the forest.

"Basil, quickly get the children into the car. I will get the food."

"But....but we haven't eaten yet."

"Just get them in the car! Hurry!"

We just managed to get in the car and started driving, when we saw *Mau-Mau* rebels all dressed in their war attire and spears approaching the road. My heart was pounding, and I started perspiring profusely, as I floored the pedal. I was trembling as I explained to Basil that we were about to be attacked by the *Mau-Mau* rebels. Basil's lips quivered when she realized that we might all have been killed, even Gregory who wasn't even baptized.

We drove silently into the night. I don't think that the children were aware of the danger that we had faced, except for Luiza. Fear etched on her face. A few hours later, Basil passed the food around. Her hands were still trembling.

As the sun peeked over the horizon, we could see the city of Nairobi, a metropolis compared to Kampala. I felt a sense of relief as we entered the city. We saw several barricades and barbed wire around commercial and government buildings as we drove through the city. The *Mau-Mau* rebellion was at its peak. The British blamed the uprising on the Kikuyu tribe since their opposition to British domination was most vocal. The *Mau-Mau* uprising was the beginning of more trouble to come. Basil suggested that we go back to Uganda. I convinced her that we would be safe as we were now out of the zone of danger.

We drove to the suburb of Eastleigh, where Custodio lived. His wife welcomed us with open arms and gave us a hearty breakfast. After breakfast, we slept until late afternoon. I had a bath after I woke up and waited for Custudio. As soon as Custodio came home from work, we had a drink and some supper. We left for the racecourse soon after that.

"Please come home early. The British have imposed a curfew starting at 7:00 p.m." Custodio's wife said.

When we arrived at the racecourse, there was a big sign on the gate. "CLOSED DUE TO STATE OF EMERGENCY". My heart sank. How could this be – those damned rebels? Don't they know that nothing will change? The British are too powerful to let them have their independence.

We went directly to the Nairobi Tailor's Club. I bought Custudio a beer and I had a scotch. We played cards and I drank away my sorrows until 9:00 p.m. We managed to avoid the police patrols by taking the smaller streets to get home. Basil and Custodio's wife were waiting at the door and burst into tears when they saw us. I could tell that Basil was dying to give me a lecture, but she remained silent.

We woke up the next morning and continued our journey to Mombasa. The sun was brilliant and the sky bright blue with cotton-like clouds. I felt rejuvenated and ready to journey on. It was not long before we passed through Nairobi National Park. It was a living tapestry of giraffes, buffaloes, cheetahs, and lions roaming in large open grass plains with scattered acacia. The children were wide-awake marvelling at the wildlife. Luiza and Matti were trying to identify the animals. There wasn't a single place that we could stop to take a break. I was forced to drive on even though I was tired. We finally arrived in Voi, a large town in the southern Rift Valley. We stopped there to stretch and eat snacks that Custudio's wife had packed for us.

The Makupa causeway was a sign that we would soon be entering Mombasa Island. The blue water on either side of the causeway felt liberating. The mixed cultural flavour became quite evident as we entered the town of Mombasa. People of Indian and Arabic decent were milling about the streets. The Indians mainly wore Western attire while the Arabs were dressed in their traditional loose white gowns and maroon fezzes. The women were covered from head to toe in black with just their eyes peeping through. The ocean, the breeze and the smell of the sea reminded me of Goa. Basil was calm and content. The children were wide-eyed taking in this mosaic of people and ancient Muslim architecture. Narrow streets and alleyways were characteristic of the old town of Mombasa. After weaselling our way through the maze of streets, we finally arrived at Ethelvinas Hotel. Basil met Ethelvina, the owner of the hotel when she first came from Goa, with Luiza and Matti.

"Come, come in, Carlit, Basil," Ethelvina welcomed us.

"How are you Ethelvina?" Basil inquired.

"I am fine. This hotel keeps me busy all day. You must be very tired."

"Yes, it has been an exhausting and scary journey."

"I hear that the Kikuyu have launched a full-scale rebellion," Ethelvina remarked.

"We were almost killed by the *Mau-Mau* rebels," Basil said.

"That must have been terrifying. Thank God you are safe."

"Yes, it was Dias who managed to get us here safely," Basil replied.

"I will take you to your rooms."

"God bless you."

The African porters carried our baggage up to the third floor. I tipped them one shilling each. Basil thought that it was too much. It was comforting to be able to bathe and rest my tired eyes. We all slept soundly and woke up early the next morning. We embarked on the last leg of our journey. The drive along the coast was exhilarating. White dhows sailed down the coast frequently. We would spot large ocean-going vessels in the distance. They must have been coming from or going to India. I longed for the day when I would be able to take my family to see *Mai.* She would be so thrilled to see all her grandsons.

We drove through the abandoned Swahili town of Gedi. A glimpse of the ruins of this once-thriving town could be seen through the forested area. Within an hour of passing Gedi, we finally arrived at Malindi. It was a town of whitewashed houses and narrow lanes. We drove past The Blue Marlin and Malindi's beach hotel, something we could not afford. We ended up staying at a quaint cottage close to the beach. We thoroughly enjoyed the warm salt water of the Indian Ocean and ate an abundance of seafood. While the children played on the beautiful white sandy beaches, I would enjoy drinking beer at the bar. Basil was in her glory wading in the ocean. Within a couple of weeks, the swelling in Basil's knees had subsided. It was time to head back to Uganda.

CHAPTER 24

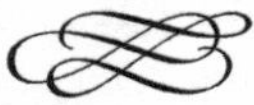

BASIL WAS CHANGING Gregory's towelling nappies frequently on the drive back from Malindi. We stopped often to air the car and dispose of the waste. In Nairobi, we decided to take him to the doctor. Gregory was diagnosed with a severe case of diarrhea. The doctor could not prescribe any medication since he was barely two months old. Basil decided to give him the age-old remedy of gripe water. This seemed to stabilize him, so we were able to continue our journey.

On the way out of Nairobi, we were stopped twice at army checkpoints. We were forced out of the car while the army searched for weapons. I was glad that I did not bring my hunting rifle with me. We only stopped at large towns to avoid trouble with the *Mau-Mau* rebels. It was a huge relief when we crossed the border into Uganda.

"Are we in Uganda?" Luiza asked excitedly.

"Yes Luiza, we do not have to worry about the *Mau-Mau's* anymore."

"Were they going to kill us?" she inquired.

"No, I don't think so. They consider the British as their enemies."

I did not want to tell her that the Asians were probably next on their list. Most of the Africans felt cheated because the Asians controlled most businesses and the economy.

Everyone in the car was more relaxed. Gregory was getting better, so we drove straight through until we reached Jinja. In Jinja, we filled the fuel tank and then had lunch at the Crystal Hotel. The last leg of the journey into Kampala seemed to drag on. I found it hard to keep my eyes open. We finally rolled into Kampala at 7:00 p.m. on Saturday. We had our baths, changed, and got into bed. Nobody stayed up for supper, even though Basil insisted that we eat. We slept in for most of Sunday. Most of us woke up between 4:00 p.m. and 5:00 p.m., except for Michael who slept right through until Monday morning.

On Monday after closing the shop, I went home since I was extremely tired. When I walked into the house, Basil had this tense and uneasy look on her face.

"Gregory has been vomiting all day," Basil said, teary-eyed.

"Did you give him gripe water?"

"He cannot retain that either. Can we please take him to see Dr. Ahmed?"

"Basil, I am very tired. I came home early to rest."

"Look at him," Basil said in desperation, as she opened the tiny blanket.

I could not believe what I saw. He was limp and languid.

"Oh my God, let's go now."

We rushed to Dr. Ahmed's office, only to find the waiting room brimming with people.

"Mrs. Ahmed, please can you take us in next, our baby is very sick," Basil pleaded.

"These people have been waiting for a long time. I

cannot......," Mrs. Ahmed stopped in mid-sentence when Basil showed Gregory to her.

"Please take him in right away."

Gregory was dehydrated. Dr. Ahmed told us to take him to Mulago Hospital immediately. He spent a week at the hospital with Basil. Mrs. Manu would take them food during the day, and I would visit every evening. Thankfully, his recovery was quite remarkable. When he left the hospital, he looked healthy and normal.

We decided to christen Gregory as soon as possible. It was necessary to choose proxy godparents for him since we were naming him after my adopted brother who had passed away. Mr. and Mrs. Mendes were kind and gentle people. They lived in Kawempe, a small town on the outskirts of Kampala. They owned a general store that catered to the local population. Basil and the children visited them regularly and got to know them quite well. They also came from the same village as us, Navelim, in Goa. We thought that they would make good godparents.

Basil and Luiza met the priest to set a date for the baptism. After the meeting, Basil was quite distraught. Father King scolded her for waiting so long to baptize Gregory since it was customary to baptize a child eight days after he was born. I could never understand why priests made such a big deal about the timing of baptisms.

His godparents had arrived late for the baptism because of the unreliable bus service from Kawempe. Although Mrs. Mendes wore a beautiful red sari with gold trimming and jewelry, she looked frazzled when they entered the church. Mr. Mendes on the other hand was quite calm and looked debonair in his grey suit. Father King gave them both a stern look. He had a frown throughout the baptism which annoyed me to no end.

After Gregory's christening, I had a hankering to go fishing.

Port Bell, a small town situated on Lake Victoria was about eight miles from Kampala. The long pier was ideal for fishing. I was hoping to take the family and my fishing buddies. Basil took the liberty of inviting all the neighbours and decided that we should have a picnic. It was our first outing since we travelled to Malindi, so the children were most excited about the picnic. We loaded our cars with plenty of food, beer, and fishing gear. It was a bright and sunny morning when the caravan of cars headed for Port Bell. Shortly after arriving, Basil and the other ladies laid down reed mats under a large mango tree. I pulled out the fishing gear and went with Jacinth and Mr. Bernard to a tranquil area along the pier. No sooner had we settled down when Basil came around with some chutney sandwiches. They went very well with the Pilsners. The serene waters of Lake Victoria were calming and relaxing. The occasional ship departed from the pier destined for Kisumu, I assumed. It was not long before the children started chasing each other. Placido and John got rid of their safari shoes and jumped into the water.

"Get out of the water now!" Basil yelled.

"Aaw.... we are enjoying the water. We won't go too far," Placido reassured her.

"No! you could drown. What's worse - you could catch Bilharzia."

"Bilha.... what?"

"The snails in the lake carry this parasite that can make you very sick," Mrs. Manu explained.

"Eeeh....okay, okay," they both shouted as they jumped out of the water.

We managed to catch over a dozen Nile Perch by noon. It was time to take a break for lunch. The women had already laid out the food consisting of pilau, chicken and pork sausages. After eating this sumptuous food, we dozed off. Our afternoon siesta lasted for over an hour, after which we resumed our fishing. We ended up catching tilapia and more Nile perch in the afternoon. Basil was pleased with the quantity of fish that we caught, surmising that it would last us for an entire week.

It was around 4:00 p.m. We had tea that the ladies poured from their thermos flasks that warmed the cockles of the heart. The women rolled up the mats and put the leftover food in containers. The men loaded the cars, including the catch of the day. We bid each other farewell and took to the road. The first part of the road was mud and gravel with the tall grass on either side. After a mile, we were on Port Bell Road, which was tarmac and relatively smooth. The mainstay of this town was the Bell Brewery. The smell of hops permeated the entire area. We wanted to visit the brewery and enjoy a few beers, but Mrs. Paes refused to let her husband stop for a drink. As we drove towards Kampala, we came across the imposing gray walls of the Luzira prison. It looked like a concentration camp with barbed wires on top of the walls. I could not fathom how my friends, Mr. Paul and Mr. Gomes worked in a place like that. The only possible reasons must have been a good salary and free housing.

On Sunday afternoons, I would take Basil to the quiet streets in Shimoni, so that she could practice driving the car. I taught her a few basics like road signs, how to apply brakes, how to change gears and use the clutch. After five weeks she seemed to be getting the hang of it. As we hummed along Port Bell Road, there was hardly any traffic. I figured it would be a good opportunity for her to test her driving skills.

"Basil, why don't you drive for a few minutes?"

"Dias, I don't think it is a good idea. I have never driven on the main road before."

"It is no different from the streets in Kampala."

"What if something happens? The children might get hurt."

"There are hardly any cars on the road. It should be safe."

Basil was nervous, but she moved to the driver's seat. She gripped the steering wheel tightly. She struggled with changing the gears. I didn't want her to strip the gears, so I helped her out. There was a large lorry about a mile away in the opposite direction. Basil's eyes widened. She gripped the steering wheel more fiercely. Her knuckles were white. Suddenly, she applied the brakes with all her might. The car ground to a sudden halt. Placido and Michael were hurled into the front seat. My head hit the dashboard and we had fish and water all over the car. I turned and looked at Basil. She was still gripping the steering and looked straight ahead.

"Why did you apply the brakes?"

"It....it was the lorry. I thought that it was going to hit us."

"It would have moved to the side, or you could have done so."

She started crying. I had to pry her hands off the steering wheel. I helped her out of the driver's seat. I heard Luiza moaning. I turned back to see that the bucket holding the fish hit Luiza. She was holding Gregory and protected him well.

"It is okay, everyone. Let's put the fish back in the pail and wipe ourselves."

Luiza managed to get a towel and passed it around. Basil did not say a word. She was trembling. I drove back to Kampala. Everyone was silent. This marked the end of Basil's driving career.

CHAPTER 25

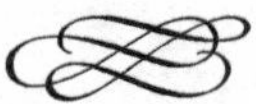

IT WAS the season of Lent. We had to abstain from eating meat on Fridays. Basil cooked the fish that we caught in a variety of ways – fish in curry, fried fish with masala, fish cutlets and grilled fish. Every Friday felt like a feast. The pleasant aroma of fish curry cooked with coconut reminded me of my homeland. I yearned to go back to Goa.

Whenever I was leaving to go to the club, Basil would remind me that it was Lent. She expected me to abstain from gambling and drinking for forty days. I paid no attention to her. The club was buzzing with the news of the Kabaka of Buganda returning from exile. It seemed like the British were making inroads with the Baganda. One of the requirements was that Buganda remains part of Uganda, even though the Kabaka, Mutesa II, was a constitutional monarch. It was a relief that the constitutional crisis was nearing resolution.

Good Friday coincided with Gregory's first birthday. Basil would not celebrate his birthday on such a solemn day. We decided to have a party for him on Easter Sunday. His godparents, my cousin Rock Santan, his family and other relatives were invited. Basil cooked all day Saturday for the party. Everyone was dressed in their Sunday best. After lunch, Luiza placed the birthday cake with a single candle on a small table with a lace cloth. She had sewn the tablecloth and the dress that she was wearing. Gregory was wide eye and smiling when we placed him in front of his cake. The party continued until teatime and thereafter we went to the club for our Easter celebration.

Nobby and his band were playing some great music for this occasion. The dance floor was packed. I had a couple of dances with Basil and then went to the bar to quench my thirst. Shortly after that, we started playing cards. Basil would keep sending the children, to remind me that it was time to go home. My answer was a consistent no. I could not quit when I was winning. I guess that my son's birthday brought me luck. I was concentrating on my game because the stakes were high. Suddenly, someone tugged at my shirt. I thought that it was one of my sons. I was about to tell him that it wasn't time to leave when I noticed that it was Kirit, Mr. Patel's son. He owned the shop next to mine. I was surprised. What was he doing here? The Hindus avoided the club like the plague. Their religion did not permit drinking or any form of gambling.

"Arrh, Kirit what are you doing here?"

"Mr. Dias, you have to come quickly, quickly." Kirit blurted out as he tried to catch his breath.

"Why, what happened?"

"There is a thief in your shop."

"A thief! How do you know that?"

"My father heard some sounds and also noticed a light go on in your shop."

"Jacinth, tell Basil that I had to leave right away. I will come back to pick her and the children later."

"Okay Carlit, please be careful."

We got into the car and drove quickly towards the shop. I went directly to Kenya Shoe Store, Mr. Patel's shop. The smell of leather filled the shop. He told me that he had already called the police. While I waited for them to arrive, I went to the rear of the shop and saw that the light was on. It would be too dangerous for me to go in and accost the thief without a weapon. Furthermore, there could be several of them.

The police finally arrived. There were three officers – a Sikh and two native Ugandans. They were smartly dressed in khaki shirts with metal buttons, knee-length matching shorts, maroon socks, and black leather boots. They asked me to open the shop. I was appalled to see papers, buttons, lace, and other trimmings strewn all over the floor. There was a box next to the counter with some fabrics, reels, and trimmings in it. The cash drawer was left open. My chest started heaving and blood rushed to my head, angered by the audacity of this thief. I waited near the counter with the Sikh officer while the two policemen started combing the shop. About ten minutes later, they came back saying that they did not find anyone.

"Maybe he got frightened and ran away," the Sikh police officer said.

"I think that he is still in the shop," I insisted. "Let us go together and look for him."

We went into the back and looked under the tables, then in the changing room and the little kitchen. There was no sign of the thief. We looked upstairs where we stored our fabric but could not find him. Suddenly it dawned on me to check the false ceiling above the showcase. I made one of the policemen shine the torch in that space. The thief was crouched in the gap that was barely three feet high. He looked like a deer caught in the headlights.

"*Toka, toka upesi*," the policeman yelled.

The thief slowly got out of his hiding place and surrendered. His eyes were full of fear. As soon as he stood up the two policemen started hitting him with their batons. The thief put his hands up to protect himself. I heard bones cracking. I cringed. They tied his hands and legs with rope. He could barely walk so they dragged him out of the shop.

As they were taking him to the black police van, several passersby kicked and beat the thief. The policemen made no effort to stop them. Within minutes, there was a crowd watching this poor man being beaten. It made me sick to my stomach but there was nothing I could do. Telling them to stop would be an exercise in futility. By the time they put him in the van, he was drenched in blood. It was sad to see how they treated their own. Once they were gone, I started putting things in order. It took me several hours to organize the mess. I suddenly realized that it was 10:00 p.m. Basil and the children would be waiting for me at the club.

I rushed over only to find them standing outside the club. Fortunately, Jacinth had stayed with them, otherwise, Basil would have been a nervous wreck. I could tell that she was upset, so I tried to explain about the robbery at the shop. Although she listened to me, it did not calm her.

On Monday morning, Lady Hutton Hall came to the shop to try on the gown. She was planning to wear it to the governor's ball.

"Good morning, Lady Hall."

"Good day, Mr. Dias, and how are you?"

"I am well except for yesterday's robbery."

"What robbery?"

"A thief broke into the shop and tried to steal money and materials."

"What is becoming of this country?"

"I don't know. It is not safe for us anymore."

"We civilized and developed this country and now that it is flourishing, they want to take it away from us."

Lady Hall tried on her black velvet gown, which graced her body beautifully. The only thing I had to do was to pin up the hem. There was no need for a second fitting. It certainly was a pleasure sewing for someone of her shape and height. She was not fussy like some of the other customers. They insisted on having their outfits altered when the real problem was their shape.

Although Lady Hall was happy with her gown, she seemed troubled when she left the shop. Her husband must have been in the heart of the political strife in Uganda. It was 1956 and Nationalism was rearing its ugly head all over East Africa. The return of the Kabaka did not quell the constitutional crises. Trouble was looming over the horizon. I wondered how much longer we could continue living in Uganda. Maybe, it was time for me to think about moving back to Goa. My last visit to Goa was almost fifteen years ago. Sadly, none of my sons had ever been to the homeland.

CHAPTER 26

I HAD ASKED MY BROTHER-IN-LAW, John Glory Pires if he could handle the shop finances when I was in Goa. While we were going through the books, he kept pointing out several inconsistencies with the bookkeeping. I didn't have the patience to listen to him droning on about inaccuracies since I wasn't a numbers person. On the positive side, Chrispin Furtado was well-groomed to do the cutting and manage the workers. He was very dedicated and diligent. I was very grateful to him.

Basil expressed her concern about affording this trip and about the business while we were away in Goa. There wasn't anything I could do to stop her from worrying. *Mai* might never get a chance to see her grandchildren if I didn't make this trip soon. In her last letter, she complained about her poor health. She asked me when I was planning to bring my sons to Goa. I was getting antsy to go back to the homeland. I was sure that Basil would be fine once she got there.

On a Monday afternoon, I went to Smith McKenzie Steamships, located on Kampala Road. Mr. Mackenzie, the owner of this prosperous company, had hired several Goans to work for him. The short one called Mr. Codeiro was the ticket clerk. He acted like he owned the business. His poorly tailored suit would indicate otherwise.

"That will be five thousand two hundred shillings," Mr. Codeiro said after tallying up the cost.

"Five thousand! You must have made a mistake."

"*Arrh, arrh* one thousand for both you and your wife, 750 shillings for each of your two daughters, 500 shillings each for your three sons. The youngest is free since he is under four years, but you must pay 200 shillings in taxes."

There was no way I could afford it. Borrowing was out of the question since I owed the bank for the car loan. Basil was right. Her trusted friend, Mrs. Manu must have given her an idea of the cost. As I was pondering what I should do, Mr. Codeiro interrupted my thoughts.

"So do you want to book the tickets?" he asked impatiently.

"Just a moment," I replied, trying to stifle my anger.

The only way I could afford this trip is if I left Luiza and Matti behind. They were born in Goa and *Mai* had spent time with them. They could stay with my cousin Rock Santan and his wife.

When I came back from the booking office, I informed Basil of my decision. She was extremely distraught. She did not like the idea of leaving Luiza and Matti behind for six months.

"Basil, at least *Mai* has seen them. She is yearning to see her grandsons."

Basil had this sad and distant look on her face.

"Rock is very strict with his daughter, Tina. I am sure that he will keep an eye on Luiza and Matti."

Basil remained silent.

"Listen, Florine will take care of their needs as girls," I said trying to reassure her.

"They may be all right with Florine," Basil finally said.

The big day finally arrived. Rock Santan drove us to the train station. He was thrilled about the idea of having my car in our absence. John Glory brought Luiza, Matti and Basil to the train station. Once the luggage was loaded, the train started moving. We waved to Luiza, Matti, Rock Santan and John Glory. Rock Santan was all smiles, while Luiza and Matti were in tears. Basil was crying too. Suddenly, I felt this sharp pain in my chest. I was overcome with a sense of guilt for leaving them behind. What was I thinking? Maybe I should have borrowed the money. The train picked up speed and soon Luiza and Matti faded into the background. Shortly after the station had vanished. We were on the outskirts of Kampala, amid the tall grass and banana trees punctuated with red mud huts.

"Don't worry, Basil, they will be fine," I said trying mostly to convince myself.

Although she nodded, I could tell that she was concerned about them. I sincerely hoped that Rock and Florine would take care of them. We finally settled down when the train attendant came in with piping hot tomato soup. Basil had brought some meat patties that went well with the soup. After supper, we lay down and were lulled into a deep slumber. The next morning, we woke up to the aroma of *Safari* coffee. There was something comforting about sipping coffee and having breakfast in the restaurant on the train. This feeling of tranquillity ended abruptly when I entered our compartment. Placido and Michael were having a wrestling match while Basil was trying to serve coffee from a thermos flask. Gregory was sulking in the corner because there was no milk. After we finished our breakfast and freshened up, we settled down and enjoyed the changing landscape. Several hours later, we could see houses with large spaces in between. I surmised that we were on the outskirts of Nairobi. I felt a tinge of excitement. The children were glued to the window as the small houses gave way to larger three-storey buildings.

As expected, Custudio and his wife came to greet us at the train station. The thought of going to a horse race crossed my mind but the train was leaving for Mombasa shortly. We waved to Custudio and his wife as the train left the station. It was well over half an hour before we got out of the city. Nairobi had developed much faster than Kampala. Not long after leaving Nairobi, we entered the arid plains of the savannah. We all drifted off to sleep. Several hours later we were in Tsavo National Park with a plethora of wildlife that included lions, leopards, rhinos, elephants, and cheetahs. In the afternoon, I went to the bar on the train and had several beers followed by an afternoon siesta. We finally entered Mombasa late in the evening. The humidity was unbearable, and the children were wilting from the heat. We were exhausted after being on the train for almost two days. We were all glad when we arrived at Ethelvina's Hotel.

Early the next morning we headed for the Port of Mombasa. It was bustling with activity. The passengers were boarding the colossal *SS Karanga,* while cargo was being loaded into the hold. The air was filled with an odour of seawater and fish. I was glad that the temperature and humidity had not yet reached intoxicating levels. We stayed on deck to ensure that all our cargo was loaded and then went down to our cabins. I did not plan to spend too much time in these stifling chambers. The children had the same game plan. Basil was the only one who would stay in the cabin and chat with the other Goan ladies for hours on end. The first couple of days we were all seasick and spent most of the time in bed. On the third day, I managed to round up a group of men willing to play cards. Luckily, this kept us entertained for the rest of the day.

After six days in the Indian Ocean, the ship finally docked in Karachi. India would not allow ships departing from any of its ports to land in Goa. This was India's way of letting the Portuguese know that they abhorred their occupation of Goa. Shortly after arriving, we boarded the *SS Lurio,* a former Portuguese military ship that was recently converted into a passenger ship. The excellent condition of the ship was a vestige of strict military discipline.

The large delta of the Indus River came into focus as we sailed from Karachi's harbour. Shortly after that, we were navigating the deep blue waters of the Arabian Sea. The pale blue sky was almost cloudless, and the sun was blazing. The serene voyage turned turbulent a few hours later, with the trade winds bringing in the monsoon rains. The blue waters became choppy and gray. We quickly took to our cabins for cover. The ship rocked. We had to hold onto the frame of the beds to avoid getting hurled onto the floor. The captain warned everyone to remain in their cabins. We were overcome with nausea. Several hours later the winds died down and the sea became relatively calm. The captain announced that an elaborate dinner would be served. It was available for all the passengers regardless of their cabin class. None of us felt like eating, so we called it an early night.

We arrived in Panjim harbour early the next morning. The ubiquitous palm trees and magnificent white churches were a welcoming site. As we got out of Panjim, the muddy and sandy terrain was covered with sprouts of plants and grass. The smell of wet earth filled my nostrils. The monsoons had a cleansing effect on the dusty atmosphere of the dry season from

November to May. Basil was all smiles. The children were in awe, taking in their home country for the first time. They found the pigs and chickens running around the villages quite amusing. Basil would mention the names of friends and relatives from some of the villages that we passed. I don't think any of that registered with the children, except for Placido. He had a sharp memory and listened attentively to everything.

"Daddy, there are so many big white churches here!" Placido exclaimed.

"Yes, son, this is Goa. The church is the centre of each village. When I was young, I used to paint the altars."

"Wow! I would like to do that when I grow up," Placido said excitedly.

It was getting hotter as we went down the winding and treacherous road towards Margao. We passed through the narrow streets which were flanked by large, whitewashed houses occupied by the Portuguese. It was the afternoon siesta time. Most of the shops and markets were closed. This made it easy for us to get through the town. We finally arrived in Navelim. The Holy Rosary Church was a joyful sight. It brought back warm memories, especially of our village feast. Basil made the sign of the cross, something she always did when we passed a church. After passing the village shops, we turned onto an unpaved narrow road and drove for a few minutes, when I saw our house come into focus. I felt a tingling sensation all over my body. Sylvain, the neighbour's daughter, ran to inform *Mai* that we had arrived. We just got out of the taxi and *Mai* was at the door to greet us. Tears of joy streamed down her cheeks.

"*Mai, Mai*" was all I could say as I embraced her.

It was good to feel the warmth of her body and inhale her scent after all these years.

"*Mai* these are your grandsons."

Mai opened her hands wide, and my sons ran up to her. She embraced them for a long time and then finally stood up.

"*Baba*, where are Luiza and Matti?" *Mai* asked, suddenly realizing that they were not around.

"*Mai*, I could not bring them since they are at school." I did not have the heart to tell her that we could not afford to bring them. She could not hide her disappointment. Although I had my regrets for not bringing Luiza and Matti, I was glad that we made it to Goa despite all the obstacles. It felt good to be home.

CHAPTER 27

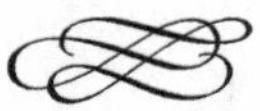

FRIENDS, relatives, and neighbours were visiting us daily. Basil spent most of her time cooking for them. I missed my friends and wished that I could move back to Goa. Occasionally, Basil would ask me to visit her relatives, but I refused. I preferred spending my evenings at Elna's bar playing cards and drinking the local liquor *feni*, derived from the cashew fruit. The bouquet and taste of this drink was exhilarating. I was expected to pay for the drinks at the bar since I was the wealthy one from Africa. I unwittingly built quite an entourage of friends, some of whom I hardly knew.

Going to a *theatre* in Goa was a must and probably the only thing that I did with Basil. She wore a new bottle-green sari and gold jewelry. I donned my black suit and we headed for Margao. The *theatre* was called "Like Father, Like Son". The temporary stage was set up on the grounds of the Holy Spirit Church. It was normally used as a playing field. We were given special seats in the front since we were from out of town. The *theatre* finally began an hour later than scheduled. However, it was worth the wait. Boyer, a famous Goan actor, played the role of the father. He exemplified a total drunk and a Casanova. Some unknown person played the son's role. I enjoyed the show more because we missed this kind of entertainment in Uganda.

Two months had flown by, and I had not visited my close friend Shamrao. I wondered what the latest developments were on the political front. There was talk about the possible occupation of Goa by the Indian government. Since Shamrao was a political activist, I was certain that he would have the inside story on the current situation.

"*Arrh* Carlit, when did you come back from Africa?"

"It's been over two months. The days just seem to fly. How are you, Shamrao?"

"I have been busy writing articles for the "V" Journal."

"Your dedication to the cause is admirable. Are you not afraid?"

"No, I believe that we should continue our fight for the liberation of Goa."

"I see that the Portuguese have not broken your spirit since the last protest."

"They haven't, but they still harass me. Last week they searched my home."

I was certain that Shamrao would keep the flame of freedom burning until Goa was free.

On the other side of the coin were the wealthy Goans who were fervent supporters of the Portuguese. Romeo and Saluzin from Navelim were actively fighting to keep the Portuguese in Goa. They feared that if the Indian Government stepped in, Goa would lose its unique identity and that they would lose their fortunes. I wondered how this would all pan out. In a way, I was glad that I was in Uganda, away from this political unrest. After leaving Shamrao's house I walked through the paddy fields.

Brilliant green stalks filled the flooded miles of endless rectangular sections, only to be broken by islands of higher ground where houses and coconut trees were situated. I could tell from the stalks of rice, that it was almost harvest time. I am sure that *Mai* would be looking forward to receiving her entitlement of rice from the community fields. As I approached the house, I could smell the burning of dried palm leaves mingled with the aroma of fried mackerel.

A month later, we were invited to a wedding in Navelim. We decided to leave the children with *Mai*.

"Daddy, why can't we go to the wedding?" Placido protested.

"Because we want you to spend time with *Mai*."

"But I already spent a lot of time with her, and she doesn't understand what I am saying."

"You cannot come because the wedding will end late – past your bedtime."

"I can stay up," he sulked.

Basil and I got dressed and walked to the church. The ceremony went on for hours on end. The bride, dressed in a traditional white sari with a sheer linen piece draped over her head, was adorned with an abundance of gold jewelry. Just before exchanging their vows, she was tilted to one side and suddenly she fainted. Thankfully, the maid of honour prevented her from getting hurt, by breaking her fall. I wondered if she fainted from the stifling heat or the fear of getting married. She seemed to be very young, probably around sixteen. Her mother ran up frantically and started fanning her.

"Don't just stand there. Get a glass of water," her mother yelled at the altar boy.

They finally managed to revive her, and the service ended with the priest reminding them that it was their duty to have children. At the reception, they served *pilau* and sausage, with an endless flow of drinks. After the wedding march, the dancing began. As usual, Basil was worried about the children, so we decided to leave early.

When we got home, the house was in darkness. As we approached the door, we saw the children huddled in a corner of the balcony.

"Mummy, Mummy we were so frightened. We don't know where *Mai* is." Gregory, who was only four, said as he rushed into Basil's arms.

"We were playing near the rice fields. When we came back the house was locked," Michael said as his lips twitched.

"Basil, stay with the children. I will look for *Mai*."

I combed the neighbourhood without success. I wondered if she had gone for a walk and collapsed. My fears were growing as I went from house to house. I finally gave up and decided to walk back to the house. When I arrived at the door, I saw *Mai* sitting in the living room having a drink. Basil was fanning her.

"Where were you?" I yelled.

"*Baba*, don't be angry with me, I had gone to the village square to talk to my friends."

"But you left the children alone in the dark. They were terrified."

"Oh, I did not think that they would be afraid since they lived in Africa. Besides I only went for a short time."

"Short time? They said they were waiting for hours. Don't ever do that again!"

Mai withdrew to her room, her shoulders drooping, and her gait slow. I felt terrible for yelling at her. I decided that I would never leave my children with her.

The next day, things were very quiet around the house. *Mai* and Basil were cooking lunch and the boys were chasing the pigs in the backyard. I decided to read the newspaper in the living room. When I looked out the window, I saw a group of uniformed men walking towards the house. I quickly put down the newspaper and went to the foyer. When I opened the door, I realized that they were the Portuguese police. A top-ranking Portuguese official dressed in white was accompanied by a *mistesse* – mixed Portuguese and Goan and two Goan constables dressed in Khaki uniforms. They were very stern. As I looked past them, I saw the neighbours peering out of their windows.

"Are you Carlos Dias?"

"Yes, that is me."

"Do you have a friend named Shamrao Madkaiker who lives in the Buticas district?"

"Yes, we are friends."

"He is being investigated for plotting to overthrow the government by distributing anti-Portuguese literature."

"He is my jeweller and a friend."

"What do you discuss?"

"Mostly about Africa. He is very interested in the political situation."

The two constables went around the house searching from room to room. One of them came back with a copy of the "V" Journal. Shamrao had given it to me during my last visit. Beads of sweat on my forehead turned into rivulets along the side of my face. My heart raced. I should have gotten rid of that.

"We strongly suggest that you stay away from this man. He is a bad influence," said the man in the white uniform.

"I am only here on holiday and will be going back to Uganda soon."

"That is good. The sooner you leave the better."

They took the "V" Journal and left.

Basil came running out of the kitchen. She was trembling and pleaded with me not to talk to Shamrao anymore.

I had my lunch and a long afternoon nap. After waking up, I went to Elna's Bar. There was a heated discussion going on, but when I walked into the bar everyone became quiet. Elna served me with my usual when I sat down. A couple of my friends cautiously approached my table.

"Carlit, you should be careful with the company you keep," Auguste said, almost in a whisper.

"Oh, Auguste, why does everyone make such a big thing out of nothing?"

"You know they could put you in prison. Look at what happened to Bento, Shamrao's friend."

I knew then that it was time for me to head back to Uganda.

CHAPTER 28

THE BROWN BRICK building with a terracotta tiled roof became visible as the train rolled into the Kampala railway station. I was relieved that the long and tiresome journey had finally come to an end. The Union Jack was flying prominently from the rooftop – a stark reminder of British domination. I felt oppressed by colonial rule. Once again, I would have to put up with some of the condescending British. My dream was to retire comfortably in Goa after having amassed sufficient wealth. Hopefully, the Portuguese would be driven out of Goa by the freedom fighters.

My cousin, Rock Santan, Luiza and Matti had come to meet us at the train station. As soon as we got off the train, Matti rushed up to Basil. She burst into tears and embraced her. Luiza stood at a distance and sobbed softly. Rock Santan helped me unload our large metal trunks and bags. Although I had told Basil to pack only a couple of bags, we ended up with seven. She did not have the heart to turn down the gifts of food from her neighbours and relatives. The boys hugged Matti and started telling her stories about Goa all at the same time. She kept moving her head around trying to pay attention to each one. She requested that they speak one at a time but that was to no avail. Luiza gradually approached us and embraced Basil, me and then the boys. Basil held onto Luiza and Matti and sighed.

"Hey Carlit, how was Goa?" Rock Santan inquired.

"Goa was fine, except for the political trouble."

"What do you mean?"

"The Portuguese are clamping down on the freedom fighters. The rights of the middle and low-class Goans are being compromised."

"That must be terrible for the Goans who are against the Portuguese."

"Yes, they have imprisoned some of them."

"My God, what are they up to?"

"I don't know. Why don't we discuss this later? We are all very tired."

As we drove home, everything felt surreal. Although Kampala had been home for many years, it felt foreign. The rice fields, palm trees and sand were replaced by red soil, occasional Jacaranda trees and large grassy areas. The mild temperatures were a pleasant change from the stifling hot weather in Goa. Although I enjoyed the good life that Uganda offered, Goa will always be home to me. As we approached our house on Salisbury Road, I thought about the challenge of getting back to work after six months of fun and pleasure. I wondered how things were at the shop. Hopefully, the workers were still around, and we did not lose any customers. As these thoughts buzzed through my mind, I suddenly noticed that Luiza and Matti were very quiet. I suspected that something unpleasant must have happened to them while we were away. I hoped that they would discuss what was bothering them with Basil.

It came out a few days later. Basil and I were having our

after-dinner chat in bed. Luiza was very upset because we left her and Matti with Rock's family for such a long time. She mentioned that there were many occasions when they were unjustly punished for things they had not done or said. I felt compelled to take some action, but I was not in a position to put my cousin to the test. It would only cause more problems, so I decided to forget about the whole affair.

I was busy trying to get things back to normal at the shop. Basil worked on getting Michael admitted to Norman Godinho School since he missed the registration period. This school, strictly for Goans, was started by Mr. Godinho, a wealthy entrepreneur. He owned Norman Cinema and several buildings on Buganda Road. He had built a sprawling home in a prestigious area on Nakasero Hill Road. The view of the city from his living room was magnificent.

A week after we arrived from Goa, Basil managed to go to Norman Godinho School. Mrs. Castelinho, from Mangalore, India, was the headmistress of the school. Her slightly graying hair was always tied up in a bun. Her metal-rimmed glasses and piercing eyes reinforced her authoritative image.

"You know that the school year has already begun," Mrs. Castelinho said sternly.

"Yes, Mrs. Castelinho. I am sorry but we were in Goa."

"You knew the school year began in January. Why didn't you come back earlier?"

"Our tickets were booked six months ago, and we could not change them."

Mrs. Castelinho shook her head in discontent. She shuffled several papers on her desk until she found the one that she was looking for. It seemed like a class list. After scanning it for several minutes, she finally said, "I will see what I can do. He had better be a quick learner."

"He is a very smart boy. I promise you that he will catch up with the others very quickly."

"Aren't you that tailor's wife? What's his name? Carlos Dias?"

"Yes, I am."

"The tailor's children are not doing so well. I hope for your sake Michael is different."

Basil was almost in tears when she told me about her encounter with Mrs. Castelinho. I was livid and wanted to confront her myself, but Basil pleaded with me to refrain from doing so. She was afraid that I would jeopardize Michael's chances of getting into the school.

Back at the shop, I encountered numerous problems. Chrispin had focused on some customers and things that interested him. He had neglected other areas of the business. The workers, Margaret, and George did not want to work with him anymore and were threatening to leave. I managed to pacify them by saying that I would deal with them directly. I needed a plan to move him out of the shop. I mulled over this for several days. I finally came up with the idea of opening a branch of Luiza Gowns. The demand for tailoring services was growing. This would be a good opportunity for me to grow my business. Chrispin was only too glad to accept my offer as he was an enterprising young man.

For the next two weeks, I was busy with an order for the National Theater. They were putting on the play "Anne of the Thousand Days". They required twenty elaborate costumes that would be extremely time-consuming. The thought of refusing this order was tempting but I could not afford to lose such an important client. Although my plate was full, my brother-in-law John kept harassing me about keeping proper records for accounting purposes. He wanted me to provide him with details of all transactions every week. I could barely manage to do this once a month.

"Carlit, I spent a lot of time getting the books in order while you were away."

"You are an accountant – that should have been an easy task for you."

"No, it wasn't. It took me over three months working every weekend to organize the books."

"The books were not in bad shape."

"Yes, they were. I had to look all over the place for the receipts and sales records."

"I put them all in a drawer."

"Listen, Carlit, I cannot work with you if you do not cooperate."

"I don't need your services. They are beginning to stifle me. Besides, it does not bring in any revenue."

"In that case, I will leave. I will withdraw my partnership in this business."

"Go ahead."

Good riddance. I had more than my fair share of problems to deal with. Later that evening, I mentioned to Basil what had happened. It seemed rather strange, but she did not say a word. That was not like her. As I thought about it, I remembered that she was against the partnership. Her words, as I recalled, were "Never mix business and family. It is bound to end up with problems." I wished I had listened to her, but at the time it seemed like the right thing to do. Besides, I could not see how she could advise me on business matters when her role was to cook and raise the children.

Once I completed the order from the National Theater, I decided to look for another shop. I walked along Salisbury Road but did not see any "To Let" signs. As I passed by *Taws Limited* –

a supplier of office equipment and furniture, I noticed that part of their shop was unoccupied. Surprisingly, the owner told me that he was considering sub-letting part of the shop. The extra space was available since they had withdrawn from the furniture part of the business. We were able to strike a deal of four hundred shillings a month for the rent. I was thrilled. When I broke the news to Chrispin he was just as excited. Thus began "Luiza Gowns Branch".

Luiza Gowns Dress Makers - Cinema Ad slide 1

Luiza Gowns Dress Makers - Cinema Ad slide 2

CHAPTER 29

LUIZA GOWNS BRANCH began prospering just a few months after opening. Chrispin was in his element. Although he was making several times the goodwill, he cleverly concealed his profits. It did not bother me since he was prompt with his goodwill payments for using the name "Luiza Gowns". When I was too busy to take on new customers, I would refer them to him. He welcomed the extra business. Although my business was doing very well, I always had a cash flow problem. I couldn't understand why this was the case. To make matters worse, Basil would ask for money to cover our living expenses. Regardless of how much I gave her, it was never enough.

It was bright and sunny. The morning air was fresh, perfumed with the scent of frangipani blooms. I walked along Salisbury Road deep in thought, wondering what was in store for me. Among the myriad papers on the newsstand "Handicap" jumped out at me. I promptly picked it up and continued on my way to the shop. I was glad that the workers had not come in yet. As I turned the sports pages, I felt an adrenaline rush. The upcoming race featured my favourite contenders including Black Knight. I felt compelled to go to the race. I could make it in time for Saturday's race – The Queen's Gold Cup. Just as I put away "Handicap", my workers strolled in. Margaret had not shown up, which made it a busy day for me. At the end of the day, I drove to the club for a desperately needed drink.

People were carrying green and white flags along Kampala Road as I drove back from the club. I presumed that they participated in a Democratic Party (D.P.) rally at Jubilee Park. I learned later that the British police had dispersed the crowds. As the struggle for independence was becoming more intense, these rallies became more frequent. The D.P. was led by Benedicto Kiwanuka. The Catholics and the Asian business community were ardent supporters of the D.P. On the other side of the spectrum was the United People's Congress (U.P.C.) led by Dr. Milton Obote. The UPC was nationally based and wanted greater African control of the economy in a federally independent state. Mutesa II, who was the King of Buganda, added another level of complexity to the political scene. His party Kabaka Yeka (K.Y.) – 'The King Alone' – was formed to represent the interests of the Baganda. Not knowing who would ultimately take control of the country was a major source of anxiety for me. I hoped that the party that won would be sympathetic towards the Asians. Our main objective was to continue operating our businesses in peace. Suddenly, I saw a police roadblock and applied my brakes. I just managed to stop a couple of feet in front of the barricade.

"Where are you going?" the policeman asked.

"Home...err.... I'm going home."

"Were you at the DP rally?"

"No, no I was at the club."

He turned his face away. I suppose that he got a whiff of alcohol from my breath.

"Make sure that you do not participate in any political rallies."

"I am not interested in politics."

"Good. Keep it that way. We do not want any trouble from you Asians."

He then waved me on.

The following day I picked up Jacinth to go to Nairobi for the race. We hardly got out of Kampala when the police stopped us. Within the next fifty miles, we encountered three additional police barricades. They would question us in detail as to the purpose of our trip and needlessly delay us. By the time we reached Jinja, we were both fed up and decided to go back to Kampala. I was extremely disappointed that we missed the Queen's Gold Cup since it took place only once every five years.

It was Saturday afternoon. I closed the shop and went home to have my lunch. I was hoping to relax. From Basil's face, I could tell that this was not going to happen.

"Dias, Michael got into trouble at school."

"What happened now!"

"He and his friends tried to steal guavas from someone's home near the school and they got caught."

"Why? Couldn't they have run away?"

Basil went into this long, drawn-out story of how the owner confiscated their school bags while they were up the tree picking the guavas. The owner handed their bags to the headmistress. Mrs. Castelinho refused to give Michael his bag unless we went to the school.

Basil went to meet Mrs. Castelinho while I took my nap.

Mrs. Castelinho warned Basil that she would expel Michael if he got into any more trouble. I decided to punish Michael by grounding him for the weekend. After a few hours of seeing Michael's sad face, I let him go out and play with his friends.

On Monday morning, I decided to check in on how Chrispin was doing. The shop was not open, which surprised me since it was 8:30 a.m. Chrispin was punctual and usually in early at 7:30 a.m. I wondered if he was hung over from a weekend of drinking and continued walking to my shop. At noon, I went home for lunch and then dropped by Luiza Gowns Branch. The shop was open but there was no sign of Chrispin. Andrew, who worked for him, informed me that he came in to open the shop but left soon after. He claimed that he was having severe back pains. That was not surprising given the long hours of standing that our kind of work entails. I had the keys, so I told Andrew that I would lock up. Andrew also told me that Chrispin had been absent on several occasions in the past.

In the afternoon, customers kept coming to pick up their dresses, so I hardly got any cutting done. Another distraction was Chrispin's absence. I decided to send George to check up on him. He grumbled about going all the way to Bakuli, an unsavoury suburb of Kampala. I continued working until George arrived five hours later.

"So, was he sick at home?"

"No, *Bwana* he was not at home."

"Where was he then?"

"At the shop."

"What shop?"

"It is a small *duka*. He was there with two workers."

I gave him one shilling and he couldn't stop thanking me.

My blood was boiling. I was enraged. I could not believe that he went behind my back and secretly set up another shop. He must have known that it would mean neglecting Luiza Gowns Branch. I had given him a great opportunity and he turned around and beguiled me. I doubt that he had any idea of what was in store for him.

CHAPTER 30

AVENGING Chrispin consumed me to the extent that Basil suspected something was bothering me. No matter how hard I tried to conceal my feelings she always sensed something was amiss. I would never tell her about winning at the horse race just in case she brought me bad luck. Somehow, she would get wind of it through the grapevine. She confronted me once when I won a sizable sum. I told her that it was not her concern and never to listen to the neighbours - their gossip and rumours would get her into serious trouble. After that, she knew better than to question me. I could tell that she was dying to ask me what was on my mind but did not dare broach the subject. By Sunday evening she could not hold back anymore.

"Dias, are you okay? You don't look too well," Basil said.

"I am fine. I just need to get some rest."

I went to bed but could not fall asleep. I couldn't understand why Chrispin would want to cheat me. Could it be that he felt I was too controlling? Was it greed? Ambition? Or was he trying to outdo me? I had given him a free hand to run Luiza Gowns

Branch. That was not enough for him. The time had come to put an end to Crispin's clandestine operation.

On Monday morning, after my breakfast, I went directly to Luiza Gowns Branch. Chrispin was busy cutting the orders for the day. He did not even look up as I entered the shop. I cleared my throat.

"Oh! Carlit it's you. I thought that Andrew had come in early."

"How are you feeling this morning? Andrew told me that you went home last week because your back was giving you trouble." I sounded genuine about my concern.

"Yes, with all the standing and cutting my back has been hurting."

"I see. *Ahuh*. I see...."

"My wife insisted that I stay at home and rest although I wanted to come to work."

"So, you were resting at home."

"Yes, I could hardly get out of bed. The pain was terrible. I was taking *aspros* every four hours."

"You are such a liar. What do you take me for?"

My chest was heaving. I felt like my head was going to explode. Chrispin's comfortable demeanour changed. He had a look of terror in his eyes.

"What do you mean? I wasn't lying.... I... I was...." and he stopped in mid-sentence. He realized that he was trapped. He was trembling.

"How could you do this to me? You ungrateful bastard!"

"I needed the extra money for the children's school fees and books."

"You shameless man. I want you out of my shop now! I don't ever want to see you again."

He put down the scissors and walked out of the shop with

his head down. The workers were walking into the shop at the same time.

"*Jambo Bwana,* where are you going?" they inquired.

He ignored them and continued to walk out of the shop in shame.

I spent the next hour making sure that the workers had sufficient work for the day. I informed them that Chrispin would not be running the shop anymore. I told them why I fired him. I warned them if they tried the same trick they would meet with the same fate.

After settling these matters at the branch, I rushed to the main shop since it was almost 9:00 a.m. The workers were waiting at the door.

"*Bwana*, what happened? We have been waiting for one hour. You seem to be upset."

"Margaret and George, just get in the shop. We will talk about this later."

Within minutes we were buzzing around doing our work. However, I was still obsessing about what Chrispin had done. Now I was landed with two shops that I could not run by myself. I made a promise that I would never enter into a partnership. I would have to close one shop. It would be difficult to decide which shop to close since both were doing well. I pondered this for several weeks. I finally decided to close the main shop and move to the branch. The rent was cheaper, and it was more centrally located. Moreover, the revenue from the main shop more than covered the goodwill that I had paid.

I spent the following month packing and moving the sewing machines and furniture to the other shop. It was a bit bigger, so I had space to accommodate the extra equipment and furniture. This certainly caused a disruption in my business and a loss of income. It wasn't a good time. My expenses were rising with all my children going to school. I also had to pay rent for both shops until my lease for the other shop ended. Furthermore, the neighbours that looked after my house in Goa had written asking for money for the upkeep. The strain of all these challenges was weighing me down. Going to the club in the evenings helped me temporarily forget about my problems.

The talk at the club was mostly about the elections. They were crucial since the winning party would lead Uganda into independence. The Baganda feared losing their political identity in an independent Uganda. As a result, they did not cooperate with the British Protectorate Government. They refused to participate in the elections and declared self-independence for Buganda. This, however, was a meaningless gesture. In 1961, the first elections were held, with only the U.P.C. and D.P. parties as contenders. The boycott by the Baganda allowed the D.P. to make a clean sweep in the province of Buganda. Although the U.P.C. won the popular vote, the D.P.'s success in Buganda gave them a majority of seats in Parliament. I was pleased with the outcome because I knew that the future of the Asians was safe so long as the D.P. was in power. This feeling of security was short-lived. The Kabaka and the U.P.C. wanted to eject the D.P. from power in the 1962 elections, and so Obote agreed to support Buganda's demands. This opened the way for the Baganda to participate in the central government through the Kabaka Yekka (K.Y.) party. In the pre-independence elections, the K.Y. - U.P.C. alliance won a majority of seats and on October 9, 1962, Uganda became an independent nation, with Dr. Milton Obote as President. This event was marked by a celebration at Kololo Stadium, where 50,000 people witnessed the unfurling of the Uganda flag and heard the country's national anthem for the first time.

I felt a sense of relief that the political turmoil had come to an end without any bloodshed. However, I was apprehensive about President Obote's position on the future of Asians. Throughout his campaign, he always referred to the tribes of Uganda and encouraged them to put Uganda before their tribal differences. Not once did he mention the existence of the Asians and their contribution to Uganda. I suspected that very soon he would expel us from the country. A major reform that he implemented immediately after independence was to raise the salaries of all the native Ugandans to be at par with the Asians. This meant doubling their salaries. I was forced to increase the salaries of all my workers in the shop and the maid at home. This only exacerbated my difficult financial situation.

A couple of months after independence, the workers at the shop became insubordinate. This included Andrew, who was not even from Uganda. He was a Kenyan. I had provided these people with secure employment and a means to improve their lives, and this was how they repaid me. This was very unsettling. The safety and future of my family were in jeopardy. The time had come for me to seriously consider going back to the homeland.

CHAPTER 31

My business was beginning to stabilize in the new location. The level above the shop was vacant so the landlord allowed me to move my family into these premises. It was convenient and the rent was much more reasonable than a regular flat. One drawback was that the children would create a racket when they played or got into fights. I had to discipline them on several occasions to be quiet while the shop was open. They obeyed me for a while. Just as I was beginning to feel that this arrangement was working, I heard some commotion upstairs. There was a thud and then the sound of things flying around. I could hear John swearing and Michael talking back to him. Thankfully, there were no customers in the shop at the time. I could feel my chest tighten. I ran up the stairs to give them a good hiding. I stopped dead in my tracks. Placido was putting the finishing touches on a painting he was working on. It was a watercolour of the "Horn of Plenty". His ability to bring life to the grapes, oranges, apples, and myriad other fruits was outstanding. Placido suddenly turned around and saw me staring at the painting.

"Dad! ... I ... thought that you were in the shop," he said, with fear in his eyes.

"Son, that is a remarkable painting. I had no idea that you could paint."

Placido's fears melted away and his face lit up.

"You, you think so?"

"Yes, the colours are vibrant, and the shading brings the fruit to life."

"Thanks, Dad. It was just something I felt like painting."

I continued admiring the painting when I sensed that he was beginning to feel uncomfortable.

"Mum told me that you used to paint altars in the churches," Placido said, breaking the silence.

"Yes, that was in Goa, when I was young. I had to stop since the paint fumes would make me sick."

I realized then how much I had missed painting. Although it seemed like an impossible dream now, I hoped that one day I would pick up the paintbrush again.

I forgot all about the fight and went down to the shop feeling elated. I was convinced that one day Placido would make a great artist.

Luiza was also artistically inclined. She had just graduated from Norman Godinho School with excellent marks in art. It was time for her to go to secondary school. I did not want her to go to Kololo Secondary School, since it was a co-educational school. She had blossomed into a young lady, and I was afraid that the boys in the higher classes would take advantage of her. The two other secondary schools – Old Kampala and Aga Khan were also co-ed schools. I could not sleep thinking about this. I finally discussed this with Basil, and she suggested that we put her in a boarding school. It was an all-girls school called Mount Saint Mary's and was run by the nuns. Several other Goans put their daughters in this school. She went on to say that it would be expensive, but I convinced her that I would find a way to pay for her fees. It was a relief to know that Luiza would be in a good school for the next four years. It was comforting that she would not be able to date boys in that school.

I was reading the Uganda Argus at the shop on Monday morning. The headlines read, "*Prime Minister Doctor Milton Obote to wed*". A few months previously, he had deposed the Kabaka, who was President and transferred all executive power to himself. As the Kabaka was the monarch of the Baganda, they lost their autonomy. The Kabaka fled to Britain when the army, led by Colonel Idi Amin, seized his palace. It was ironic that Obote's wife-to-be was a Baganda woman. Her name was Miriam Lule, and she had been educated in England. She was full and well endowed, attractive attributes for native Ugandans. I scanned the sports section. Emerald had won the gold cup horse race in Nairobi. This was something I had predicted but I did not get a chance to place a bet. I put the newspaper away regretting that I did not attend the race.

I had just come back to the shop after my afternoon siesta when a couple of policemen walked in. I panicked at first and then realized that they were escorting a well-dressed lady. She was probably the wife of an MP.

"Mr. Dias, I hear that you are the best tailor in Kampala," the lady said with a British accent. She must have come from a wealthy background and was most likely educated in England.

Saturday, July 2nd. 1966. Page 17

By Sheila Newick

THE WEDDING

by Luiza Gowns

THIS long established business — since 1949 — is in Salisbury Road, Kampala. Here customers can either buy ready-made clothes or have them expertly cut and fitted by the owner, Mr. Carlos Dias, and suberbly made by his staff of five dressmakers, all of whom have been trained by Mr. Dias. Luiza Gowns makes dresses, women's suits and bridal wear and customers may bring a magazine picture of the style they like or select from the many magazines and pattern books in the shop from which Mr. Dias will magically transform it into your fitting. He will advise customers on the choice of material especially for bride's and bridesmaid's gowns.

LUIZA GOWNS sells imported wedding veils and headdresses and will make a veil and crown of the bride's own design.

Below. Mr. Dias at his cutting table.

Left. A wedding dress of white brocade with a cowl neckline. This dress was specially made to fit the model, Joyce Mulanda, and for the 'People' photograph and we should like to thank LUIZA GOWNS for their co-operation. Veil and headdress are by LUIZA GOWNS. Bouquet of white carnations and ferns, also made specially for the photograph, by MARJORIE MOORE, florist, Kampala Road, under Nommo Gallery.

Wedding article - Luiza Gowns

"As you may have read in the paper, I am getting married," she continued.

"You.... are President Obote's wife, I mean wife-to-be?"

"Yes, I am Miriam Lule. I would like you to sew my wedding gown."

"Madam Lule, it would be an honour for me."

"I have an idea of what I want but need your advice on the type of fabric and trimmings."

We spent an hour selecting the fabric, lace, and accessories. I was relieved when she left. I took several deep breaths and was finally able to relax. I could not believe that I was going to be sewing for the President's future wife – not just any dress, but her wedding gown. It was the opportunity of a lifetime.

Luiza was accepted into Mount Saint Mary's School. My brother-in-law John took care of all the arrangements. He had to pull a few strings to get her in. Basil was busy putting together care packages for Luiza to tide her over for three months at the boarding school. She packed tins of crackers, Kraft cheese, biscuits, pickles, and oodles of other non-perishable food in her trunk. I would have sewed some new clothes for her, but I was busy with the bridal gown order and other work at the shop.

The materials for the wedding gown were putting a strain on my financial situation. The gypio lace itself cost one thousand shillings, not to mention the satin and crinoline. Furthermore, I needed most of these materials in a hurry if I was to meet my deadline. The supplier in England required a significant advance deposited in their account. This was beyond my means. Fortunately, my brother-in-law came to my rescue and put up a financial guarantee for the order. Once all the materials arrived, I worked diligently on the gown. At one time, all the employees of the shop were working on different parts of this gown. I even refrained from going to the club in the evenings. After weeks of working on the dress, it was finally ready for a fitting. Miss Lule arrived at the shop escorted with her bodyguards.

"Mr. Dias, it is tight around the waist and the bust."

She had put on weight during the past four weeks, probably due to all those state dinners she attended. I cut the gown according to her measurements.

"Yes, I noticed. Don't worry, I will open the seams and make it a little bigger."

As I was saying that I wondered if there was sufficient material to cover the extra two inches she had added to her figure. Beads of sweat formed on my forehead as I pinned up the hem.

When she left, I turned the gown over and measured the inseam. There was an inch and a quarter on either side. The quarter-inch seam would be risky since it could open easily. I made sure that I reinforced the seam and prayed that it would not split during the wedding ceremony. The day finally came when the gown was ready for the final fitting. I anxiously waited for her to step out of the fitting room. She strolled out with a smile on her face.

"It is magnificent. The gown fits me perfectly."

"Thank you, Madam Lule. The gown suits you well." I breathed a sigh of relief.

"You certainly are the best tailor in Kampala."

What a compliment from the future President's wife. At that moment, thoughts of leaving Uganda and going back to Goa evaporated. My opportunities in this great country were endless.

CHAPTER 32

It was a warm sunny day with blue skies. The bells tolling at Namirembe Cathedral signalled an auspicious event. The Anglican missionaries had built the earthen brick cathedral at the turn of the century. It was situated on Namirembe Hill – one of the seven hills of Kampala. The dome at the center rose high above the rest of the cathedral. On the top of the dome was a cross – a strong sign of Christian influence in Uganda. Slim, tall stained-glass windows punctuated the brick walls at regular intervals. The well-kept grounds were a vibrant green with calla lilies and poinsettia shrubs in garden beds. Majestic palm trees surrounded the cathedral. President Milton Obote and his newlywed, Lady Lule, emerged from the stately wooden doors to shouts of joy from guests and numerous onlookers. The celebrated couple waved to the crowds. Several newspaper photographers were vying for the best spot to take the perfect picture. After posing for the photographers, they stepped into an elegant black convertible Mercedes Benz and were whisked into the heart of the city. Crowds flanked the sidewalks of

Kampala Road. I managed to get a glimpse of the couple, and waved, hoping that Lady Lule might notice me. The ultimate reward was seeing Lady Lule glowing in her wedding gown. I felt a great sense of pride. It was time for a celebration with my friends at the club.

"Here he comes gloating over ordinary people like us," Lino announced as I entered the club.

"Hey Carlit, you are famous," Jacinth said as he patted me on the back.

"Yay! Yay! Carlit," they all cheered.

I felt uncomfortable with all the attention. I did not know what to say. My lips went dry. I had to think of something quickly to say.

"I am buying drinks for everyone."

"Viva! Viva!" was the response from the club members.

I noticed that Chrispin was a couple of tables away when I sat down to play cards. He chose to ignore me. I did not want to have anything to do with him. I was here to celebrate, and nobody was going to stop me. The card game got intense as time progressed and I forgot all about Chrispin. The ante kept rising after each game. I placed a bet that was four times the last one.

"Carlit, what are you doing? – a hundred shillings!" Jacinth complained.

"I feel like a winner today. What is a hundred shillings?"

"It takes some of us a week to make that kind of money," Bernard said.

Several people including Bernard could not handle the high stakes. They backed out. Only three of the die-hards stuck with me. One of them was sweating profusely. People from the other tables stopped playing and came to watch our game. I could see from the corner of my eye that Chrispin had joined the crowd. I focused on playing well but there was not much I could do with the hand that I was dealt. To my chagrin, I lost the last game and the hundred shillings.

"Every day is not Sunday," Chrispin said under his breath.

I wanted to tear him apart. It took a huge amount of restrain not to lunge forward and strike him. I gave him a piercing look; he quickly turned away and walked towards the bar.

The following morning, on the front page of the Uganda Argus, was a picture of President Milton Obote and his wife. Several heads of state attended the reception held at the Apollo Hotel. Although my name was not mentioned in the article, the news had travelled far and wide. Orders from several famous and wealthy people started flowing in. I was surprised when the Princess of Bunyoro came to the shop. The kingdom of Bunyoro in Western Uganda was very powerful at one time. I had to hire some part-time help to cope with the additional workload. Working late nights aggravated my sore back. Basil would massage my back with coconut oil. It was soothing and provided well need relief. The scent of the oil reminded me of Goa.

Uganda was developing in leaps and bounds, which was good for my business. Several of the Asians were building factories, businesses, hotels, and shops. A notable family, the Madwanis, owned a sugar factory in Jinja, a biscuit factory just outside Kampala and several sugarcane plantations. In addition, the expatriates continued to own large companies and extensive farms dating back to colonial rule. The Uganda government was faced with the problem of trying to correct the imbalance in favour of the Africans. In the government and Statutory Boards, implementation of Africanization was well underway. Some of the Asians that worked for the government were feeling threatened. A few of them decided to leave and go to India or England. Africans were given easy access to loans to start their businesses and buy farms. Only a few took advantage of these opportunities. It concerned me that my business could be taken over as part of a drastic nationalization program. Kenya had already issued a government policy statement entitled *African Socialism*. Although their policy was cautious, Tanzania had categorically stated that it aimed to develop a true Socialist State. If Uganda chose the same approach, it would be the end of all the Asian business owners, including myself.

I focused on the enormous amount of work at the shop to cope with my worries. Andrew would act up whenever I put pressure on him to complete orders quickly. On several occasions, I was on the verge of firing him, but I could not afford to lose any workers at this time. It was difficult to find reliable Africans who were skilled at sewing.

One evening, I decided to close the shop early because I was exhausted. When I got home, Basil handed me a letter. It was from Cresence Carvalho, our neighbour in Goa. She looked after *Mai*. Her letter stated that *Mai* was very ill and stayed in bed most of the time. That was not like *Mai*. The letter ended with an appeal to send money for her upkeep. I wondered how much money Cresence kept for herself.

The next day, I went to the bank. I asked for a bank draft of five hundred shillings, which I sent via registered mail to Goa. I was relieved that I had done my duty. However, I was concerned about *Mai's* health. When I went home, I asked Basil to write a letter to Cresence requesting that she get the doctor to do a thorough check-up on *Mai*. I instructed Basil to tell her that money was no object. I felt torn that I could not be with *Mai* when she needed me most.

There were times when I just wanted to throw in the towel and go back to Goa, but I had to think of the children. Placido was flourishing here, winning prizes for his excellent work in art at Kololo Secondary School. His collection of paintings and sculptures had grown. Although he was only seventeen, he organized an art exhibition, where he sold 9 out of his 17 paintings. A man named Paul Faulker who had come from Canada bought one of his paintings. What would he do with all this talent in Goa? Luiza had just been accepted into the Royal College of Art at the University of Nairobi. She had been quite an inspiration for him. All my other children were doing well in school and were very much at home in Uganda.

I felt confused and depressed. I decided to go to Neeta Cinema to take my mind off this dilemma. The movie *Seconds,* starring Rock Hudson, was playing. The melodrama and suspense provided a well-needed escape from reality. The turmoil resurfaced in a few hours. I figured that the best way for me to get over this difficult time was to go to Nairobi. Coincidentally, the Triple Crown Sweepstakes was on this coming weekend. It would help me clear my mind and get out of the doldrums. I felt reassured that everything would fall into place after the race.

CHAPTER 33

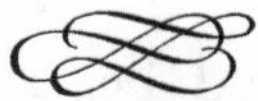

I DRAGGED myself out of bed. My eyelids felt like lead, and I struggled to open my eyes. As I laboured with my razor, I wondered why I was even bothering with this mundane activity. Darn! I cut myself just below my lip. I quickly pressed the towel on the cut. I continued with my daily ablutions. It stung as I soaped the area around the cut. Thoughts of what had to be done were buzzing through my mind. What day was it? - Thursday. Oh no! I had to go to the shop. It suddenly dawned on me that I would be leaving for Nairobi tomorrow to see the Triple Crown. I put on my favourite shirt – white with navy blue pinstripes. I waltzed into the kitchen, whistling. Basil was busy rolling out *chapatis* and tossing them onto the hot cast iron pan that sat over the hibachi. The aroma of the roasting *chapatis* in ghee made my mouth water.

Basil wondered why I was in such a good mood and looked at me quizzically. It didn't take her long to figure out that I was going to Nairobi for a horse race. She complained about the unnecessary cost and went on to lecture me about the ever-growing expenses, especially with Luiza's fees at the University. As much as I tried to explain to her that money was no issue, she was not convinced. I quickly lost my appetite and told her that I had to go to the shop.

I got into my car and drove towards the shop. Basil always put a damper on anything exciting. *Mai* was never like that. I had to go to the bank and get a draft made at lunchtime. Hopefully, the money would be used to buy medication to restore her health. The thought of her being ill and alone saddened me. I wiped away my tears and got out of the car when I arrived at the shop. It was important for me to maintain composure in front of the workers, so I took a deep breath and walked in.

Instead of waiting until lunchtime, I went to the bank at 10:00 a.m. I withdrew one thousand shillings with the intent of sending it to *Mai*. Just as I was going to inform the clerk of the amount, I realized that I needed money to bet at the horse race in Nairobi. My account balance was just a few shillings over one thousand. After debating what I should do, I decided to send *Mai* five hundred shillings. It would go a long way toward her medical expenses. Besides, if I won the race, I could send her a lot more money.

The drive to Nairobi seemed much longer than usual. As we rolled into Nakuru, I was overcome with extreme fatigue and struggled to stay awake. It did not help that Jacinth was fast asleep. I tried focusing on the road, but my vision was blurred. When I blinked the fuzziness went away for a few moments. I shut my eyes for what seemed like a split second. When I opened my eyes, the car was off the road. I quickly tried to steer it back onto the road, but it was too late. We ended up in the ditch.

"Whoa, what! Carlit......what happened?" Jacinth yelled as he woke up in a fright.

I was in a state of shock. I opened my mouth to speak but no words came out.

"What do you think happened? I dozed off."

"Dozed off! You could have killed us."

"Oh, Jacinth, stop exaggerating. Besides, you were no help, sleeping comfortably."

"I was not the one driving."

"Well, now it is your turn to take over the wheel. I desperately need to get some sleep."

When I got out of the car I was engulfed by the chilly night. I trembled from the cold and my fear of confronting wild animals. My body ached from the bruises. I was glad that the ditch was shallow. We managed to push the car onto the road with some difficulty. I was thankful that it was the dry season; otherwise, we would have been stranded deep in the soft mud. Jacinth started driving and I must have fallen asleep shortly after. I only woke up when we entered Nairobi.

It was liberating being at the races. I bet a hundred shillings on Arabian Prince, a sure winner. I was shocked and disappointed when he was second last. I kept on betting on the next three races determined to win. To my dismay, I lost all of them and was down to the last one hundred shillings. Jacinth had stopped betting after losing the two hundred shillings that he was allowed to bring. His wife controlled how much money he spent. I refused to give up and bet my last hundred shillings. Horse number nine had to be the lucky one. That was my daughter Luiza's birthday. I waited in great anticipation. Number nine was leading. My heart started thumping and my palms were sweating. Thirty seconds before the end of the race, I was cheering at the top of my voice, joined by Jacinth and several other spectators. Suddenly, number nine collapsed, and the jockey flew off the horse. He barely escaped being trampled by another horse. I was dumbfounded. The winning horse was Arabian Prince. My spirit was crushed, just like number nine who languished on the ground.

The drive back to Kampala was long and uneventful. We exchanged very few words. Our journey ended very late at night. I crawled into bed trying not to wake up Basil, but that was to no avail. She got up and went into the kitchen to heat some food for me. I realized that I had not eaten in over fourteen hours. Well fed and exhausted, I slept soundly that night.

I picked up the Uganda Argus on the way to the shop. The news was all about President Obote. He had conveniently rewritten the Constitution to substantially increase his powers. His efforts to create a Socialist state in Uganda were gaining momentum. Many people were upset by the left-wing turn that the government had taken. Obote openly stated his intent to make all businesses the property of the state. It seemed like everything that I had worked for would be taken away in one swoop. I found it difficult to focus on my work during this period of uncertainty. My workers Margaret, George and Andrew kept to themselves. They sensed from my body language that I was troubled by the current state of affairs.

For the next several days I was not my usual self. The card games at the club were not as exciting. I played less and drank more. Basil would cook my favourite dishes to try and lift my spirits. Whenever the children did well in school, she would share the good news. I sensed that she was trying to keep something from me. One night, she broached the subject.

"Dias, I just got a letter from Luiza."

"Oh! And how is she?"

"She's well. She is very busy working on her projects at university."

"So, she should be. It is her last year."

"Yes, it is. Now it is time for her to marry."

"Why do you bring up the subject of marriage out of the blue?"

"She...she... has...er...met a boy."

"Met a boy? How could she? I thought that she was focusing on her studies."

"She is, but don't you think it is time for her to get married?"

"Yes, but only when she finishes university. It must be someone that we can trust."

"You are right. I was hoping that we could arrange to find someone nice for her."

I finished my drink and Basil brought me my supper. We both ate in silence.

The next morning, the news on the radio focused on President Obote. He was accused of promoting members of his tribe, the Lango. He also favoured the Acholi people, many of whom served in his army. His actions and policies were divisive. It would lead this country into severe political upheaval. He considered his opponents as criminals and threw them into jail. I felt sorry for the other Ugandan tribes, especially the Baganda, who lost all their rights.

I had lost my appetite for work. I closed the shop early one afternoon and went to Norman Cinema. Richard Burton, my favourite actor, was starring in the movie – Anne of The Thousand Days. It was about the birth of Protestantism. It certainly opened my eyes to the side of Christianity that I knew very little of. I was brought up to be a devout Catholic. *Mai* used to say that they were not real Christians since they did not believe in Jesus' mother.

When I got home, the house was extremely quiet. Not a sound from the children. I immediately suspected something was wrong. Basil came out of the kitchen holding a letter in her hand. Her eyes were red, and her lips were quivering. I immediately noticed that the four corners of the envelope were coloured black. My chest tightened and my breath was laboured.

"Dias, Dias I am sorry... so very sorry."

Basil came and hugged me. She did not have to say anymore. I felt a sharp pain in my chest. Tears welled up and flowed freely down my cheeks.

"*Moji Mai, Moji Mai*," I cried out.

The pain in my chest turned into a great void. I felt that a part deep within had died. It was too painful to read the letter. The following morning, I asked Basil to read it to me. She struggled to keep her composure as she read the letter. Cresence, our neighbour had taken care of all the funeral arrangements. She ended her letter by saying that my bank draft had arrived on the day that *Mai* had passed away.

CHAPTER 34

The emptiness persisted. My guilt mushroomed as the days went by. I should have gone back to Goa as soon as I found out that *Mai* was ill. Winning money at the races to provide *Mai* with a comfortable life was fruitless. How could I have been so fickle? It was high time to take stock of my life. If I continued gambling on horse races it would ruin me and my family. However, I knew that Basil would never let the family go without the necessities of life. I wondered how she managed to keep the family going. She always had food on the table and took care of all the children's needs. I hardly provided her with any support when it came to the children. Being a father was foreign to me. I suppose that was because my father was never around. When I was a child, he was at sea and when I was four, he passed away. I wondered what he looked like. The only photographs that *Mai* had of him were eaten by white ants.

As it was customary, I wore a black band around my shirtsleeve. Black pants and a white shirt would be my attire for the rest of the year. Customers and friends at the club would offer their condolences. Although they meant well, they kept bringing back the painful memories of *Mai's* lonely death. Visits to the club were starting to lose their allure. I stayed in the back room of the shop and asked Andrew to take the orders. Unless they were important customers, I gave Andrew strict instructions to tell them that I was not available.

A couple of days later, we received a letter from Luiza, saying that she was coming down with a friend during Easter break. Her friend was a young man called Felix. I wondered if this was the same person that she wrote about in her last letter.

"And where is the Felix guy planning to stay?"

"I don't know as yet," Basil replied nervously.

"Well, he is not staying here!"

"I will ask around to see if someone will be willing to put him up."

Basil asked the neighbours and friends if they would be kind enough to host Felix. All the neighbours turned her down. Finally, Mrs. Siqueira from 'Louis & Company' offered to put him up. Her daughter, Florrie was a good friend of Luiza.

It was Good Friday. Basil informed me that Felix had arrived and was staying at Mrs. Siqueira's. I had just come home, after working for half the day, and decided to take a nap after lunch. I was jolted awake from a deep sleep when I heard Basil shouting.

"*Baba! Baba!* Are you okay?" she cried out.

"Basil, I am sorry, but I tried hard to avoid the other car," her brother said.

"Oh! Look at him .... He looks lifeless."

I jumped out of bed. My heart was racing, wondering how serious the problem was. When I walked into the kitchen, Basil's brother John was holding Gregory while Basil was trying to shove a raw egg into his mouth. Poor Gregory – he was in a daze.

"What did you do to my son, Gregory?" I demanded.

"I took them out for ice cream and on the way back we met with an accident."

"You could have killed him. How could you be so careless?"

"Carlit, I am sorry, but it was an accident."

Basil took Gregory to his bed and put some smelling salts under his nose. Within a few minutes, he came to his senses. The first thing that he asked for was a glass of milk. This child loved his milk. One Christmas he asked for four pints of milk as a gift. As John left, I noticed that he grimaced and limped as he walked. The next day Basil informed me that he had fractured his knee. I felt bad for telling him off. After all, he often took the children out for a drive or ice cream.

On Easter Sunday, Basil had invited Felix, Mrs. Siqueira, and her daughter Florrie over for lunch. She had cooked *pilau*, *sorpotel*, rice cakes and several other side dishes. We ate well and then settled down in the living room. After an hour, Mrs. Siqueira and Florrie left, but Felix stayed behind.

"Mr. Dias, I would like to talk to you," he said.

I felt uneasy.

"Yes, Felix. What is it?"

"I am interested in marrying your daughter. I have come to ask you for her hand in marriage," he blurted out, all in one breath.

"Marry.... marry my daughter?"

"Yes, we have known each other for four years now."

"You have taken me by surprise. She...she has not finished her university yet."

"She only has one year left."

"What about you? Have you completed your studies?"

"I am working as a Trainer at East African Power and Lighting."

"Will you be able to provide her with a good home?"

"Yes, I am making a good salary and the company will provide me with a house."

"This is all too sudden. I have to think about it."

Felix seemed relieved and disappointed at the same time. He bid the family farewell and said that he would come back tomorrow. I assumed that he expected an answer by then. Basil and I discussed Felix's proposal later in the evening. He seemed like a capable man. If there was a family scandal, I would have heard about it during my frequent visits to Nairobi. Basil seemed to like him, although she was worried about the size of the dowry. I barely slept, thinking about this proposal all night. Luiza would end up living six hundred miles away from us. When she was barely a teenager, she went to boarding school at Namagunga. After that, she went to the University of Nairobi. It seemed like she hardly lived with us.

Felix showed up the next day as planned. After exchanging a few pleasantries, I told him that we accepted his proposal. His face lit up, but I suspected that he tried to conceal his excitement. Basil insisted that we have an engagement party and invited all the neighbours and family. During the following several weeks, Basil, Luiza and Matti were busy preparing and shopping for the wedding. Luiza was designing her dress while Matti worked diligently on her chief bridesmaid's dress. Every day a new item was added to Luiza's trousseau. Basil visited the goldsmith regularly to ensure that the elaborate necklace and earrings for Luiza would be ready on time. When it was finally complete, she proudly showed it to Luiza.

"*Mai* it is pretty, but I cannot wear it."

Basil's smile disappeared and her face fell.

"But...but why not? I thought you would like it. You know that it is pure gold?"

"I do, and it is nice, but it will not go with my dress."

"So, what are you planning to wear?"

"A simple silver chain with a pearl."

"But you know that it is our custom to wear gold jewelry, especially for your wedding", Basil said as she shook her head in dismay.

She looked at me, hoping that I would intervene. I was not going to get involved. Basil walked out silently with tears in her eyes.

Luiza's wedding gown was based on a Danish design. She asked if I could sew her gown. It was time for her to go back to Nairobi to make the church and other arrangements for the wedding. Although the overall design of her gown was simple, it required hundreds of pin-tucks, giving the fabric an embossed appearance. I spent several days sewing the pin-tucks. I finally managed to complete the whole ensemble after a week. Unfortunately, Luiza was not around to try on her gown. The rest of the family had already left for the wedding. The realization that Luiza would be leaving the family hit me. The void inside me grew and I felt very alone. I went to the club hoping that it would lift my spirits. The rest of my evening was a blur. Next thing, I remember waking up and dashing to the train station. I had forgotten to take Luiza's wedding gown, so I had to rush back to the house and pick it up. When I arrived at the platform of the station the train was pulling out. I tried to jump onto the train with my bags, but the porter pushed me off. It was the first-class cabin.

CHAPTER 35

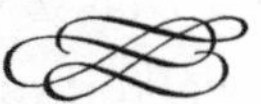

I RAN from the platform to the ticketing office, hoping that there might be another train leaving later the same day. There was only a cargo train leaving at midnight. I might have bribed the conductor to let me board this train, but it would not arrive in time for the wedding. What should I do? My car was in the garage being repaired. I dashed out of the station, sweating profusely. I stood helplessly outside the station, not knowing what to do. Just then I saw a taxi stopping in front of the station to drop off his passengers. I lugged my bags towards the taxi, but a couple of locals beat me to it. I approached the taxi driver and flashed a ten Shilling note in front of him.

"Take me to Jinja! *Haraka! Haraka*!"

"*Bwana*, Jinja is far away. It will cost you a lot of shillings," the taxi driver replied.

"Don't worry, I will pay you whatever it costs. I need to get there in a hurry."

I pulled out another ten Shilling-note. There was a twinkle in his eyes, and he smiled, revealing his set of white teeth. The driver asked the passengers to get out of the car. They grumbled and argued but they eventually got out of the car. As soon as I got into the taxi, the driver floored the gas pedal creating dust clouds behind us. He drove onto Coryndon Road and then turned right onto Jinja Road. Within thirty minutes, we were out of the city on our way to Jinja.

I took a deep breath, relaxed, and fell asleep. I dreamt that I kept telling the driver to speed up, but he was deliberately driving slowly. I suspected that was his tactic for trying to garner a larger bribe. When we arrived in Jinja I had just missed the train. I was furious.

"*Bwana! Bwana!* Get up! We have arrived in Jinja."

I was jolted awake from my terrible dream. I still had a chance to catch the train. I grabbed my bags. I gave the taxi driver a hundred shillings.

"*Bwana*! What about *bakshishi*," the taxi driver yelled.

"What *bakshishi?* I gave you twenty shillings in addition to the fare. Go away, you ungrateful man."

I slammed the door of the taxi and hurried towards the station. As I looked west, I saw a train approaching the station. I could not believe my eyes. I paid for my ticket and boarded the train. I put my bags in my compartment and headed directly for the restaurant car.

As I lay down in my compartment, I started thinking about how different things would have been if my daughter Luiza had gotten married in Goa. The dowry would have been part of a major negotiation process between the two families. The parents of the groom would try and maximize the value of the dowry since they would stand to benefit. In this case, neither Felix nor his family broached the subject of a dowry. Basil, on the other hand, provided a sewing machine and gold jewelry as part of the dowry.

Traditionally, the night before the wedding, the groom and bride would have been given a bath with coconut juice. This was a purification rite. Providing a special meal for the poor in the neighbourhood the day before the wedding was another custom. Finally, the day after the wedding, the entire trousseau and items of the dowry would be displayed in the hall of the groom's home. The guests would take great pleasure in viewing the articles. None of these rituals and traditions would be observed for Luiza's wedding. Sadly, this generation had embraced the Western lifestyle. It was a sign of the demise of our Goan traditions.

The train rolled into Nairobi at 10:15 the following morning. Felix had come to pick me up from the station. I gave him the wedding gown and my luggage, and I asked him to drop me at the Tailor's Club. It was a pleasure seeing my old buddies. I thought about going to the races with my friend Custodio. He convinced me not to do so. If I went to the racetrack, I would most likely miss the wedding. After playing a few games of cards, I went over to Custodio's place and rested. I got dressed and took a taxi to St. Austin's Church in downtown Nairobi. My stomach rumbled as I walked into the church. I saw Felix and his brother standing at the altar. I waited anxiously at the entrance of the church. Luiza, Matti and Cedric, the pageboy, finally arrived. The music began. I walked towards Luiza fighting back tears. It was hard to fathom that my little girl would soon be a married woman. I realized that I hardly spent time with my children. Luiza spent most of her young adulthood away from home – I hardly knew her. The moment I gave her away to her husband-to-be, I made a vow to spend more time with my children. If their Uncle John took them on various outings, then I should find the time to do the same.

Basil sobbed throughout the ceremony. I refused to look in

her direction. I looked up when the priest announced that Felix and Luiza were officially man and wife. Luiza looked magnificent. Her wedding gown suited her perfectly. She was glowing as she walked with Felix toward the kneeler. At the end of the service, I was congratulated by numerous people, most of whom I had never met. After greeting their guests, Felix and Luiza climbed into the back of a 1940 vintage car owned by one of their eccentric university friends, Anil. He was dressed in purple bell-bottoms, a pink satin shirt with bells around his neck. He cranked the car. It started after a couple of tries, but then it sputtered to a halt. Placido and a couple of other guests had to push the car to get it moving again.

The reception was at the Stima Club in Ruoaraka, a suburb of Nairobi. Felix's mother had baked the wedding cake. She decorated it meticulously based on the design of the invitation cards. They were red bookmarks with their initials forming a logo in gold. Felix and Luiza broke tradition by inviting the guests themselves. Although the speeches interested some of the guests, I could not identify with what was being shared. I felt like a fish out of water. Hardly any of my friends were around. I was getting antsy as the evening progressed. Toward the end, I could not take it anymore. I slipped out of the reception and took a taxi to the Tailor's Club. My friends were surprised to see me.

The next morning, we met at Felix and Luiza's new flat. We had breakfast together and then bid them farewell. They were going to Mombasa for their honeymoon. Later that day, Basil, the children, and I boarded the train destined for Kampala. We slept for most of the journey. The emotional roller coaster had come to an end. I was looking forward to getting back to my routine in Kampala.

CHAPTER 36

I HAD FALLEN behind on my orders at the shop. At the same time, I was getting new customers. I considered sending some of them to Nadya Gowns to cope with my workload. However, I could risk losing these new customers permanently. Hiring another tailor from Goa would help with handling the additional work. I decided against that idea when I thought about the bad experience with Chrispin. Local unemployed and experienced tailors were non-existent. My only option was to work longer hours.

My promise to spend more time with the children fell by the wayside. I barely saw them. The odd evening when I had the energy to listen, Basil would update me on what they were doing. I was surprised to know that all my sons including Gregory were in secondary school. It seemed like only a few years ago we had celebrated his first birthday. Basil informed me that he was doing very well at school. This did not surprise me – he was always into his books. He must have taken after Basil's father, Isidore. Another interesting piece of news was Placido's second art exhibition. He was only seventeen. I was very proud of him. Sadly, I could not attend the opening night of his exhibition because I was busy at the shop.

It would be nice to go for a family vacation once the work was under control at the shop. We could visit Luiza and Felix and then go to the coast. Basil had been complaining about her swollen knees. The saltwater in the Indian Ocean would help alleviate her suffering. None of this would come to pass. Basil had to rush to Goa to visit her ailing mother. Furthermore, since *Mai* passed away, the house was not being maintained properly. Cresence, our neighbour in Goa struggled with trying to manage two homes. It did not help that her husband was working in Bombay.

I booked Basil's ticket on the *SS Haryana* and she left shortly after that. She had hired a male servant called Yowana to do the housework and cook for the family. He was highly recommended by her friend Linda DeSouza. While Basil was away, Yowana ran the household. He would serve my lunch promptly since he knew that it was important to keep the *Bwana* happy.

One evening when I came home late from the club, Matti was waiting up for me.

"Daddy, we got a letter from Luiza," she said.

"How is she?"

"She's fine. So is Felix."

"What else did she say in her letter?"

"She said that...that...she was having a baby."

"A baby, a baby! That is good news."

I was going to be a grandfather. Was I ready for that? The term grandfather seemed foreign to me.

The next day at the club, I announced the good news, and we toasted my future grandson.

The political situation in Uganda continued to deteriorate.

Obote was becoming unpopular. His only supporters were from Lango and the Acholi people whom he recruited for the army. Colonel Idi Amin joined the King's Riflemen as a cook during British rule. He rose to the rank of lieutenant, taking part in British actions against Somali rebels in the Shifta War and then the Mau Mau rebels in Kenya. Although most people thought that he was from Acholi, it was rumoured that he came from Sudan. This was probably true because he was a Muslim. Most of the Ugandans were either Catholic or Protestant. The Baganda gave up their dream of an independent state since Obote had completely killed their spirit. The Democratic Party, supported by the Asians had minimal representation in the Parliament. Uganda could be considered a one-party state controlled by Obote. The situation for Asians was getting worse as Africanization progressed. Obote was using the army to prop up his regime. Resources were being redistributed through nationalization. Obote unilaterally increased his power in the central government. Sooner or later, the Asians would have to leave this beautiful country.

Basil returned from Goa exhausted. She spent most of her time nursing her mother back to health. The rest of the time, she struggled with the maintenance of the house. As soon as Basil arrived, she took over the kitchen. She spent most of her time telling Yowana off. He was a nervous wreck and terrified of Basil. Although the plan was to keep Yowana for two more weeks, Basil fired him the day after she arrived. A few days later, Basil complained that she was finding it hard to cope, so we had to go through the tedious process of hiring another servant.

To take my mind off the dire political situation, I decided to go quail hunting with my friend Jacinth. I finally got my car fixed at Cooper Motors. It cost me three hundred shillings. We drove past the Kakira sugarcane factory and continued to the nearby

Mabira forest. Our morning hunt was rather unsuccessful. We drove to Jinja where we had lunch and drinks at the Goan Institute. We continued hunting in the afternoon. Luckily, we managed to shoot a dozen quail.

Basil cooked the quail in sumptuous gravy with coconut and spices. We ate it with relish, except for Gregory. He did not like the fact that I had just killed these small birds. After Jacinth left, we washed up and went to bed. I almost fell asleep when Basil decided to talk. She informed me that she was planning a trip to Nairobi, to help Luiza with the birth of her baby. When I told her that I didn't have any cash to give her, she said that she had saved some money from the sewing lessons that she gave. It escaped me how she found the time to do that.

I picked up the Uganda Argus on my way to the shop. The headlines read: BAGANDA TRY TO ASSASSINATE OBOTE. This was shocking news! He was shot in the mouth as he left the U.P.C. conference. He had just introduced his policy of moving to the left. At the same time, the leader of the army, Idi Amin, was accused of desertion. A few days later, Brigadier Okoya, the person who made this accusation, was murdered. The army went on a rampage in Kampala as tension increased in Uganda. Obote's popularity was declining rapidly. Murders were becoming commonplace. All this unrest in Uganda was a great source of anxiety for me.

Basil was busy preparing for her trip to Nairobi. I was glad that she was going away, albeit for a short period. She was in a constant state of fear and worried about the political situation. I drove her to the train station and unloaded her luggage. As always, Basil started crying as she waved goodbye. I could not understand why she always got so emotional.

The internal strife in Uganda that extended beyond its borders to Sudan weighed heavily on my mind. I spent most of my evenings at Pedro's Bar. Drinking helped to diffuse the worry and anxiety. When I got home late from the bar one night, surprisingly, none of the children were in bed.

"What is going on, Matti? How come the boys are not in bed?"

"Oh, Daddy, they are too excited. They can't sleep."

"What do you mean they can't sleep? They have to go to school tomorrow."

"Luiza had a baby. A baby girl!"

"A girl? But...I thought it would be a boy."

"I am an aunty," Matti cried with joy.

At that moment it did not matter whether it was a boy or a girl. This was my first grandchild. I was overcome with a warm feeling of gratitude. All my worries melted away. A few days later Basil came back from Nairobi. She was beaming.

CHAPTER 37

GUNFIRE KEPT me awake and my fears grew as the night wore on. I shuddered to think of what might be in store for us in the morning. Surprisingly, when I awoke, everything seemed normal. The children were getting ready to go to school. Basil was busy in the kitchen rolling *chapatis* while the coffee was brewing. She complained that Sara, our maid, had not shown up. I expected Sara to be late because her village was quite a distance from Kampala.

It was eerily quiet on Salisbury Road which was not normal at 8:30 a.m. on a weekday. *Cake and Candy*, the shop where I normally bought the newspaper was closed. I wondered if the owner was sick. I missed reading the *Uganda Argus* – one of the first things I did when I arrived at the shop. I hardly spotted any cars or people during my walk to the shop. Was this the calm before the storm?

As soon as I got to the shop, I started cutting the dresses for the day. I completely lost track of time until I glanced at the clock. It was already 9:30 a.m. Surprisingly, nobody had shown up, not even my workers. I went to the front door and looked outside, only to see several jeeps driving down Salisbury Road. There was a large crowd of Ugandans on the sidewalk cheering and waving at the soldiers in their jeeps. The crowd was getting louder and started throwing stones at the shops. I quickly locked the front door from the inside, picked up the money from the till and made a quick exit through the back door. I hurried down Rosebury Lane. I was thankful that there were no soldiers on this street.

When I got home, I breathed a sigh of relief. I was glad to see that my children were back from school. I went into the bedroom, only to find Basil sobbing. She looked up and opened her mouth to say something, but no words came out. I went into the children's bedroom. They were engrossed in a game of Monopoly. Gregory was not with them.

"Where is Gregory?"

"He is at school," Michael replied, barely looking up. He was busy buying hotels since he landed on Park Lane.

"We were told to go home as soon as we got to school," John said.

"The headmaster mentioned something about trouble in the city," Placido added.

"Yes, there is. I saw several soldiers driving in their jeeps and waving their guns on Salisbury Road."

Gregory was a student at Kololo Secondary School. It was in a suburb about ten miles out of the city. He used to get a ride from one of his friend's parents. I doubted that the buses were running so he would have no way of getting home. I cautioned the children not to step out of the house. I warned them that it was very dangerous on the streets. I went back to our bedroom.

"Basil, don't worry, Gregory will come home," I said hoping

to comfort her. I was concerned about his safety. The soldiers would not think twice about killing Asians.

I turned on the radio, hoping to find out what was going on. It was difficult tuning into Radio Uganda. Most likely John had damaged the radio. His favourite pastime was experimenting with electricity and radios. When I confronted him, he swore that he had not touched the radio. I turned on the television and none of the channels were operational. This country had to be in serious trouble if both radio and television were shut down. At around 3:00 p.m., I switched on the television again. There was noise for several seconds followed by a few minutes of a scrambled screen, and finally, a clear picture emerged. It was that of a large soldier dressed in full military regalia. I did not recognize who it was but assumed that he was a high-ranking military officer.

"I am not a politician, but a professional soldier," he said with a heavy Ugandan accent.

"My name is General Idi Amin. I am the leader of the Uganda Army."

Although he struggled with his English, he managed to explain that his army had taken over the country through a military coup. He went on to justify why he had to liberate Uganda from the reins of President Obote, who coincidentally was away at a Commonwealth conference in Singapore. He promised that a proper government would be formed shortly and that everything would return to normal. He encouraged all the people to go out and celebrate because Uganda was now a free country with a bright future.

It was almost 3:30 p.m. and Gregory had not come home. There was no way he could contact us because we did not have a telephone. Basil could hardly function and stayed in bed, sobbing. I listened to the radio and caught snippets of the news.

According to the reports, it was a bloodless coup, which I did not believe for a moment. Was it safe to stay in this country with the army in control? It worried me to think about what might happen to my family. At around 4:00 p.m., Basil finally got out of bed to make some tea. We had barely sat down to have our tea when Gregory walked into the house. He was pale and distraught. Basil dropped her cup, ran up and hugged him. I was relieved. We were all together and safe, for the moment. He sat at the table and told us what had transpired. The school dismissed all the students soon after the morning assembly. He met his friends and did not know where to go. Then he remembered that Augustine Dias, a good friend of ours lived a couple of miles away from the school. He was not sure how to get there. As he walked with his friends, they came across several army tanks and hid behind bushes to avoid being shot. The Israeli government had donated these old tanks to the ill-equipped Uganda army. They hurried towards Augustine's house and managed to get there in one piece. Lydia, Augustine's wife, cooked and fed him and his friends. Finally, when things had settled down and the streets were safe, his friend's father came and picked them up. Basil said prayers in thanksgiving and then went into the kitchen to prepare dinner. It was her way of celebrating the safe return of her son.

As Idi Amin promised, things were back to normal. Business was booming once again, and Uganda prospered. As time went by, Idi Amin became vocal about his belief in Islam. He passed a new law prohibiting women from wearing short skirts or dresses. He warned that any woman caught wearing a skirt above her knees would be severely punished. Matti was in a state of panic. She frantically started sewing long skirts and dresses. At times, we would hear stories about women being attacked and beaten for wearing skirts barely an inch above their knees.

Although Idi Amin was friendly with the Israelis, he turned against them. They had refused to give him the Phantom fighter jets that he planned to use to wage a war against Tanzania. Idi Amin owed Israel tens of millions of dollars for weaponry and work carried out by private Israeli companies. His requests to cancel the debt or ease the repayment schedule were turned down. In an interview with a BBC correspondent, he said the Jews were the cause of war and human suffering. Amin started making serious anti-Semitic statements. His behaviour was becoming more and more irrational as time went by. Although I was concerned about our future, I was confident that Idi Amin needed the Asians. Without them the economy would collapse, and the country would be in turmoil.

One night when I came home from the club, Basil informed me that Luiza was planning a visit to Uganda with our granddaughter, Dawn. As much as I was looking forward to their visit, I was afraid because they were travelling without Felix.

"Make sure that you inform her about the new law."

"Yes, I will call Luiza from Mrs. Paes's house and let her know."

"She must wear a long dress when she is travelling and only pack long skirts and dresses."

The day Luiza and Dawn were expected, I went to the train station well before their scheduled arrival time. The train station was buzzing with military personnel. This was commonplace in most public places of importance. I went to the café, picked up the newspaper and ordered a coffee. Once again, Idi Amin was on the front page. He had ordered the Israelis to leave Uganda within ten days. This was a huge shock for the Israeli government and the Israelis living in Uganda. They ran most of the large construction companies in Kampala. It would be extremely challenging for them to liquidate their businesses and sell their personal belongings in such a short time. I put the newspaper down and looked at my watch. It was almost time for Luiza's train to arrive. I walked down to the platform in time to see the train roll into the station. A couple of soldiers were patrolling the platform. I tried to stay calm. In the distance, I saw Luiza struggling with the luggage and carrying Dawn at the same time. One of the soldiers was walking towards her. My chest tightened and my stomach was in a knot. I raced up to her and grabbed her suitcase. The soldier swore and continued walking down the platform. Dawn threw her arms around my neck and clung to me. I was filled with the warmth of her affection. It was a moment of bliss. Luiza hugged me. As we separated, I could see the fear in her eyes. We did not say much but hurried to the exit and got into my car.

It certainly was a joy having my granddaughter around. The only thing I resented was the stream of visitors that would come to see her every day. In the evenings, after I left the shop, I could not wait to get home. I had neither the desire nor interest to go to the club anymore. Dawn would greet me with a wonderful smile that filled my heart with joy. When I was with my granddaughter nothing else mattered. Basil sewed a new outfit for Dawn and cooked Luiza's favourite meals and desserts. Dawn's uncles and aunt doted on her. Sadly, their two-week visit came to an end too quickly. It was sad to see Luiza and Dawn leave. I wondered when we would see them again.

CHAPTER 38

ALTHOUGH IT WAS LESS than a week since Luiza and Dawn left Uganda, I missed them. I wished that Luiza and her family lived in Uganda. Travelling to Kenya was becoming unsafe during this time of political upheaval. I frequented the club since I could not go to Nairobi. While I was at the club, my worries would disappear. Sadly, my drive home would take me on a downward spiral. Fear of what lay ahead under the tyranny of Idi Amin consumed my thoughts.

Placido had started a club with a group of his friends, appropriately named "The Teen Club." Basil worried that they might get into trouble with the parents whose daughters joined the club. I was not too concerned, so long as my daughters were not involved. My sons were perfectly capable of handling themselves. They were busy preparing for their annual dance to be held at the hall in Christ the King Church. Matti designed shirts for them with a frill running down the front. They were the latest fashion sported by stars such as Englebert

Humperdinck and Tom Jones. Placido was busy gathering materials to decorate the hall and organizing the event. He even managed to hire the up-and-coming band "The Scorpions", to play at the dance.

It was a Saturday night. There was a lot of excitement as the four of them were getting dressed to go to the dance. I had just come home from the club and Basil served supper. The boys skipped supper and left for their dance. I washed up after finishing my supper and decided to turn on the radio to listen to the news. Eddy Wamala read the headlines and then announced that there would be a special broadcast. There was a pause, followed by a crackling sound, and then I heard the voice of Idi Amin. I shook my head in despair. What crazy scheme would he be up to now? He stated that the Asians were milking the economy of Uganda and that it was time for Ugandans to take control of their destiny. He ended his broadcast by saying that it was time to expel the Asians from Uganda. According to Idi Amin, he received this message in a dream. I was aghast, dumbfounded, and shocked. Just then, Basil walked into the living room.

"Dias, what is it? You look worried."

"Basil, I can't believe it. This cannot be happening!"

"What...what is happening?"

"Idi Amin just announced that he is going to throw us out of the country."

"Oh, you know him. He is crazy. It is probably one of his scare tactics."

"Basil, I think that he is serious. Please ask one of the neighbours to call the children home."

"But their dance just began an hour ago."

"I don't think that it is safe for them to be out there. You never know what the army will do after this announcement."

I was in a state of shock. I tried reading the newspaper but was stuck on the same line. Fortunately, I had a bottle of Johnnie Walker whiskey. Although I normally drank it with club soda, I decided to have it neat. I calmed down when the boys got home. They looked disappointed and concerned. There was very little I could say to reassure them. Uncertainty was all that lay ahead for us.

I woke up the next morning, convinced that it was all a bad dream, only to have a rude awakening when I read the "Uganda Argus". The headline read "THE FUTURE OF ASIANS IN UGANDA"; followed by a sub-headline: "It will be Britain's responsibility". General Idi Amin stated that there was no room in Uganda for 60,000 Asians holding British passports because they were sabotaging Uganda's economy and encouraging corruption. He made this announcement when he addressed officers and men of the Airborne Regiment at Tororo. He told the soldiers that he wanted to see the economy of Uganda in the hands of Uganda citizens, especially "Black Ugandans".

After putting the newspaper down, my head was buzzing with a flurry of thoughts. A part of me felt that Idi Amin would not go through with his threat. The British would certainly reject his proposal. On the other hand, I suspected that Idi Amin would not back down on his demand to expel the Asians. There had always been an intense hatred for Asians among Africans. They felt that the Asians filled jobs that rightly belong to them. Idi Amin must have shared the same sentiment.

I showed Basil the paper. She started trembling; her lips quivered as she looked at the headlines. It was hard for her to deny it now that it was in print.

"What are we going to do?"

"Basil, I don't think that we have much of a choice."

"What about the children? Michael only just began his studies in England."

I did not even think about that. Michael had come back to Uganda for his holidays after completing his first year at the Hull College of Art.

"We will have to send him back to England. As for the rest of the children, they will have to come with us to Goa."

Although I was giving Basil all the logical answers, the reality of this dire situation had not sunk in. Wishful thinking would take over at times, hoping that Idi Amin would change his mind.

Every week, Idi Amin would make a new announcement exacerbating the plight of the Asians. His latest announcement was to include 23,000 Asians who had secured Ugandan nationality on the list of those to be expelled by November 9th, 1972. We were in constant fear that Idi Amin and the military would make our lives a living hell until we left the country. Britain, on the other hand, did not want to take the influx of Asians. There was talk that Britain would reject Amin's ultimatum. At the same time, India stated that it would not accept any Asians with British passports. Fortunately, Basil and I had Indian passports. Placido had a British passport, so he would have to go to England once he received his voucher.

Basil started clearing the house of clothes and other items that we could not take with us. The Africans would come around looking to buy things, fully expecting to get them for a song. Basil would complain every night that she had to give away good clothing, kitchenware, and furniture. The Africans knew that we were desperate and had to leave in a few months.

I had stopped taking new customers and orders except for Idi Amin's wives. When they came to pick up their dresses, they were always escorted by heavily armed bodyguards. They would walk out of the shop without paying a cent. Asking for payment could put my life at risk. I heard stories about the army confiscating shops belonging to Asians. I was in constant fear of meeting the same fate. It was difficult for me to wind down my business expeditiously. Margaret and George, my workers, realized what was going on and were concerned about their jobs. This affected the quality of their work.

It was September 25th, a little more than a month before the deadline. I needed to get out of the shop for a break, so I decided to go to Jeffery's Bar for a coffee. As I stepped out of the shop, I saw a group of soldiers walking down the street. Within minutes, they would be at my shop. I quickly turned back, went into the shop, and locked the front door. I rushed to the workroom at the back of the shop.

"Margaret, George they are coming. We need to get out of the shop right away."

"*Bwana, Bwana,* who is coming?"

"It's the army. George, quickly give me a hand with the machines."

We managed to get two of the sewing machines out through the back door. I could hear the soldiers breaking down the front door. Both George and I were sweating profusely. We hurried down the rear stairs carrying one machine at a time. George was grunting with every step we took. I told Margaret to run away. We just managed to hide at the bottom of the stairwell when we heard one of the soldiers pushing open the back door. At this point, both George and I were trembling. I prayed that they would not come down the stairs. We waited for what seemed like a long time. When there was no noise above us, we gradually got out of our hiding spot and walked down Rosebury Lane with the machines.

That was the last I saw of my shop. Margaret came to the house a few days later to find out when I would be re-opening the shop. I told her that was not going to happen. The army had ransacked the shop and taken all the cash that was in the till.

"*Bwana*, I need money to feed my children," she pleaded.

I gave her all the cash that I had, three hundred shillings, which was more than her monthly salary.

"*Asante sana, Bwana, asante sana*," she kept saying with tears in her eyes.

I was choking, knowing that this would be the last time I would see her. She was a dedicated and loyal worker. Why did Idi Amin have to do this?

It was September 28th. With everything that was going on, I had completely forgotten, it was the day Michael was leaving for England. On our way to Entebbe airport, we encountered several army roadblocks. They kept threatening to beat us if we did not surrender our money and valuables. We were forewarned about this, so I carried little money. Although I reminded Basil to keep all her jewelry behind, I had forgotten to remove my wristwatch. That was the first thing they confiscated it. By the time we arrived at the airport at Entebbe, we were nervous wrecks.

Michael managed to get through customs since he hardly had any cash or valuables. He did, however, manage to smuggle a twenty-pound sterling note that he carefully inserted in his pen. As he was walking towards the runaway, we were waving to him from above. Basil was sobbing uncontrollably as she clung on tightly to Gregory. Placido suddenly pulled a gold chain from around his neck and flung it over the railing. Michael managed to catch it and quickly slipped it into his pocket. Fortunately, none of the soldiers saw this since Michael was surrounded by a crowd of passengers. I was about to smack Placido for potentially endangering Michael's life. I stopped myself when it dawned on me that we were sending a seventeen-year-old teenager to a foreign country with hardly any money. I felt a lump in my throat and fought hard to hold back my tears. I quickly turned away, pulled out my handkerchief and dabbed my cheeks hoping that nobody noticed me.

It was almost two months since Idi Amin had imposed the November 9th deadline. To date, only a few thousand Asians had left the country. Although President Amin expected the Asians to be airlifted to England, there was no sign of that happening. He was imposing new directives daily, causing even greater hurdles for the Asians. He stated that each Asian family was only allowed to take fifty-five American dollars out of the country. The latest directive was that all requests for airline tickets for travel outside East Africa had to be cleared by the Bank of Uganda. This would prevent Asians from getting money out of the country by buying expensive round-the-world tickets, which they could turn in for a refund later. I was glad that we were only planning to fly to Kenya, and then take the ship to India. We did not need to get approval.

For the next five days, Placido and a couple of his friends were busy packing and crating valuable items that we owned. The plan was to sell these items in India and live off the proceeds. Mrs. Alfonso, one of our neighbours, happened to know the soldiers responsible for guarding the railway station. She had made arrangements with them to allow the baggage handlers to load these crates late in the night. To facilitate this process, we had no choice but to bribe those involved.

I was buying staples, such as coffee and canned foods that we would need in India. Most of the shops had run out of their stock since they were winding down their businesses. After doing my shopping, I stopped at the Caltex petrol station only to find out that they too had run out of petrol. The African attendant told me that the Asians who normally delivered the petrol had left the country. As I was driving off, I heard him say that he would be glad when all the Asians had left Uganda. He thought that he would become the owner of the petrol station. Little did he know that it would probably be shut down, as the economy would grind to a halt after the departure of the Asians.

It was October 18th; the house was practically empty. Our belongings were reduced to three metal trunks. Basil managed to sell or give away whatever was left. Gregory had made several trips to the post office to mail his books and other small items. I had my doubts that these parcels would make it to India. I knew that Gregory would be devastated if they got lost. His books meant the world to him – especially his Phillips World Atlas and his Reader's Digest Encyclopedia. We woke up the next morning, had only coffee for breakfast and headed to the airline office next to the church. Placido and Matti had left for Jerome DeSouza's house the night before. Their daughter, Gemma, was going to Canada so she convinced them to apply for entry into Canada. The plan was for them to stay with the DeSouza family while they waited for their Canadian Immigrant Status.

We boarded the bus for Entebbe. Fortunately, the soldiers at the roadblocks let us pass through without any hassle since the bus was guarded by the police. Besides the fifty-five American dollars that I converted at the Bank of Uganda; I had one hundred pounds that I smuggled in a thermos flask. I warned Basil not to say a word as we went through customs at the airport. When we arrived at the airport, she started experiencing palpitations. We were thoroughly searched at customs after which we boarded the East African Airways Super VC-10. My heart felt heavy, and I was overcome with sadness knowing that

I would never return to Uganda. Fifty-five minutes later, we landed at Embakasi Airport in Nairobi. Felix, Luiza and Dawn were at the airport to greet us. It was a delight to see them. I breathed a sigh of relief, knowing that we were finally out of Uganda, which was an extremely dangerous place for any Asian to be.

CHAPTER 39

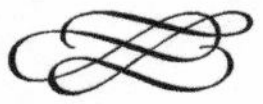

FELIX WAS WELL CONNECTED with the Kenyan Customs and Immigration officer. As an instructor at East African Power & Lighting College, he knew several influential Kenyans. It was a well-known college and Felix's reputation as an adept instructor spread quickly in government circles. Although the Kenyan government had set up maximum border security to prevent any Ugandan Asians from entering Kenya, we were allowed to enter the country after mentioning Felix's name to the immigration officer. He stamped our passports and waved us through. What a pleasant change it was from the way we were treated in Uganda.

We squeezed into Felix's orange Volkswagen Beetle and headed for their home in Rouaraka, a suburb of Nairobi. Luiza had prepared a delicious supper, which we thoroughly enjoyed. After supper, I decided to go to the Tailors Club in Nairobi. On my way back from the club it occurred to me that I might never go back to Uganda. I had spent thirty years, practically all my adult life, there. My four sons were born there. I had great memories of the Tailors Club in Kampala, and I revelled in the success of my business. I wondered what would become of it. Uganda was my second home, but now I was considered undesirable. It felt like the rug had been pulled from under my feet. I was in a state of limbo.

The morning after, we said our goodbyes and then went to the airport to catch our flight to Mombasa. The flight was barely thirty-five minutes. As we exited the terminal, extreme humidity and heat engulfed us. The temperature must have been at least 90 degrees Fahrenheit. Within minutes, I was covered in sweat. My damp shirt clung to my body. At the airport, we were met by Rosario, Ethelvina's husband, who took us to the hotel owned by his wife. Most of the Goans who passed through Mombasa would stay at Ethelvina's hotel. It was a place of unmatched hospitality with the comfort of authentic Goan food, a place to rest before embarking on the long journey to and from India.

The following day, we boarded the *S.S. Haryana*. We were pleased to see all our friends from Uganda. They told us how badly they were treated by the Kenyan police and army. As they exited the train, the army escorted them to the docks. This was to ensure that none of the Uganda Asians would attempt to stay in Kenya illegally. Our friends expressed their contempt for being treated like prisoners. Thankfully, we were treated in a dignified manner.

The voyage from Mombasa to Bombay was six days. Our futures looked bleak with only fifty-five dollars and no possibility of finding a job. None of us knew how we were going to survive in Goa. Although it was a difficult time for us, we shared a special bond since we were all in the same situation. I played cards with my friends after lunch and dinner. Basil was happy since she did not have to cook. She enjoyed chatting with her friends and reminiscing about the good old days in Uganda.

John and Gregory instantly joined a group of teenagers who

got to know the crew very well. Every night they would party on the upper deck. For a change, Basil did not worry about them staying out too late. This short-lived easygoing time came to an end when we arrived in Bombay. The pristine blue waters of the Indian Ocean turned into an unpleasant brown colour. As we docked in the harbour we were overcome by a putrid odour. The lineups quickly disintegrated into crowds of people filling the grimy and grey stone customs hall. After waiting for over six hours, we finally arrived at the customs counter. The officer on duty sported a bushy mustache - neatly twisted and curled at both ends. His tan-coloured shirt with black epaulets and a crest on the pocket was perfectly pressed. He wore a black hat with the Indian emblem of three lions embroidered in gold. The badge on his shirt pocket read "Arun Mujumdar".

"How many pieces of luggage are you bringing into India?" he asked authoritatively.

"Nine, three suitcases and six crates," I replied in Hindi, hoping to break the ice.

"Nine! Why so many? What do you have in the crates?" he asked in English.

"We have two refrigerators, six chairs, a table, and other personal belongings."

"Are you planning to settle in India?"

"Yes, in Goa. We were expelled from Uganda."

He had a look of disdain as soon as I mentioned Goa. A few seconds later I noticed a twinkle in his eyes.

"I hear that the Indians living in Uganda were very rich. Did you bring something for me?" he said rubbing his thumb against his index and middle fingers. Gauging from his hand gesture I realized that he was asking for a bribe. I was enraged. How dare he ask for money when we practically lost everything.

"We were not allowed to take any money with us. I do not have anything to give you."

"I cannot let you take any of your luggage unless it is thoroughly inspected and cleared through customs."

"How long will that take?"

"It will take at least four weeks. You will only be allowed to take your suitcases with your clothing."

We left the hot and humid customs building and were bussed to a local school. An Indian charitable organization arranged for us to stay in the school for a few days. There were about seventy-five of us travelling to Goa, but the bus had a capacity of only sixty. Most of us managed to squeeze into the seats, but several people had to stand. Gregory happened to be one of them. It felt good to get some fresh air and stretch my legs when the bus stopped for refuelling. The long and winding journey to Goa took seventeen hours. We finally arrived in Goa, totally exhausted, and famished.

It felt strange not having *Mai* to welcome us. I could just imagine her running to meet us and trembling with joy. As I entered the house, I choked with emotion and had to suppress my tears. Although I mourned the loss of *Mai* when I was in Uganda, it hit home now. I was overcome with grief and a deep sense of loss. Basil was unaware of what I was going through. She was already in the kitchen getting it organized so she could start cooking. John and Gregory walked around the house exploring the rooms and then ventured into the backyard.

A few days later, we received a letter from Matti and Placido. Thankfully, it was good news: their application to go to Canada was approved. They were leaving for Montreal in a couple of days. What a relief it was to know that they would not be stuck in Uganda after the deadline.

After a month, we had settled in, and it felt like I had never left Goa. Basil had gone to Bombay with her friend Irene to get our luggage held in customs. She spent a week there and went to the customs office daily. They kept refusing to release our luggage. She finally went with her uncle, Manu. He spoke *Hindi* well since he had worked in Bombay for a long time. Manu tried his best to convince the customs officer to release our luggage. He finally told Basil that she had no choice but to bribe them. Basil reluctantly gave them the last hundred rupees that we had, and they released our luggage.

While she was in Bombay, she went to the University of Bombay to present Gregory's original "O" Levels certificate. This protocol was mandatory due to the rampant forgery of documents in India. He had applied for admission to Chowgele College in Goa, which was affiliated with the University of Bombay. After reviewing his application and certificate, they accepted him into the two-year Science program.

Back in Navelim, I visited Elna's Bar daily where I met my old friends. One evening, a friend brought a tiny puppy to the bar, and I immediately fell in love with him. I wasn't sure what breed he was, but I decided to buy him for 10 rupees. "*Toto*" which means little boy in Swahili was the perfect name for him. Although I missed Uganda and my car, I enjoyed the fresh evening air as I walked back to the house. The smell of burning palm leaves and twigs as the people prepared their dinner gave me a warm and fuzzy feeling.

Selling the refrigerators and small appliances generated some income that allowed us to buy food and some necessities. My concern was that this money would soon run out. I desperately needed to find a job. Matti and Placido would not be able to support us since they were just starting their lives in Canada. In their letter, they stated that the Canadian government paid them a stipend while they learned French. Michael was in

England struggling to make it through college. Fortunately, he had received a government grant.

Gregory started his first year in college. It was quite a struggle for him. He had missed half the year and had to catch up quickly and prepare for his exams. He would frequently study late into the night. I would pray that his hard work would pay off. John was not interested in studying, so he was trying to find work. After months of being unemployed, he managed to get a job as a substitute teacher for a couple of weeks. Then one day, out of the blue, he was contacted by the construction company that he used to work for in Uganda "Bawa Singh Bharj". They had set up their business in New Delhi and asked if he would like to work for them. He was ecstatic about the idea of working in New Delhi. He did not waste any time packing his bags. Although we were sad to see him go, we knew that getting a permanent job in Delhi was the best thing for him.

I was getting anxious about finding a job since we were practically out of money. There were no jobs in Goa. Sadly, the economic situation had hardly changed during the thirty-plus years that I was in Uganda. I could set up my own business, but I needed capital which was in short supply. In addition, renting a place was a challenge. The waiting list for even the smallest of shops was quite long. At the bar, people talked about going to work in the Middle East. I spoke to some people whose children or spouses had succeeded in getting a job in Bahrain, Dubai, and other countries in the Arabian Peninsula. None of them were able to give me a clear answer. There were job search agencies in Bombay, but I had heard stories of how they took the finding fee and disappeared.

It was the feast day at *Fatrade*. I was obliged to attend since Basil was born there. Saint Roch was the patron saint of their village, and Basil had a lot of faith in him. After going for the long service followed by a procession, we went over to Basil's mother's house for lunch. We hardly sat down for the meal when we heard a knock at the door. Isabella, Basil's mother went to the door and escorted the visitor into the dining room.

"Basil, do you remember this man?" Isabella asked.

"No, I don't. Is he from our village?" Basil replied.

"From our village. Of course, he is your cousin John Pires.

"Oh, yes, I remember him. He lives in the blue house close to the Village Square. Hello, John."

"Hello, Basil, it has been a long time since I last saw you."

"I have been living in Uganda with my husband Carlos Dias."

"Hello, Carlos. It is a pleasure meeting you."

John Pires happily joined us at the table for lunch. He certainly had a big appetite, which explained his size. After lunch, we went into the living room. He was quite an entrepreneur. I was thrilled to find out that he ran an employment agency for jobs in the Middle East. We hit it off and I decided to invite him over for dinner the following week. After dinner, I informed him that I was very interested in working in the Middle East. He was most willing to help and informed me that he charged only 10,000 rupees. I only had half that amount. Basil had saved 6,000 rupees which she was glad to part with, knowing it would be a ticket to getting a job. Within a couple of months, John Pires got my work permit and completed all the necessary paperwork. I went to Panjim and got my visa. I was thrilled when I boarded the plane destined for Muscat. This was the dawning of a new chapter in my life.

CHAPTER 40

I LOOKED out through the small oval-shaped window and saw an expanse of blue, with white foamy slivers floating on the surface. A few minutes later, the sea of blue was transformed into a sandy plain. In the distance was red-rippled terrain that extended as far as the eye could see. Separating the land from the sea was a mountain range. I was startled when the drone of the engines was interrupted by an official-sounding voice over the PA system.

"This is your captain Clive speaking. The land mass that you see on your right is the Arabian Peninsula. Oman is situated at the south-eastern tip. We will be landing in Muscat, the capital of Oman, in about twenty minutes."

I felt my mouth go dry and my hands became moist. I suddenly realized that I knew very little about Oman, where I would be working for the next two years. Images of what it might be like formed in my mind's eye. I heard that Oman was a monarchy and predominantly an Islamic nation. They probably had strict laws banning the consumption of alcohol. I was suddenly overcome with fear about how I would cope in this foreign country. In Uganda and India, I enjoyed the freedom to drink, gamble and practise my religion. The "fasten your seatbelt" sign was illuminated. I could feel my heartbeat accelerating. I rubbed my hands together hoping to get rid of the dampness. I heard a thud when the wheels of the plane hit the runway. The captain welcomed us to Seeb International Airport and announced that the temperature was 102 degrees Fahrenheit.

As I walked out of the plane, I felt a blast of hot air and I squinted in the blinding sun. I was expecting it to be hot, but this was unbearable. I quickly took off my suit jacket and within seconds rivulets of sweat formed on my forehead and then all over my body. I was pleased when I entered the main terminal building. It turned out to be extremely modern and cool. The revenue from oil royalties afforded them this luxury. It felt foreign seeing signs in Arabic. The customs and immigration line-up consisted mostly of people from India and Pakistan. The officers wore white floor-length shirtdresses with a tassel hanging from the neckline. Their heads were covered in tightly wrapped white turbans. As I exited the airport, I saw a man dressed in traditional Arab clothing carrying a sign with my name on it. I approached him with caution.

"Are you Carlos Dias?" he asked in a heavy Arabic accent.

"Yes, yes. I am. Are you...em ... Mr. Akhmed?"

"Yes, *Salaam-alekoum*. Welcome to Oman. My driver is waiting for us."

He waved to his driver and within seconds a car pulled up. What a relief it was to be picked up at the airport. I would have been at a loss when dealing with the taxi drivers since I hardly spoke Arabic. Occasionally, I would see camels walking majestically on the side of the road. This was an extraordinary sight since I had never seen camels before. In the distance were several mountain ranges varying in colour from red, brown, and grey. Tall date palms bearing large, sprawling, green fronds at their peak lined the newly paved road. Mosques, each with distinct cupolas and architecture kept appearing intermittently. An old fort caught my eye just as we entered Muscat. It resembled Fort Jesus in Mombasa and Fort Aguada in Goa, both built by the Portuguese. I learned later that the Portuguese had occupied Muscat in the fifteen hundreds, around the same time that they colonized Goa. Close to this fort was a grandiose palace surrounded by perfectly maintained lawns and beautiful gardens. It resembled an oasis in the desert. The architecture, although modern, was Arabic and opulent. After passing the palace, we drove south on a major boulevard and then entered a suburb of Muscat, called Sidab. We stopped in front of an elegant whitewashed two-story house. It had a long balcony on the second floor and a terrace above.

"Here we are, Mr. Dias. This is my home. You will be my guest."

"Thank you for your hospitality, Mr. Akhmed."

As I walked into the foyer, two children popped their heads out of the back doorway and then promptly disappeared. A woman whose face was covered in a black veil stood at the rear of the foyer. Mr. Akhmed did not introduce me to her. I assumed that was his wife. He took me upstairs to my room. It looked bare, with only a bed, a small dresser, and a bedside table. I was overcome with a sense of loneliness at the thought of spending two years in this place without my family.

The next morning, Mr. Akhmed took me to his shop. It was in a *souq* - on the outskirts of Muscat. He showed me the type of garments that people typically ordered. The men's outfits were traditional long shirtdresses made from light purple, white and gold fabrics. They were loose and comfortable, designed for the hot weather. He referred to them as *dishdashas.* The second part of the outfit was a piece of fabric wrapped around the waist like a sarong. Although I had only sewn for women in the past, I figured that the *dishdashas* would be simple to sew. The women's clothing consisted of colourfully printed *dishdashas* which were accessorized with even more colourfully printed shawls and veils. I was surprised. I thought that women mostly wore black cloaks and veils. Mr. Akhmed informed me that was true for most of the other Gulf countries, but Oman was the exception. He also had customers who were expatriates from England, India, and Pakistan. They typically wore Western clothing. I told him that I specialized in women's clothing. He reassured me that he had very few requests for western menswear.

After work, I would venture out into the streets to get some fresh air. The temperature in the evenings was cooler, more bearable than during the day. The town was like Mombasa. Although this surprised me initially, I recall that the Omanis had ventured down the East African coast. They controlled Mombasa and the island of Zanzibar in the early eighteen hundreds. The streets were lined with small stalls selling coffee. I enjoyed this strong and flavourful coffee since it reminded me of East Africa.

Most of the orders I sewed were for the traditional *dishdashas*. It was a change for me, but I did not mind. However, I missed the creative aspect of my work. Occasionally, Arab men would bring in fabric for their wives and Mr. Akhmed would give me a standard pattern that came in three different sizes – small, medium, and large.

Eid al-Fitr is a three-day celebration marking the end of Ramadan – the month of fasting. Five days before this big celebration, an Arab man walked into the shop with his wife. I could tell from the way he was dressed that he was a wealthy man. His wife, who walked behind him, wore a long colourful embroidered cloak and baggy trousers. Her face was covered with a black veil. Mr. Akhmed had stepped out to buy some coffee since it was time to break the daily fast. The Arab man spoke some English, so we managed to communicate. He explained that his wife needed a special outfit for Eid al-Fitr since he was entertaining some very important businessmen from abroad. She hesitantly produced the design cut out from a magazine. It looked like a traditional Indian outfit. I told the man that I could sew it and then proceeded to take her measurements. I barely threw the tape behind her waist when the man yelled something in Arabic and then shouted in English.

"Don't touch her. You will defile her."

I just dropped the measuring tape and moved away from her. I was terrified. Just then, Mr. Akhmed walked into the shop with his coffee and tried to calm the man.

"I.... I am sorry. I did not mean any harm," I managed to say. My heart was pounding.

The man grabbed the fabric and motioned his wife to leave. He strode out of the store cursing and swearing. I was trembling. Once they left the store, Mr. Akhmed cautioned me never to touch or go close to an Arab woman.

As time went on, I started picking up Arabic. Mr. Akhmed and some of the customers were surprised at how quickly I had learnt the language. I had to be careful not to offend anyone by inadvertently using the wrong choice of words. My attempts to improve my Arabic by reading the local newspaper were in vain. Understanding the Arabic script was a challenge. I would invariably purchase the *Times of Oman* – a newspaper written in English. One day I came across an article on the "Dubai World Cup". It boasted a purse of $1.5 million U.S. of which $1 million went to the winner. That is why horse racing is known as "the sport of kings". It had to be the world's most lucrative horse race. I could not believe this! This was an opportunity of a lifetime. The race was to take place in three days. I put the paper down and went to talk to Mr. Akhmed. He informed me that Dubai was five hundred miles away from Muscat. The bus between Muscat and Dubai operated only twice a week – on Saturdays and Wednesdays. This meant that I would have to stay in Dubai for four days. I was only off on Fridays. Yet another obstacle was that my work permit allowed me to travel within Oman only. Dubai was in the United Arab Emirates. My only hope for doing something exhilarating was dashed.

It was almost five months since I had started working in Oman. I did not have much money left after paying for room and board. Making a lot of money by working in the Middle East did not seem to be the case for me. Whenever I had extra money, I would send it to Basil for the upkeep of the house. I could not look for another job since I had signed a two-year contract with Mr. Akhmed. I felt trapped.

It was the sixth month since my arrival. Mr. Akhmed handed me my paycheque. I had to pay him back sixty percent of it for rent and board. I decided then to call it quits. Mr. Akhmed made a big deal and stated that he was very disappointed with me. He told me that his business would be ruined if I left before my contract ended. I offered to stay one more month and convinced him that he would be able to find a replacement quite easily. Many unemployed tailors in India would be willing to accept this job. Thankfully, a month later, a tailor from Bombay arrived to replace me. I booked my ticket and within a week I flew back to India.

I decided to stay in Bombay for a few days before going to Goa. I stayed at the Navelim clubhouse which was the equivalent of an army mess hall. It was great to be back with my fellow villagers. Every evening after supper, we drank and played cards. Most of the people that stayed at the clubhouse worked on the ship. Duty-free alcohol was easily available. It was a relief to be able to drink and play cards after seven months of being dry.

After a couple of days, I took the bus to Goa. When the taxi dropped me in front of the house, Cresence, our next-door neighbour came running out of her house.

"*Irmao, Irmao*, when did you leave the Middle East?" she asked gleefully.

"A few days ago."

Just then Basil came to the front door. She just stood there in a state of shock. She was trembling. Cresence quickly took her to the bedroom and made her lie down. Basil's chest was heaving, and she had difficulty breathing.

"*Irmao*, I think you should call the doctor."

I dropped my bags and walked quickly towards the village doctor's house. Fortunately, he was in, so we rushed back to the house. He checked Basil's vital signs. Her heartbeat was rapid, and her blood pressure was high. She had palpitations. The doctor asked if anything unusual had occurred recently that might have brought this on. I was embarrassed and ashamed. I informed him that I had arrived unexpectedly from the Middle East.

CHAPTER 41

BASIL'S HEALTH gradually improved two weeks after I arrived from Muscat. I finally told her in detail what life was like for me in the Middle East. Although she understood that I had a difficult time, her main concern was our financial situation. Matti and Placido would send us money sporadically but it was not sufficient to cover our expenses. Basil decided to dig up a patch adjacent to the house, where she started a vegetable garden in May. She had built a tall bamboo fence around the patch and cleverly intertwined the branches to form a perfect barrier. As expected, the monsoons started promptly in June and after two months of heavy rain, we were blessed with an abundance of squash and cucumbers. This certainly helped since we did not have to buy expensive vegetables from the market. She was not the only one plucking the vegetables from her garden. The cows and other animals would stick their heads through the fence and eat the leaves and vegetables. She had to constantly keep driving them away.

We could not live on vegetables only. Chicken and pork were

outrageously expensive, so buying meat was out of the question. Thankfully, Basil had salted and dried some fish before the monsoons. I thought about going fishing with my friends in the nearby River Sal but couldn't see myself doing so during the monsoons. It was easier to go to Elna's Bar for a drink and chat with my friends. After a few drinks, I would forget my financial woes and ward off the loneliness at home. The house felt empty with Jonathan being away in New Delhi and Gregory busy studying at the college library.

It was a Sunday afternoon after the monsoons. I was taking a nap when I heard a knock on the door. I was too lazy to get out of bed. Thankfully, Basil got out of bed and went to the door.

"*Arrh*, *Baba* Johnnie, what happened!" I heard Basil say.

"Nothing! I just decided to come back to Goa for a break," John replied.

"But what about your job? Are they going to keep it for you?

"I don't think so. It was too tough, so I gave it up."

I could not believe what I was hearing. At that moment I jumped out of bed and went into the foyer.

"You gave it up! How could you?" I asked.

"Sorry, Dad but I could not take it anymore. The living conditions were horrible, and the pay was dismal. I could hardly pay for my expenses."

I was overcome with a sense of desperation. We had no source of income. He was our last hope. When I looked up at John, he had tears in his eyes. I realized how difficult it must have been for him to live in New Delhi. The temperature would rise to over 40 degrees Celsius, making it unbearably hot. Furthermore, he must have felt very lonely and depressed. While John and I were talking, Basil slipped away and started preparing a meal.

John was like a lost soul for several weeks. He would spend

his morning in the village square talking to others who were unemployed. In the evenings he would go to Margao with his friend, Albert. During one of his visits to Margao, he met Richard Colaco, Crescence's nephew. He had started a school specializing in Radio and TV repair. I was glad when John registered for a radio technician's course at Richard's school. As a child, he would tinker around with old transistor radios. I hoped that he would do well in this field. Although his chances of getting a job here in Goa were impossible, he may be able to get a job in Bombay.

A few weeks before Christmas, we received a letter from Placido. He stated that he had filed applications with Canada Immigration to sponsor John and Gregory. They were thrilled with the possibility of starting a new life in Canada. Gregory was doing his second year in Science at Chowgele College. Just before his final exams, Gregory and John were called for their interviews in Bombay. This was a challenge for Gregory since it took away two crucial weeks from his study time.

We were now well into the dry season. It was hard for Basil to maintain her garden because of a lack of water. Very little grew during the summer, except for mangoes and jackfruits. Sadly, we did not have any fruit trees on our property. Vegetables were replaced with more rice, part of our staple diet. I did not like the rice grown in Goa. It was bulky and unrefined. I preferred the long-grain basmati rice grown in other parts of India. Basil kept reminding me that we could not afford to eat expensive rice. Although I knew that she was right, I refused to make this sacrifice. I decided to sell the last couple of bottles of coffee that I had brought from Uganda. They fetched a good price in the black market.

It was June and water was in short supply. The local well had dried up too, so we were forced to get water from a deep well located more than a mile away. Sylvain, our neighbour's daughter, was kind enough to carry the water for us. Gregory would help her with this arduous task on some occasions. As a result of a lack of rain and extreme heat, the ground was parched and the shrubs, weeds and grass turned brown. To keep the house cool, all the doors and windows were left open during the day. A natural draft caused by the high peaked roof made it a little more bearable.

One afternoon when I came home from the bar for lunch, I noticed two official-looking envelopes. They were addressed to John and Gregory. I was tempted to open them but decided to wait until they came home. John was in Margao attending his radio technician course and Gregory was at college. I wondered what it could be. The stamps were Indian, so my initial conclusion was that it was probably from a local government agency. While I was looking at the envelopes our family dog, Toto came running up to me. As usual, he was barking and running around my feet. I could tell from the look in his eyes that he wanted something to eat. I gathered that Basil had not fed him. She never liked him since he always caused her trouble. I came home one time to find her chasing "Toto" with a broom and shouting insults at him. He was running away with a string of sausages dangling from his mouth. Basil had put the sausages out to dry in the sun. I managed to stop "Toto" in his tracks and yank the sausages from his mouth and handed them back to Basil.

When I woke up from my nap, I saw Gregory's books on the bench in the foyer. From the aroma, I suspected that he was in the dining room eating a late lunch. I picked up the envelope and walked into the dining room. He was busy wolfing down his food. It always amazed me how someone as skinny as Gregory could consume such large quantities of food.

"Gregory, you have received some important mail."

"Mail? Is it from Placido and Matti?"

"No, I don't think so. The stamps on it are Indian."

I handed him the envelope. He ripped open the envelope and started reading the letter. His eyes lit up, but he did not volunteer any information. He just continued reading the letter. The suspense was overwhelming.

"Gregory, who is it from? Is it good news?"

"Good news, good news...oh yes. It is great news!"

"What is it?"

"It is from the Canadian Embassy in New Delhi. I can't believe it. My application for entry into Canada has been accepted!"

He jumped out of his chair and started dancing and waving the letter around. He ran up to Basil and hugged her. She looked very confused.

"*Baba, Baba*, what is it?"

"I am going to Canada!"

"Canada... so soon? How... what... what about your studies?"

"I can continue my studies in Canada. I can even work full-time and study part-time. The possibilities are endless."

I had never seen him so happy and excited. He had a perpetual smile on his face for the rest of the day.

When John came home, he was even more excited than Gregory. He ran all over the neighbourhood announcing that he was going to Canada. We did not see him for the rest of the day. He staggered home late that evening. I gathered that he was celebrating with his friends. Although I was happy for them, it saddened me to think that they would not be around. Canada was at the other end of the world. At least England was within reach, and a place that I could consider visiting. I hoped that being young might make it easier for them to adapt to this distant land, especially the harsh winters. With that thought in mind, I drifted off to sleep. That night, I dreamt that I received photographs of John and Gregory all bundled up standing in front of a mountain of snow.

John and Gregory went to Bombay for their medicals. Their entry into Canada was contingent upon passing all the medical requirements prescribed by the Government of Canada. After coming back from Bombay, Gregory wrote his final exams. Soon after that, he was busy packing and getting all the paperwork done for their departure. Placido had sent them their tickets. I felt bad that I could not give them any money for their expenses. When the time came for them to leave, I asked Basil to accompany them to Bombay. She arranged with one of her cousins to take them to the airport. After she bid them farewell, she took the bus back to Goa. I could tell from her eyes that she cried all the way back. That evening when we sat down for supper, we hardly said a word to each other. The house felt empty.

CHAPTER 42

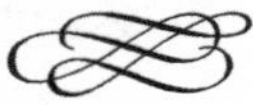

ALL MY CHILDREN were thousands of miles away, dispersed in Africa, Europe, and North America. Luiza, my oldest daughter was in Kenya with her family. I did not have to worry about her because her husband, Felix had a good job. However, I missed not being able to see my only granddaughter, Dawn. Although Luiza would send photographs, it was not the same as being able to cuddle up and play with her. Matti, Placido, John and Gregory were in Canada, probably struggling to adapt and make ends meet. Canada was a young country, abounding in natural resources with unlimited potential for industrial growth and development. I was hopeful that once they found their niche they would do well. On the other hand, I was concerned about Michael, who was studying in England. I wondered how he was surviving. I felt guilty for not being able to help him financially. I was not sure that his government grant would cover all his expenses.

My life felt empty without my children. Not having a job made me feel helpless. On the financial front, we were struggling. I was delighted when Placido and Matti sent us thirty Canadian dollars. I could not wait to go to Margao to convert it into Indian rupees. On either side of the narrow road leading to town were endless rice fields. The monsoons were at their peak with heavy rains and flooded paddy fields. Luminous green stalks covered acres of land, divided by rectangular dams of mud that held the water. Slender, tall palm trees swayed in the wind. This tranquil beauty ended abruptly as soon we entered the town of Margao. At the entrance of town were unsightly commercial buildings heavily stained with black and green mildew. The terra cotta tiles were dark green with weeds sprouting in between the tiles. People flocked to this small but important town in the south of Goa. As we approached the centre of town, the crowds grew, and traffic was chaotic. I got off the bus and went to a local jewelry shop, where I exchanged my Canadian dollars for Indian rupees. I managed to negotiate a much higher exchange rate than the official bank rate. It worked out to one thousand rupees. I felt rich as I stepped onto the bus heading for Navelim. The conductor was trying to garner as many passengers as he could. Some passengers were jumping onto the bus as it was moving. A man selling lottery tickets hopped onto the bus too. I was the first person he approached, so I decided to buy twenty tickets for forty rupees.

I was getting antsy since we had not heard from John and Gregory. It was almost three weeks since they had left India. We only received a short telegram – "ARRIVED SAFELY, RGDS. JOHN & GREG". I was glad when we finally received a long letter from Gregory. He talked about how happy they were to be in Canada and how surprisingly warm it was. Placido had told them to enjoy the weather since it was going to get very cold in a couple of months. I was amazed to find out that both John and Gregory had found jobs. They worked in a factory doing twelve-hour shifts packing Styrofoam cups. Although it was long and monotonous work their hourly wages were good. Gregory promised to send us some money. In the meantime, he had to pay off his loan for the ticket and buy some clothes. Basil was in tears when I read the letter to her. I tried to convince her that she should be happy for them. At least they could find work – something that was impossible in Goa.

The monsoons had finally come to an end. A few months later, we celebrated a very quiet Christmas without the children. Thankfully, carnival time would be in a couple of months. Basil was feeling down. I decided to lift her spirits by taking her to the carnival dance. It usually is a grand outdoor event with a large band providing music and entertainment. Some of the guests dressed in elaborate costumes, making it a festive occasion. When I mentioned it to Basil she was elated. I suppose that was not surprising since she probably hadn't been to a dance or party in over four years. She spent several days going through her wardrobe and trying out different *sarees*. Cresence, our neighbour, would help her with adorning these *sarees*. After a week of doing this, she asked me if I liked the royal blue sari that she planned to wear for the carnival. I agreed that it was a good choice. On the day of the dance, I came home from the bar only to find her dressed in an ivory saree. I did not bother to ask her why she had changed her mind. I got dressed in my suit and called for a rickshaw, which was a scooter converted into a small taxi for two people. We squeezed into the back, and the driver sped off towards the large field in Sinquetem, where the dance was being held. As we approached the area, we could hear the music blaring. Basil was in her element since she loved being around people. It was crowded and everyone was having a good time. We danced and partied until the wee hours of the morning. When the dance ended, I called for a rickshaw. The driver reeked of alcohol and the rickshaw swayed from side to side. He drove recklessly and at one point he missed the narrow road, and we landed in a ditch.

"Dias! Dias! ... Are you okay!" Basil shouted.

I was being crushed under her weight. I could barely reply.

"Dias say something! Are you hurt?"

"You..you are crushing me," I managed to say.

She climbed out of the rickshaw that was on its side with great difficulty.

"You idiot! You drunken fool!" she yelled at the driver who was groaning.

"Sorry...I hope you are not hurt," the driver mumbled.

"Hurt, what are you talking about? You almost killed us!"

Within minutes, we were surrounded by people from the neighbourhood. One family took us into their home and offered us some tea. They called another taxi who took us home safely. I was sore for the next several days.

We would receive letters from our children in Canada quite regularly. They were now well settled with good jobs. The money that they sent kept us afloat. Basil and I missed them, but we were getting used to it. One day we received a letter from the Canadian High Commission stating that Placido and Matti had sponsored us. Although I was excited about the thought of going to Canada, Basil had concerns.

"Dias, if we go to Canada, squatters could move in and take over the house."

"Oh, Basil you always worry about things that may never happen."

"You can't blame me. I have heard so many stories about properties being usurped by squatters or tenants."

"But we don't have any tenants. I will make sure that Cresence looks after the house."

We went for the interview, and the Canadian interviewing me was very impressed that I operated a successful business in Uganda. He informed me that I would do very well in Canada since there was a demand for experienced tailors. The interviewer also stated that our chances of getting accepted were good since our children were already working in Canada. A month later, we received a letter from the Canadian High Commission informing us that we were accepted and that we should proceed with our medicals.

When we packed our bags, I was overcome with sadness. Once again, I was leaving my childhood home. My dear mother had built it with great hardship over fifty years ago. Although I was looking forward to starting a new life in Canada and being with my children, I felt sad about leaving the homeland. It was too late to change our minds. Our children had already spent a lot of money buying our tickets and getting all the paperwork done. We left Goa with mixed feelings and anticipation of what lay ahead.

CHAPTER 43

"WELCOME TO DORVAL INTERNATIONAL AIRPORT. It is sunny and the temperature is 72 degrees Fahrenheit." Her voice was clear and pleasant. I looked out the oval window and saw a large building with a sign on the top – "DORVAL INTERNATIONAL AIRPORT". I never thought that I would ever visit Canada. I turned to Basil to make sure that I was not dreaming. Her eyes were shut as she slipped rosary beads through her fingers. She was whispering the "Hail Mary" with a sense of urgency. My excitement suddenly turned into fear when I thought that my children might not be at the airport to meet us. Basil would be in a frenzy. I would have no idea how to navigate through the airport. I prayed that they would be there. After travelling for over twenty-four hours, we finally arrived. As the door of the aircraft opened, I inhaled the crisp fresh air.

I had some difficulty understanding the customs officer since he had a French accent. After repeating the same question three times, I finally understood what he was saying.

"No, officer, I do not have any alcohol or tobacco," I answered.

I had warned Basil not to utter a word. He believed me since he politely directed me to the lineup at Immigration. Everything was so orderly and well organized. This was a remarkable change from Bombay Airport where pushing, shoving and long queues were commonplace. The immigration officer asked me some routine questions and then signed and stamped our pink landed immigrant forms.

"Welcome to Canada. I hope that you will enjoy living here."

"Sir, you can go to the carousel and collect your luggage."

"Are we done? You must have some more paperwork to do."

I was bewildered. Has he finished already?

"No. Mr. Dias, that is all. Just make sure you do not lose that pink slip. It is proof of your landed immigrant status. "

It was hard to believe that we were now officially landed immigrants in Canada.

We went to the luggage carrousel and picked up our suitcases. The airport was spotless, and the air was fresh. When we exited the luggage area, there was a sea of excited people waving. All I could see was a crowd and did not recognize any familiar faces. I was in a daze when I suddenly heard – "Dad! Dad! Over here."

I turned around and saw Matti, Placido, John and Greg smiling and waving to us. I breathed a sigh of relief. They rushed over and hugged us. Both Basil and I were choking with emotion. It felt good to see my children after all these years.

Our first week in Canada was a blur. We slept for most of the time. I did not expect jet lag to take such a toll on our bodies. As we got back to our daily routine, I began observing my surroundings. The apartment was spacious, with four bedrooms and a large patio in the back. The walls were covered with different designs of wallpaper. I had never seen such beautiful walls before. We were used to pastel paint on the walls. Every morning after breakfast, Basil and I would go for a walk on Wellington Street. We enjoyed seeing so many different stores with merchandise neatly displayed in the windows. On a good day, we would walk to the Atwater Market. We were amazed to see such an abundance and variety of vegetables and fruits. They even had mangoes. Although the price was exorbitant, we would sometimes indulge and buy two mangoes.

After taking it easy for a month, I got restless and decided to look for a job. I started scouring the classified section in the newspapers. Most of the jobs were for piece work in factories. There were some openings for tailors, but none of the companies were interested in interviewing me. Their excuse was that I did not have Canadian experience. I expressed my frustration and disappointment at the dinner table. Matti decided to talk to one of the buyers at Zellers. He suggested that I contact Mrs. Vanelli, the owner of "Vali Designs". When I called Mrs. Vanelli, she asked me some routine questions over the telephone, and then gave me a date for an interview. I was very nervous since this was my first job interview. I was grateful that Mrs. Vanelli was very pleasant, and I felt at ease talking to her. I told her about my work experience and how I had established and operated a thriving business in Uganda for 23 years. She was impressed and astounded when I told her that I had sewn the wedding gown for the Prime Minister's wife in Uganda. I was relieved when the interview was over. Three days later, I got a call from Mrs. Vanelli offering me a job as a senior tailor. I was ecstatic!

It was August, the peak of the summer months. The hot and humid days reminded me of India. I never imagined that temperatures would soar in Canada at any time of the year. It was hard to fathom that in a few months, it would be getting cold. The sidewalk sale was in full force on Wellington Street. Basil and I thoroughly enjoyed rummaging through the clothes and other items looking for good deals. Even after converting the prices into Indian Rupees the clothes were relatively inexpensive. Matti explained that the stores were liquidating their summer merchandise to make room for their fall and winter wear. This concept of seasons was foreign to me. I was quite content to take advantage of the low prices and stock up on shirts, socks, and other clothes. Basil was buying clothes for her and all her relatives back in Goa. Friends would drop by on a Saturday morning to do their shopping. Basil delighted in cooking and feeding them after they finished their shopping sprees.

Carlos and Basilia, Canada

I found my new job challenging. The work itself did not pose a problem, except for the jargon. However, I managed to pick it up within a few months. I found it difficult working for someone. For the past twenty-three years, I ran my own business except for a brief time in Muscat. In this new job, Mrs. Vanelli would insist on doing things her way. We would disagree on several occasions. In the end, I would give up in frustration and do it her way.

The cold weather of November began to set in. Placido had lent me a jacket that I wore to work. The stores displayed darker clothing, winter coats, hats, and scarves. Although the cold weather was unpleasant, I was looking forward to the winter since I had never seen snow. My only experience of cold weather was on the way to Nairobi when the train passed through the highlands in Kenya. The temperature would drop below 60 degrees Fahrenheit.

Placido had applied to sponsor Michael, who was studying in England. He made several visits to the Immigration and Manpower office at Atwater during his lunch hour. Fortunately, his place of work, *Simpson's,* was reasonably close to the manpower office. I did not realize how much paperwork and time was involved. Making telephone calls to England was quite expensive, so we communicated with Michael through regular mail. After six months, Michael finally received his acceptance letter.

Barely two weeks after Michael had been accepted, Luiza wrote to us saying that Felix and she had applied to come to Canada. This was exciting news. If their application was accepted, we would finally be united in Canada. I focused on working harder at my job and learning more about Canada. The "Montreal Star" was a joy to read with ten different sections. On Saturday mornings, I would read every section of the paper. Basil and I stopped going for walks because the weather was getting cold. I was willing to brave the cold, but Basil would refuse to do so. She would complain that her nose would run, and she was afraid of catching a cold.

The winter started with a major snowstorm – 15 centimetres of snow. Although the slush on the streets was an ugly sight, the pristine snow on the trees and rooftops was a delight. However, the strong winds made it quite unbearable to be outside. After four weeks of cold temperatures, the excitement of winter and snow had petered out. Basil refused to step out of the house unless it was necessary. She would tread very carefully for fear that she might slip and fall. I was getting used to the winter since I went to work during the week. It always felt good to come home to a warm place. Towards the end of November, I noticed the stores putting up their Christmas decorations. I found this odd. The stores in Uganda would usually decorate a few days before Christmas.

Being homebound in the evenings was starting to get to me. I was grateful to have a group of friends around my age with similar interests. We would meet every couple of weeks to play either *truque* or *sol*. We would invariably congregate at our apartment. Placido decided to form a club for Goans and held the first event in our apartment. He decorated it with artifacts and posters from Goa and asked Basil to cook a traditional Goan meal. He invited several Goan families that lived in Montreal. The event was such a great success that everyone wanted to continue this tradition. As the Montreal Goan Club got bigger, they decided to use the church hall in our neighbourhood for special events. With all these activities, the winter went by very quickly and before we knew it, Michael arrived from England. What a joy it was to see him after five years.

It was almost nine months since I started working. As time went on, Mrs. Vanelli was giving me more responsibilities. I was too proud to ask her for a raise, even though I felt that I merited it. At the same time, my creativity was being stifled. I was forced to stick to the company's production plans. Their designs were run-of-the-mill and did not keep up with the latest fashions. When I discussed this issue with Mrs. Vanelli, she told me that was the way she ran her business and considered my suggestions too risky. I could not work in such an environment and decided to quit my job after ten months. I was glad that my children supported my decision.

I took a break for several months to ponder what I should do next. One possibility was to set up my own business, taking sewing orders at home. The only problem was space and the fact that we were living on the second floor. Basil was happy to have me at home for company, and we resumed taking our long walks. We were pleasantly surprised when we received a letter from Luiza. She mentioned that she had given birth to a boy named Denzil. I was blessed with a second grandchild. Furthermore, their application for entry into Canada had been accepted. I was overjoyed, knowing that our family would finally, be reunited.

CHAPTER 44

THINGS WERE FALLING INTO PLACE. Luiza and her family had just arrived and were settling in quite well. Placido managed to find them an apartment on Wellington Street in Verdun, fairly close to our apartment. I would visit them regularly. On my way to their home, I would pick up candy from the convenience store. It was a pleasure seeing the joy on Dawn and Denzil's faces when I gave them the candy. I would take them to the park in front of their apartment that faced the St. Lawrence River. They would play on the swings and run around in the park, happily consuming their candy bars. When I took them home, Luiza would check their teeth and ask them to brush immediately. While the children were brushing their teeth, Luiza would reprimand me for giving them candy.

We were beginning to feel cramped in our apartment, since Basil and I had accumulated clothing and other items. Now that the children had jobs, they could afford a bigger place, so Placido took it upon himself to house hunt. I would save the "Classifieds" section of the newspaper so that he could check the listings after work. It was difficult to find apartments larger than the one we rented, so the only option was to buy a house. We did not have sufficient money for a down payment. After scouring the ads for weeks, an interesting alternative caught Placido's eye. Duplexes in LaSalle were selling for around $60,000. One advantage of buying a duplex was the rental income from the unit above would cover about 40% of the mortgage payments. Although most of the duplexes were selling for $60,000, Placido spotted one that was going for $55,000. He called the real estate agent, who was happy to show him the house. The owner happened to be Indian and was desperate to sell the house since he was going through a divorce. Placido made an offer for $53,600 and it was accepted. Everyone in the family contributed their entire savings towards the down payment. After anxiously waiting for two weeks, we were thrilled when the bank finally approved our mortgage.

We moved into our duplex in July. Basil was in her element since the kitchen was large and the backyard had room for a garden. Within a couple of weeks, she dug up a patch, where she planted tomato, cucumber, and zucchini plants. The patio in the back was covered with a large grapevine–a perfect place to enjoy a cool beer on a sunny afternoon. The basement was large enough to have parties - something I was sure that Placido couldn't wait to host. In the evenings, it was a pleasure to sit out on the front balcony and enjoy the warm summer.

I started exploring the neighbourhood by visiting the stores that were located on Dollard Street. Although it was not as quaint as Wellington Street in Verdun, some of the shops were interesting. "Fabricville" got my immediate attention. It was a large brightly lit store with a huge assortment of fabrics and sewing notions. I informed Basil about my discovery, and from then on, we would visit the store regularly. Occasionally, we would see a tall grey-haired man, whom we befriended. To our surprise we found out that Mr. Morgan was the owner. He was easy to talk to, so one day I told him about my business in Uganda.

"Mr. Dias, have you ever considered setting up a tailoring business in Canada?"

"I have thought about it, but I do not have the capital."

"You don't need much money. All you need is a couple of sewing machines and a small place that you can rent. I am sure you could find something on Chabanel Street."

"I don't even own a sewing machine and I doubt that I will be able to afford the rent."

"My wife is looking for a good tailor. The last one she tried did not work out very well."

I went home feeling down. I wanted very much to start my business, but the challenges were overwhelming. In the evenings, Basil and I would lie in bed discussing how I could set up my business. I would drift off to sleep and dream that I was operating my own business on Chabanel Street.

It was August, and the weather was unbearably hot and humid, so I went to the basement to escape the heat. I decided to read my newspaper in the family room. I noticed the ads for the horse races at the Blue Bonnets Raceway, but the urge to go for a race had evaporated. I realized that had I not gambled on horse races back in Kenya, I would have been wealthy today. In the business section, I came across a story about a successful Montreal designer, Elena Friedman. It described the expansion of her business into the United States. I was surprised to read that she had started her business in the basement of her parent's home. It occurred to me that I could do the same thing. There was ample space behind the garage. That evening, I spoke to Placido, and he thought that it was a great idea. He loved doing renovations, so he spent several weeks building a false floor and drywalling the area. He also installed shelves for storing fabrics and notions. Jonathan did the wiring and installed a couple of fluorescent lighting fixtures. I could not believe the transformation from an empty drab concrete space to a bright and spacious sewing room.

Matti took me sewing machine hunting on Chabanel Street, the center of the rag trade district. The suppliers sold many kinds of sewing machines, from light-duty home use to industrial types. Most of the shops carried machines that cost way over my budget of three hundred dollars. We finally came across a small store; it was the back end of a house owned by a Chinese gentleman named Quang Do. Although his English was limited, we managed to communicate. He was willing to sell a used commercial sewing machine for $250. The price was right, but my only problem was that it was an unknown Chinese brand. All my sewing machines back in Uganda were made by Singer and were very reliable. Matti informed me that the Singer machines in Canada were not as robust as the ones we had in Uganda. I decided to try the machine out and was surprised at how well it worked.

I was anxious to put my sewing machine to use, so I went to Fabricville to purchase some fabric. As I rummaged through the box of shirting fabric, I sensed someone approaching me.

"Mr. Dias, it is good to see you again."

"Oh..., hello Mr. Morgan. How are you?" I was embarrassed that he caught me going through end pieces of fabric. I quickly dropped the fabrics back in the bin.

"I am fine. Anything interesting happening in your life?"

"There is, my son, has set up a sewing room for me in the basement."

"That is good news. So now you can get back to your sewing. Will you be taking orders?"

"That is my goal, but for the next week or so I will be trying out my new sewing machine."

I barely finished my sentence when I heard the cashier paging Mr. Morgan.

"Well, I must go now. Good luck and let me know when you launch your business."

The machine was much faster than the ones I was used to. Adjusting the tension of the stitch was yet another challenge. I tested it on a piece of cloth which flew off the machine and I nearly ended up stitching my finger. After struggling for almost an hour, I managed to adjust the stitch and sew my first shirt. By the time I had completed my second shirt, I was getting the hang of it. I got very excited and decided to sew a dress for Basil. I picked up the fabric for Basil's dress and decided to stock up on thread, buttons, and zippers. I was getting quite enthusiastic about starting my business. My son Michael had designed business cards for me, so I decided to leave some with the cashier at Fabricville and asked her to give one to Mr. Morgan.

Basil was working in her garden when I called out to her.

"What is it, Dias? Can't you see that I am busy in the garden?"

"Yes, I know but I need to talk to you."

Basil stomped out of her garden fuming because I interrupted her favourite pastime.

"It is not even lunchtime. What is it?"

I handed her a bag. She looked confused and then decided to open it.

"A dress? For whom is it?"

"It's for you. I made it on my new machine. Try it on."

As she walked towards the bedroom to try the dress, she was teary-eyed.

A week later, the telephone rang, it was Mr. Morgan stating that he got my business card and would like to come by with his wife. She needed a new dress for a wedding in a couple of weeks. I was both excited and nervous about my first order.

I told Basil to finish cooking supper early. Spicy food tends to leave a lingering aroma. Thankfully, it was summer allowing us to keep the windows open to air the place. As expected, Mr. and Mrs. Morgan showed up precisely at 7:00 p.m. After we exchanged pleasantries, I took them down to the basement. Mrs. Morgan showed me the pattern and the fabric. I did not think that the fabric was suited for the pattern that she chose but I did not want to offend her. I would have to find a way to make it work. I took her measurements and told her that the dress would be ready for fitting in three days."

That same night, I marked up the fabric and cut out the dress. I was grateful that my trusted Sheffield scissors worked like a charm. I had ordered them from England almost thirty years ago when I set up shop in Uganda. As I was cutting the dress, I thought about my business in Uganda and how it had flourished. It was hard to believe that I was starting all over again. I doubted whether I would attain the same level of success. After cutting the dress, I put the fabric away and planned to sew it first thing the following morning. With that thought in mind, I went to bed.

Mrs. Morgan struggled to get into her dress. I was sure that I had taken the right measurements. She looked in the mirror and was visibly upset. Mr. Morgan shook his head disapprovingly. Although the basement was cool, I could feel sweat dripping down my forehead and back. I opened my mouth to say something in my defence, but the words eluded me. My first order was a disaster. What was I to do? Mrs. Morgan was almost in tears.

"Dias, Dias wake up! You are trembling."

I woke up with a start, my heart was racing, and my body was covered in sweat. As my mind focused, I realized that it was all a bad dream. What a relief!

"Are you okay? Do you have a fever?"

"No... no I am fine. It's warm in the bedroom. Just go back to sleep."

I turned around and I fell into a deep slumber.

Three days later, as scheduled, Mrs. Morgan came in for her fitting. I was extremely nervous and waited anxiously while she tried on the dress. As she stepped out of the changing room, I looked at Mr. Morgan's face. He initially had a serious look on his face. This concerned me. Then he gradually broke into a smile. It was only then that I ventured to look at Mrs. Morgan.

"Mr. Dias, it fits me perfectly. I love it."

"Thank you," I said, thanking God at the same time.

I pinned up the hem, making sure that Mrs. Morgan was comfortable with the length of the dress.

A couple of days later, Mr. and Mrs. Morgan came to pick up the dress. Mrs. Morgan told me that she was looking forward to going to the wedding. The hat that she bought matched the dress and the whole ensemble looked very classy. They thanked me once again and as they were leaving, Mr. Morgan placed an envelope in my hand. When they left, I opened it expecting to find $70, the price that we had agreed upon. I was amazed to find a $100 bill. What a way to start my business! It felt good to be back in business.

CHAPTER 45

PLACIDO WAS DATING JUDY, a Goan girl, who was formerly from Uganda. They met at the Queen's Hotel in Montreal where the federal government temporarily lodged some of the Ugandan refugees. They were *Brahmin*. We were *Sudras,* lower than *Brahmins,* according to the Indian caste system. Back in India, the *Brahmins* would never associate with any other caste. When the Goans immigrated to Uganda, they continued with this rigid system of social stratification. I was skeptical about the future of Placido and Judy's relationship. I wondered if the Goans had done away with the caste system now that they lived in Canada. It seemed like social class was not important in North America. I was amazed to find out that plumbers and construction workers made more money than office workers. It was liberating to know that one was not hampered by an archaic class system. To succeed in this country, all you needed was skill and a desire to work hard.

Judy would visit on weekends and I was getting to know her. She was a very caring person, always inquiring about my health.

Basil was a bit more cautious about accepting Judy. Her experience with the Goans in Uganda was not pleasant when it came to the caste system. She decided to keep her distance. Deep down, we hoped that her parents would be more open-minded and put aside their differences in social standing.

Basil had started catering for events held by the Quebec Goan Association. Her reputation as a chef was spreading rapidly in the community. As a result, several people suggested that she start a catering business. Michael used his talents to design an attractive flyer which was distributed at the following Quebec Goan Association event. It was not long after this event that she started getting orders for weddings and house parties. Our kitchen was converted into a production line on weekends when Basil catered for events. She was fortunate that all the children would give up their weekends to help her out.

As expected, my sons would have parties in the basement. John accumulated quite a collection of albums and tapes and would DJ for the parties. Placido would convert the basement into a discotheque with a mirror ball, running lights and decorations. Late in August, Placido and John held their end-of-summer party. I was surprised to see the number of people that attended it. There must have been over fifty people, some I hardly recognized. Basil and I stayed in our bedroom hoping that the blaring music wouldn't keep us awake. We were restless and hardly slept that night. Basil sat up in bed several times during the night saying her prayers.

The next morning, I ventured downstairs to check the aftermath of the party. The floor of the main hall was littered with empty beer cans, cigarette butts, paper napkins and some of the decorations. A stale smell of smoke and alcohol permeated the basement. I was hoping that they did not damage my sewing room, so I walked towards it praying that it was intact. I tried to push open the door to my sewing room only to find out that it was locked. I breathed a sigh of relief. I found out later that Placido was wise enough to lock it before the party began. When the children woke up, they headed downstairs and started cleaning up the place. They accumulated five bags of garbage.

By now, Placido had been dating Judy for almost nine months. He decided to invite her parents over for dinner. I gathered that their relationship was getting serious. I was concerned for Placido. I did not want him to find out the hard way that Judy's parents would not allow their daughter to marry him. Although Judy's dad, Eustache, sometimes put on airs, her mother, Laura, was very pleasant and down to earth. In our discussions, I found out that she was from a village called Betalbatim, which was close to our village.

"Mrs. Dias your sorpatel is delicious," Eustace said.

"Thank you, Mr. DeSouza, why don't you have some more?"

"All the food is delicious. You certainly are a good cook," Laura added.

This broke the ice. Placido breathed a sigh of relief. After dinner, we reminisced about the good old days in Uganda and the people that we knew in common. We ended up talking about Idi Amin, the uncertainty and fear that we faced during the last days in Uganda. When we said our goodbyes, I felt that Judy's family had accepted Placido.

It was the beginning of fall, and the trees were starting to lose their leaves. On the bright side, the changing of the colours was a sight to behold. On a negative note, my business had slowed down. I was afraid that it would take longer to save for my trip to India. Although Basil was disappointed about putting her garden to sleep, she was proud of her harvest of tomatoes, cucumbers, zucchini, and peppers. Every time we had visitors, she would proudly show off the fresh produce from her garden. She ended up making several batches of tomato sauce with spices and herbs. Although the concept of freezing food was foreign to her, Luiza convinced her to do so. I was skeptical about this idea myself. I was pleasantly surprised to find out how good the sauce tasted when Basil had thawed it for the first time.

In the evenings, Basil and I would watch the news on TV before going to bed. On the political front, a new party was emerging. It was the Parti Quebecois, the main opposition to the Liberal party that was currently in power. The Parti Quebecois was rapidly gaining popularity. This was of great concern since we had a strong allegiance to the provincial and federal Liberal parties. Pierre Elliot Trudeau, the leader of the Liberals and Prime Minister of Canada had compassion for the Uganda refugees. It was a scary thought that the Parti Quebecois might win the elections and possibly divide the country.

It was a Saturday night. The boys would usually go out to a party or the movies with their friends. This time, Placido was going out by himself. He was well-groomed and looked quite dapper. I don't know what time he came home, but when I woke up at around 2:00 a.m. and checked his room, he was not in bed. The next morning, he slept in and skipped breakfast but joined us for lunch.

"Mum and Dad, I have something to tell you."

"What is it, son? Is everything okay?" Basil inquired nervously.

"Don't worry mum. It is good news."

"Good news? Tell us! Please."

"I proposed to Judy last night and she has accepted. We are planning to get married."

Basil was in shock. Tears flowed freely from her eyes. She got up slowly from her seat and hugged Placido. I was choking with emotion too but managed to conceal my feelings.

"Congratulations, Son. That is great news."

Basil finally stopped crying and wiped her tears.

"When are you planning to get married?" she asked.

"It will probably be next summer."

"Next summer, that is a long time away. In Goa, people usually get married a month after being engaged."

"It is different over here Mum."

"I suppose, everything is different here. However, we should never forget our customs and our roots."

It was hard to believe that only a few years ago Placido was just a young man. Soon he would be a husband and start a family of his own. He always carried the burden of our family on his shoulders. He was the one that packaged and shipped appliances to India when Idi Amin was expelling us from Uganda. It was due to his foresight and courage that we were able to live off the proceeds of these goods in Goa. He was the one that purchased this house and helped me start my business.

Basil and I had managed to save enough money for one ticket to India. I was extremely grateful that the rest of the family offered to pay for the second ticket. The only problem was that we did not have money for our expenses. We needed money for the maintenance of the house and to purchase household items during our six-month stay. I estimated that we would need at least another five hundred dollars.

It was October 9th, Placido's birthday. I decided to buy a lottery ticket hoping to make some quick money. Three days later I went to the convenience store to check if I had won.

"Sir you won something," said the store clerk.

"That is great! I need the money. How much is it."

"Just a moment I am checking it on the computer."

I was trembling with excitement. This was going to be my lucky break.

"You won five dollars and a free ticket."

To say that I was disappointed would be an understatement.

A couple of weeks later, I got a call from a customer referred by Mr. Morgan. She wanted me to sew her wedding gown and dresses for three of her bridesmaids. I was ecstatic. She wanted them in three weeks which was a challenge for me. I enlisted Luiza's and Matti's help in the evenings and I worked twelve to fourteen hours a day. My back was sore, but I continued working long hours. One day short of three weeks, we completed the order. The bride-to-be was very pleased with the outcome. She paid me a tidy sum of $480. This amount would go a long way to cover our expenses in Goa.

We finally booked our tickets. Most of December was spent purchasing clothing, household items, and non-perishable food to take to India. Basil was buying gifts for the neighbours and relatives in Goa. I purchased several jars of Maxwell House instant coffee since they fetched a good price in India. Our suitcases were bulging and had to be reinforced with special straps. Michael and Placido complained about the weight as they dragged our suitcases to the taxi. It was minus 25 degrees Celsius. The winds were howling, and the snow was almost knee-deep. Basil was crying as she said her goodbyes. I felt sad leaving the children, but at the same time, I was anxious to go back to India. I prayed that Canada would be in one piece when we got back from India. We boarded Air India flight 1107. The aroma of the food and the mixture of scents made me feel like I was already in India. As the plane took off, I exhaled, looking forward to spending the next six months in my beloved homeland.

CHAPTER 46

THE BLAZING SUN WAS BLINDING. We squinted as we exited the plane. We rummaged through our bags for sunglasses and quickly shed our sweaters. It was quite a transformation from minus 25 degrees Celsius and snow to plus 30 degrees and sand. I inhaled the warm air and felt the strong allure of Goa deep within my psyche. Although we were exhausted after a long journey, we were content to have finally arrived. It was worth the hard work and sacrifice back in Canada.

At our house, the musty smell brought back a flood of childhood memories of the monsoon season. We put our suitcases down in the foyer and I looked up at the altar.

Sacred Heart Image of Jesus

I was pleased to see the large picture of Christ that I had drawn almost thirty-five years ago was still intact. I thanked God that the termites had not destroyed it. I expected *Mai* to emerge from the kitchen in her soft white saree and greet us at any moment.

After all these years, I still found it hard to believe that she was gone. Tears welled up in my eyes as I thought of how she had built this bungalow as a widow. It must have taken a lot of courage on her part to undertake a challenging project of this nature.

Cresence, our neighbour, had done her best to clean the house, but the dampness that had set in during the monsoons lingered on. Basil opened all the cupboards, closets, and windows. She emptied the closets and hung out the linen and clothes in the warm sun hoping to kill the mildew. She also started making a list of things that we needed. Most of what we took for granted in Canada was hard to find here. Paper towels and dishcloths were unheard of. However, Basil, being a resourceful person, was able to use local substitutes and alternatives. For example, she used the husk from the coconut as a scouring pad for the dishes.

My first visit to Elna's Bar in Navelim was a joyous one. I was warmly welcomed by Elna and the patrons of her bar.

"Elna, a round of drinks for my friends to celebrate my return to Goa."

"Viva! Viva! Carlit. Welcome back! We missed you," my friends chanted.

I sometimes wondered whether it was me they missed or the free drinks.

"How is Canada? I hear that it gets very cold. What does snow look like?" Jacinth inquired.

I spent several hours answering questions and trying to describe Canada. It was hard for people who lived in a warm country to fathom how cold it got. The only tangible example I could give was that of holding ice cubes in their hands and sticking their heads in the refrigerator.

The village of Navelim was recently connected to the electrical grid, but only one wealthy lady in the neighbourhood managed to get electricity in her home. She walked around like she was part of the elite of the village. Basil complained about cooking without electricity. I decided to go to Margao and apply for our electricity connection. After waiting in line for over two hours, I was told to fill out several forms. As much as I hated filling out forms, I did not have much of a choice. It would be a difficult six months without electricity. Besides, I didn't think that the children would ever consider visiting Goa if we did not have electricity.

I was enjoying the great weather – sunny and warm. It was liberating to step out of the house dressed in a shirt and a pair of trousers. I decided to go fishing with my buddies. Our fishing expedition was not as much fun as I had hoped. The fish were not as abundant as when we were younger. After three hours of fishing, we managed to catch only five fish among the three of us. I was embarrassed to take the small quantity of fish home, so I offered them to Jacinth. I suspect that he would brag to his family that he caught all the fish.

Although *Mai* had built a big house, the surrounding property was owned by Mr. Alfonso, who lived in a mansion in Margao. He was very elusive and rarely visited the property. I had gone to visit him, but the maid informed me that he was out of town. I told her to let Mr. Alfonso know that I was visiting from Canada and wanted to talk to him about buying the property.

When I told Basil about my visit to Mr. Alfonso's she was delighted.

"Dias, at least this might entice the children to visit and probably settle in Goa."

"Basil don't raise your hopes too high. After all, they are used to the lifestyle in Canada."

"I know, but they should never forget their roots. This is their homeland."

I felt the same way, but I wasn't sure that the children had similar aspirations. Regardless of how they felt, it was my duty to provide them with ample property so that they could build their own houses and enjoy living in Goa.

To my surprise, our application for electricity was approved. It helped that I submitted four times the required fee with my application. Our house would be connected to the electrical grid in a month. After evaluating several electrical contractors, I hired one that I could trust to do the wiring and install the lighting. He also happened to be the lowest bidder. I was on a roll. I decided to build a new Western-style toilet and shower. A good paint job was next on the list.

We finally got our electrical connection two months after the approval date. Basil was in her element. One evening, as I was walking home from Elna's bar, I was surprised to see the house in darkness except for a small oil lamp which flickered near the doorway. Basil was sitting on the balcony chatting with Cresence. She informed me that the electrical box burst into flames when she turned on the stove to cook supper. I suspected that the electrical contractor had used substandard wiring or fuses. I was forced to hire another electrician to re-wire the entire house. I should have known why the first contractor bid a low price for the job. He was nowhere to be seen.

A month later, I received a message from Mr. Alfonso. He was interested in meeting me, so I dropped everything and went to see him. We talked for a long time about our families. He wanted to know all about my children. I was glad to tell him that they were all doing very well and that my youngest son was very interested in Goa. This was one of the reasons why I wanted to purchase the property. Mr. Alfonso promised me that he would give my offer to purchase serious consideration. However, he also wanted all the neighbours to buy the rest of the property at the same time. He did not want to be left with a mosaic of unsold lots.

I spoke to the neighbours, none of whom were interested in buying the property around their homes. They probably expected Mr. Alfonso to get tired of waiting for them to purchase their lots and finally give them the property.

"Mr. Alfonso, I tried to convince the neighbours to buy their lots, but they claimed that they did not have the money."

"That certainly complicates things. I may just have to wait things out."

"Please, Mr. Alfonso it would mean a lot to my family if you sold us the property."

"I understand, but like I told you, I do not want to be stuck with odd lots."

"I am certain that once you sell me the property, the neighbours would want to buy their lots."

"I need to think about this a little more."

My hopes for purchasing the property were dashed. We only had a few weeks left before leaving for Canada.

Basil was busy cooking all kinds of traditional Goan sweets to take back to Canada. I also started purchasing items that were not available in Canada. Goan liquor called *feni* made from coconut was something that I cherished. I decided to take three bottles although Canada Customs allowed only one per person. I did not think that the extra bottle would cause any problems. Almost everyday Basil's relatives would come with a parcel for our children or some relative in Canada. It did not matter that some of them lived as far away as Vancouver.

"Basil, the suitcases are full of parcels, and we have not even packed our stuff."

"Dias, how can I turn these people down? They are my relatives."

"You better inform the others that we cannot take any more parcels. If they insist, we will just have to leave them behind."

Mr. Alfonso had sent a message with his maid stating that he would like to see me. This was the week before our departure. I decided to take a taxi to Margao since I did not have any time to spare. When I arrived at his residence, he was out. I waited for over an hour and was about to leave when he walked in the door.

"Mr. Dias, I have been thinking about your offer to purchase the property."

"Mr. Alfonso, I am sorry about the neighbours being uncooperative."

"I think that it is important for Goans overseas to take an

interest in Goa. Some of them have been away for generations and their children probably know nothing about Goa. I think that is sad."

"I agree with you. My children have always been interested in Goa especially my youngest son, Gregory."

"After careful consideration, I have decided to sell you the property. "

"Thank you. Thank you. My family will be thrilled to hear the good news."

I was surprised at how quickly we closed the deal. The day before our departure, we went to the lawyers and signed the deed of sale. Basil was trembling as she signed the deed. I could not help but think about *Mai*, smiling and joyous, nodding in approval. I wished that she was here to witness this special moment. Basil was beaming and for the first time, she seemed truly happy. We were now owners of the property. Although *Mai* had never mentioned it, I believed that her dream had been realized. As Air India flight 1867 took off, I looked out the window, content that we finally had a foothold in Goa.

CHAPTER 47

A RAGING battle in provincial politics was brewing in Canada. After four years of being in power, the Parti Quebecois, led by Rene Levesque, finally called a referendum proposing that Quebec negotiate for sovereignty. Placards and posters were placed on every street corner. A sign in blue read: “OUI POUR LA SOUVRENITE.” The red sign next to it read: “FOR A UNITED CANADA VOTE NO”. Claude Ryan, backed by the federal government, was leading the “NO” campaign. There was endless debate about how the question should be posed to the voters. Both sides accused each other of misleading the public and causing confusion. The date set for the referendum was May 20th, 1980. I was concerned about our future in Quebec. We barely had a chance to get used to the time difference when we were faced with the political strife in Canada.

Despite this, we were glad to see the children, after six months. We could not wait to break the good news about the property in Goa. Sadly, they were not as excited as we had expected. I suppose that Goa was a foreign and distant land for them, lacking the amenities of a country such as Canada. They had not developed an affinity for Goa since they had lived most of their lives overseas. I still hoped that in time they would go back to their roots.

Placido and Judy set their wedding date for June 2nd. Placido asked if I could sew Judy's wedding gown. It certainly was an honour, but time was not on my side since the wedding was only a month away. I was glad that Luiza was doing the bridesmaids' and flower girl's dresses. Placido set up a committee of family members and friends to help organize his wedding. The Dorval Community Center was the venue that he booked through friends of his, who lived in Dorval. Although he hardly gave me enough time to do the wedding gown, I was pleased to take on the challenge since it was the only tangible way that I could contribute towards his wedding. His guest list comprised three hundred and twenty-five people. I wondered how he was going to manage financially. He had only been working for five years and none of his siblings were able to help.

Basil received a letter from Cresence, our neighbour in Goa. The monsoons had attacked the Goan coastline with a vengeance. Strong winds accompanied by heavy rains blew off some of the tiles from the roof. Cresence managed to get labourers to cover the exposed area with dried coconut palms, which cost two hundred rupees. Cresence asked if we could send her money as soon as possible. She also mentioned that she served them *kanji*, water drained from cooked rice. I suppose that she expected us to send a few extra rupees for this, too. I was glad that Cresence was looking after the house since all the other neighbours were against us. One of the neighbours asked Cresence why we bothered acquiring the property since we hardly lived in Goa. They resented the precedence that we set.

Their concern was that the landlord would pressure them into purchasing their lots.

Placido and Judy finally picked a pattern for her wedding gown. I had a few designs in mind, but they insisted on the pattern that they had chosen. The lace had a hint of silver, so they decided to go with silver trimmings. They asked Matti to make the headdress and the boutonnieres from the same fabric. I spent several days marking and cutting the fabric. It was quite a long time since I had made a wedding gown, so I had to be extra careful. I could not afford to make a mistake, since the fabric was very expensive.

Basil was busy cooking the traditional *sorpotel* for the wedding. It was a sumptuous dish made from three different cuts of pork. Placido had taken her to Enkins, the butcher shop on St. Laurent Street. They came home with over fifty pounds of meat. The kitchen was transformed into what resembled a commercial kitchen. Some of Basil's friends came over to help cut this large quantity of meat into thousands of small cubes. The whole process took several days.

As the day for the referendum approached, we were bombarded with ads from both the "Yes" and "No" campaigns. The Liberals were using scare tactics through their ads, stating that separation would spell disaster for Quebecers. Arguments would break out in bars and offices over the best option for Quebec. The Parti Quebecois proclaimed that a separate Quebec would be more successful economically and that Quebecers would have the freedom to promote the French language and culture. I could see the strain that this referendum was causing my children. Our fears during Idi Amin's regime, which lay dormant for eight years, resurfaced. We could not bear another era of political instability. I prayed that this country would remain intact so that we would be spared the anguish that separation might bring.

Meanwhile, Placido had several meetings with his committee to ensure that everything was in order for the wedding. It amazed me to see how easily he got their cooperation. They were given several tasks before the wedding and on the day of the wedding itself. I fully expected that he would go to town when it came to the decorations. He had already purchased over a hundred yards of white sheer fabric and many strings of lights. The basement was packed to the brim with all these items.

It was May 20th. I had just completed the main part of the wedding gown. I was anxious for Judy to try it on, but she could not make it because she had to vote. My children had come home early from work and rushed to the polls. The queues were extremely long. Our polling station was at Laurendeau Dunton School which was just across the street from where we lived. I sat on the balcony watching the people going to cast their votes. This was one time when I wished that I was a Canadian citizen. My Landed Immigrant status did not give me the right to vote. I went to my sewing room to continue working on the wedding gown but found it hard to concentrate. I was anxious about the results of the referendum. It was only 6:00 p.m. The polls were closing at 8:00 p.m. It was hard to believe that the fate of this great country would be decided in two hours. I went upstairs to turn on the TV. Basil was very nervous.

"What is it, Basil?

"I don't know what it is, but I am afraid. I am getting palpitations."

"Why? What are you so worried about?"

"It is about the referendum. What will happen to us if they separate?"

"No worries, Basil, it will not happen. Our friend Pierre Elliot Trudeau will never allow it."

These words rolled off my tongue, but I did not believe them. Visions of us packing up and leaving this country flashed through my mind. Fear engulfed me as I tried hard not to think about this possible outcome.

As usual, Basil and I sat down for dinner together. We ate silently. Basil took the dishes away and I went back to the bedroom and switched on the TV. Over eighty percent of the polling stations had counted their votes. The regions of Saguenay–Lac St. Jean and the St. Lawrence north shore voted solidly "Yes". The island of Montreal, especially the west voted "No". Every time it seemed like the "No" side was winning, results from polling stations that just closed would put the "Yes" side in the lead. Basil decided to stay in the kitchen because she could not bear the suspense. Finally, all the results had come in. The "No" side won with 59.5% of the vote. I was ecstatic and Basil's tears of joy flowed down her cheeks. The children were elated. What a relief! For the time being, we were safe in this country. While a sad Rene Levesque conceded that Quebeckers had given the federalists a second chance, a restrained Trudeau talked about having meaningful discussions on constitutional reform with the provinces. I hoped that this desire for separation would wither away in time.

Judy came over a few days later and tried on her gown. She looked magnificent and surprisingly there was no need for alterations. I pinned up the hem and continued working on the rest of the gown. Placido received confirmation that three hundred and ten people would be attending the wedding. Every evening, Luiza and Matti worked feverishly on the centrepieces in the basement. They had to make thirty of them in less than two weeks. Placido was up late every night making plans and drawing sketches of the decorations and the layout of the hall.

The day had finally arrived. Placido had spent the morning with his committee decorating the hall and rushed home just in time to get dressed. In keeping with the Goan tradition, Basil and I bestowed Placido with our blessings. After the service at St. Thomas à Becket, we took photographs outside the church and proceeded to the hall. It was a glorious day. At the entrance, was an archway of hundreds of white balloons. The ceiling of the hall looked like soft white clouds. Placido had managed to create this effect with yards of white sheer fabric that he hung in swags. The centrepieces on the lace tablecloths made the place look festive. Everyone was in awe as they entered the hall. Basil was in her glory, and I was beaming with pride. At the end of the reception, I was suddenly overcome with sadness when I realized that Placido and Judy had become part of the Canadian fabric. Would their children ever be able to identify with their Goan ancestry? I couldn't help but feel that they would lose their heritage altogether.

CHAPTER 48

THE HUDSON'S Bay Company realized that Placido could not work effectively as a Visual Presentation Manager, due to his limited knowledge of French. They valued his talent and decided to offer him a job in Toronto. His options in Quebec were limited, so he was forced to accept the transfer. Although Toronto was only six hundred kilometres away, the thought of him going away saddened me. By now Placido and Judy had three sons, Tyler, Andrew, and Lucas. I would miss my grandsons. It seemed like the family just got together after being apart for over five years. Basil was down in the doldrums since she saw this as the beginning of the family Diaspora and was in tears every time the subject came up. It reminded me of the time when I moved from India to Africa. I clearly remember *Mai* crying bitterly when I broke the news to her.

"You are my only son. I have no one else. I may never see you again. Please don't go to Africa." she pleaded.

I felt guilty and sad to see her in that state, but I knew that

East Africa held a lot more promise than Goa. The journey that began fifty years ago finally brought me to Canada.

After much thought and consideration, Placido finally decided to accept the job in Toronto. The Hudson's Bay Company paid for his relocation expenses. We were sad to see him, and his family go, but Placido convinced us that he would visit us regularly. They decided to settle in the suburb of Scarborough. A couple of months later, Gregory drove Basil and me to Toronto. I was glad when Placido told me that the Goan community in Toronto was quite large – well over two thousand. Almost every month, they celebrated the feast of one village or another. The feast of "Our Lady of the Holy Rosary" had been celebrated by the villagers of Navelim for nineteen years in Toronto. The first one, with barely forty people, was held at Ornel Vaz's home – a long-time friend of mine. Ever since then, the celebration of the feast had grown by leaps and bounds. The competition between different village feast celebrations in Toronto was mushrooming. The most recent Navelim feast in Toronto was celebrated in an elegant banquet hall with over three hundred people in attendance. There weren't as many Goans in Montreal, so none of this competitiveness existed. The only feast celebrated in Montreal was that of Saint Francis Xavier, the patron saint of Goa. In Toronto, Placido was becoming known in Goan circles for his ability to decorate and organize events. This year would be the 20th anniversary of the Navelim feast and Placido was elected as president. He did not waste time putting together a committee of hardworking and talented people.

Continuing to operate my business had become a challenge. I found it difficult to cut straight since the strength in my hands was waning. Feeding thread through a needle was becoming a chore. My eyesight seemed to be getting worse and the doctor informed me that I had cataracts in both eyes. I dreaded the thought of an operation but knew that I would have to get it done. The Morgans were very disappointed when I informed them that I was closing the shop. My other customers were equally disappointed but, in a way, I was glad to pack it in, since I believed that it was time for me to take it easy. From a financial standpoint, I was able to get by with my Canada Pension.

This year had certainly been one of change, not only on a personal level but also on a national and international level. It started with Placido and his family leaving for Toronto. Then, I decided to retire from my business. I had time to watch more TV and every time I turned it on, the news was about the O.J. Simpson double-murder case. It seemed to dwarf other significant international issues, such as the genocide of the Tutsi tribe in Rwanda and the dawning of a new era in South Africa, its first multi-racial election. My hope in humanity was restored, seeing Nelson Mandela's struggle for freedom was finally paying off, after thirty years.

"Dias, turn off the TV. I cannot bear to see O.J. Simpson's face."

"Basil, I realize that the media is paying too much attention to O.J. Simpson, but I do not want to miss the other news."

"What other news? I only see O.J. Simpson's face and that of his poor deceased wife."

"They have some coverage on South Africa. The system of apartheid is finally crumbling, something I never thought would happen in my lifetime."

"Well, at least that is good news. I wonder if the situation in Uganda will improve."

"Basil, Uganda will never be the same since Idi Amin

destroyed the country. I don't think that it matters anymore, at least not for us. We will never go back to Uganda. "

One afternoon, I was sitting on the balcony when I thought about composing a song about our village, Navelim. I worked diligently on the lyrics and every time I came up with a verse, I sang it to Basil. After several weeks, I finally finished writing the whole song. One weekend when Luiza and Matti came over for dinner, I sang the song. They were surprised that I had composed it.

"Dad, why don't you sing it with the grandchildren at the Navelim feast?" Matti suggested.

"That is a good idea, but how can I teach them the song?"

"We could send the words and a tape of the song to Toronto. Judy could teach them to sing it."

"I don't think that they will be able to learn it. They hardly speak any Konkani."

"Dad, I think that it is worth a try."

"I suppose that I could write out the song phonetically – it might help."

The next day, I mailed the lyrics to Judy, trying not to get my hopes too high about my grandchildren learning the song.

It was Friday, November 20th, the weekend of the feast. Basil and I packed our bags and waited for Gregory to come home from work. He quickly ate his supper and put our luggage in the car. We hardly drove for a block when Basil started fidgeting. She kept questioning whether we had locked the front door properly. Although I told her that I did, she did not believe me. Gregory knew that Basil would not be at peace during the six-hour journey. He turned around and drove back to the house. I checked the front door only to find out that it *was* locked. I opened it and checked the iron and the oven too.

"So, was everything okay?" Basil inquired.

"Yes, as I expected. The door was locked, the iron unplugged, and I even checked the oven. Let's just go now."

We had just passed Brockville when large flakes of snow started falling. It was a beautiful sight. By the time we arrived at Kingston, the highway was covered in snow. Gregory, who normally drove over 120 kilometres per hour slowed down to 60. Several cars were lying in the ditch. The snow was falling in sheets – it was virtually impossible to see the car ahead. I was sitting on the edge of my seat. Basil was praying the rosary. A huge truck passed us at high speed, splashing slush over the windshield and exacerbating the limited visibility. The car was starting to slip and slide, and it seemed like we were heading for the ditch. Gregory was struggling to control the car. Suddenly red brake lights of a car shone through the snow-covered windshield. I was certain that we were going to crash. Basil started praying loudly. I was sweating and braced myself for the collision. Gregory kept pumping the brakes and steering to prevent the car from sliding into the ditch. He managed to stop the car barely six inches from the car ahead. We were silent for the rest of the journey.

I was pleased when we finally arrived in Toronto. Placido welcomed us and made sure that we were comfortable. I was not able to see my grandchildren because they were asleep. They were anxious to see us, so they waited up, but by 10:00 p.m. Judy insisted that they go to bed. I was happy to get to bed after a tiresome seven-hour journey. I woke up to voices that sounded like they came from the television. I went into the family room and my grandson Tyler came running up to me. I held him close to me, enjoying the embrace of this little boy. Placido was already loading his minivan with all the decorations. Judy prepared a wholesome breakfast which we ate with relish. After breakfast, I decided to go for a walk and ended up in a shopping mall. I was quite surprised to see the amount of Asians in the neighbourhood. Judy informed me that immigration from Hong Kong had increased significantly since the takeover by China was imminent. Most of the Asians that immigrated were well off and did not want to lose their wealth if China decided to impose Communist rule after the British left Hong Kong. It reminded me once again of the time when we were forced to leave Uganda. I could certainly empathize with the Asians from Hong Kong.

Later that morning, I practiced the song with my grandchildren and was surprised to see that Tyler knew all the words perfectly. After having our tea, we got dressed and went to the feast. It was held in a large hall in Mississauga, almost a sixty-minute drive from Scarborough. I was amazed to see the constant traffic on the eight-lane highway 401. Toronto was far more modern and larger than Montreal. When we entered the hall, there were at least five hundred people. I was overwhelmed. People from different parts of the hall came to greet Basil and me. It was such a pleasure seeing old friends, some I had not seen for over ten years. I even met my best man, Mr. Gonsalves, and his wife.

The feast began with the Holy Rosary, recited in Konkani and English, followed by a Mass. They managed to get a Goan priest who hailed from Navelim to lead the service. After the service ended, we wished each other a happy feast and settled down to dinner. On the way to the bar, I was greeted by several people, some I hardly recognized. People started dancing as soon as the band started playing. After several songs, the band decided to take a break and The M.C. took the microphone.

"We have a special presentation tonight. It is a song composed by one of our fellow villagers about Navelim. Ladies and Gentlemen, please help me welcome, Mr. Carlos Dias."

There was applause. My heart started racing and my mouth went dry. Judy gave me a glass of water, which I gulped. I was trembling but tried hard to conceal it. Sheer excitement was replaced with fear. Judy gathered Tyler, Andrew and Lucas and led me to the stage. My knees felt like they were going to give way at any moment. I was handed the microphone as my grandsons gathered around me. One of the musicians from the band started strumming his guitar and gave me the signal to start. I cleared my throat and started singing. When I got through the first verse, I was able to calm down. I was well into the second verse when I had to hit a high note. My chest tightened and for a moment I thought that I was going to collapse but I continued all the same. I could hear my grandsons' voices faintly in the background. I ended the song with a triumphant "Viva! Viva!" The applause was deafening. At that moment I felt euphoric. I walked to my table and sat down, but had difficulty breathing, so I got up and walked as fast as I could to the exit. The tightness in my chest got worse. I could feel my chest heaving. I walked out to the parking lot and took several deep breaths. A vision of me lying unconscious on the ground flashed through my mind. I prayed and continued breathing deeply. I gradually calmed down and started feeling better. I took a deep breath and walked back to the hall.

"Dias, Dias where were you? I was worried. People were asking for you."

"Oh, it was nothing. I just had to step out for a breath of fresh air. It was getting stuffy in here."

I could tell from the look on Basil's face that she did not believe me. I was just getting comfortable in my seat, when I sensed someone behind me, so I turned around to look. There was a group of people standing and smiling.

"Congratulations Carlit. That was a great song!" Mr. Gonsalves said.

The rest of the gang congratulated me one at a time. Led by Mr. Gonsalves, they all sang a traditional Goan blessing in my honour. For a moment, I felt like I was back in Goa, and I was hopeful that our Goan traditions would continue to live on.

CHAPTER 49

I TRIED HOLDING the newspaper at a distance, but the words were blurry. Additional light from a lamp did not help either. Besides my walks, reading the paper was something I cherished, but now it was becoming a chore. It was my way of keeping abreast of the events in Canada and the world. When I immigrated to East Africa it was difficult for me to communicate in English since I only knew Konkani and Portuguese. I learned English by reading the newspaper. I could not fathom what my life would be like without my eyesight. The doctor informed me that the cataract in my right eye had progressed to the point that it would require surgery. I was terrified of having the surgeon cut into my eye. My fears were quelled when the doctor explained that the operation would be done with laser technology. When I told Basil about my operation she was beside herself.

"Dias, what would happen if they made a mistake?" she asked nervously.

"Oh, Basil you always worry. The doctors in Canada are very

good. They are using the latest technology for the operation. They call it laser surgery."

"Whatever you say, Dias. I will pray that your operation goes well."

To take my mind off the operation, Basil suggested that I organize a game of cards with my friends. I called Neru and Jerome, who were most willing to accept the invitation. Basil was thrilled and already started planning the dinner menu. I went to the liquor store and picked up a bottle of Johnnie Walker whiskey. Neru and Jerome enjoyed drinking scotch. I had stopped drinking several years ago because of my diabetes. Strangely enough, I had no desire to drink alcohol anymore. In the past, it just seemed like the natural thing to do when playing cards. Playing my favourite game, *Sol* was so invigorating that I wondered why I had not arranged this session earlier. This game certainly required a sharp mind. Jerome and Neru were in top spirits. We stopped briefly to have dinner. Neru kept singing Basil's praises and she kept serving him additional helpings. We played until 3:00 a.m.

It was the night before my operation. I tossed and turned, finding it difficult to sleep. I could sense that Basil could not sleep either. She got out of bed on several occasions. I could hear the kettle boiling in the kitchen, so I gathered that she was making herself a cup of tea. The second time, I decided to join her. She prepared a bowl of cereal for me, which I consumed within minutes. I guess being nervous made me feel hungry.

"Dias don't worry. Your operation will go well. I have been praying for you."

"You are right. There is nothing to worry about."

Gregory drove me to Hotel Dieu Hospital at 7:00 a.m. Over ten centimetres of snow had fallen overnight and it continued snowing in the morning. The traffic was bumper-to-bumper. I was afraid that we would not arrive at our scheduled time of 8:00 a.m. After struggling through traffic, we finally arrived at the hospital at 7:55 a.m. in a frazzled state. Gregory wished me well and then the nurse took me into the operating hall. All I could see was bright lights. The doctor was talking to me, but I found it hard to concentrate on what he was saying. I just wanted to get through this ordeal. The lights became a blur and I heard the nurse asking me to stay still. Fortunately, I did not feel any pain. I was wheeled out of the operating room into another hall. The doctor spoke to Gregory, giving him some post-operative care instructions. When we arrived home, Basil had piping hot coffee and *chapatis* waiting for me.

After the operation, I decided to make a will. It dawned on me that if I had not survived the operation, Basil and the children would have had a problem settling my estate. In India, there was no need for wills, since all the property would be divided equally among my wife and children according to the law. I thought about my will for weeks and finally decided to talk to Gregory, who agreed to take me to his lawyer. She was a pleasant lady who put me at ease immediately. I did not realize how simple it was. My request was to divide my assets equally among my children. I expected Basil to continue with her pension and I knew that the children would look after her. A great burden had been lifted from my shoulders after I signed my will. I enjoyed the summer and felt great spending time outdoors, reading the newspaper and going to the park.

I was glad that the August heat and humidity had finally come to an end. The cool and crisp temperatures of fall were a welcome change. I enjoyed this time of the year, going for long walks and admiring the vibrant colours of the leaves. I marvelled at this phenomenon – something I would certainly miss once I settled down in Goa. I would pick up the beautiful multicoloured leaves and put them in between the pages of the phone book. I planned to frame them and put them up on my living room wall in Goa. They would be a pleasant reminder of Canada.

It was early November when Matti called to inform us that she was planning a Christmas family gathering at her condominium hall. She wanted all the family members and in-laws to be there. Now that the family was getting larger by the year, it was getting difficult for us to celebrate Christmas together. I thought it was a great idea. I wanted to do something special for my children this Christmas. They all seemed to be managing well on their own – what could I offer them? One night I prayed for God's guidance. To my surprise, the next morning the answer to my question was clear - I could give them money. I had put some money aside hoping that when my children visited Goa I would spend it on making their visit comfortable. It did not seem likely that any of them would be making the trip to Goa in the near future. They simply could not afford it.

"Are you sure that you want to withdraw such a large sum of money?" The teller asked.

"Yes, I am. It is for something special."

"Please give me a moment, while I check with my manager."

I waited patiently for the teller to get back. I was afraid that the manager would prevent me from withdrawing the money.

"Mr. Dias, would you like us to wire the money to an institution or a specific person? It would be safer for you," The manager asked.

"No, I need the cash."

As soon as I got home, I put the money in a fireproof box and hid it in the closet under boxes of Basil's shoes and summer clothing.

I was surprised at how much my vision had improved after the cataract was removed. It was such a pleasure reading the newspaper. I happened to read the sports section of the newspaper and my eyes fell upon the big race at Blue Bonnets. My heart raced when I saw the amount of the purse. It was two million dollars. I could use some of the money that I withdrew and place a bet on this race! Although I was out of touch, I could research and catch up with potential favourites. I could see myself at the races, jumping for joy when my pick made it to the finish line. Suddenly I caught myself. What was I thinking? This was my chance to show my appreciation to my children and I was about to blow it away. I quickly came to my senses and put the paper away. That day, I vowed never to think about betting on horse races. Deep within my psyche, I felt that chapter in my life had come to an end. The desire to gamble had left me. My only regret was that I had not given it up earlier.

It was Christmas Eve. I went to midnight mass with Basil and Gregory. I was tingling with joy, listening to the Christmas carols sung by an angelic choir. It was a special and uplifting service. When we arrived home, I put the money I had withdrawn from the bank in envelopes with a card for each of my children. There was so much I wanted to say, but I could not find the words to express how blessed I felt to have such dear children. All I could do was sign the card. We woke up late on Christmas morning. Basil had prepared a special breakfast of eggs, bacon, sausages and toast. After breakfast, we rested for a while, changed, and then headed to Matti's condominium hall. It was decorated magnificently with a head table set up at the back of the hall. Luiza was putting some finishing touches on the centrepieces. John was playing Christmas carols. Matti was busy making sure that the food table was set properly while Placido was rearranging the poinsettias and candles. All my children, their spouses, grandchildren and in-laws were there. We were almost fifty. I was sitting at the head table next to Eustache, Judy's father, together with Basil and Judy's mother, Laura. We had three grandsons in common. There was a lot of hustle and bustle, while pleasant aromas emanated from the kitchen.

"Isn't it wonderful to see how well they get along?" I said, turning to Eustace.

"Yes, it is. We are lucky grandparents," Eustace replied.

"Eustace, we are more than just lucky, we are truly blessed."

"I suppose that you are right when you consider that we survived Idi Amin's regime."

After dinner, the grandchildren started opening their presents. The noise level and excitement in the hall were overwhelming. Then my children started opening their gifts. John was the first one to open the card that I had given to him. I anxiously awaited his reaction. He swallowed, and then I could see tears streaming down his cheeks. He came up to me and we embraced.

"Thank you, thank you, Dad," he kept whispering. Then, one by one, my other children came up – all of them in tears. We hugged. I felt their warmth in a way that I had never felt before. We had connected at a level that was beyond description.

We had trifle and rainbow cake for dessert. As I sipped my coffee, I thought about the time when I was an only child living in Goa with *Mai*. Gregory, my adopted brother, was my only companion for a few short years before he moved to Bombay. After he died, I felt very much alone. Sixty years later, here I was in Canada with my six children and my ten beautiful grandchildren. My journey in life took me to Uganda, where I prospered and did many things that brought me joy, my successful tailoring business, attending some major horse races and playing cards at the club, just to mention a few. My wife

Basil always let me enjoy this freedom. She was the glue that held the family together while I was away. She instilled a strong sense of family unity in our children.

"Come on everybody, it is time to dance," Matti announced.

Jonathan played my favourite song – *Lucille*, by Kenny Rogers. As I waltzed with Basil, my thoughts drifted to my past. I had travelled across the great oceans and lived on three continents, Asia, Africa and North America. All my life, I kept searching for something that would be fulfilling. I had chosen the gambling route in the hope that I could give *Mai* a good life. This addiction continued even after I had a family of my own. I realized now that all I ever had to do was to share in the joy and successes of my children – something that I had neglected, especially when they were young. After the song ended, I was out of breath, so went back to the head table and sat. Looking out into the hall, seeing my family joyous and in perfect harmony, I could not help but feel fulfilled. This Christmas celebration would be etched in my mind – one that I would always remember.

THE END

GLOSSARY OF TERMS

1st Dando - a district (ward) of Navelim
Altar – Every Christian house in Goa had a picture of Jesus and the holy family with candles in their foyer.
Askari – security guard (Swahili)
Aspro – Pain medication usually taken for headaches
Baba – term of endearment for a child (Konkani)
Bhel puri – a savoury Indian snack
Bwana – Sir (Swahili)
Chaiwala – A person who makes and serves tea (Hindi)
Chapatis – flatbread (Konkani)
Contradance – dance made up of a long line of couples at weddings
Cosnem – Firecrackers (Konkani)
Dhows – Lateen sail-rigged boats used in the Red Sea and Indian Ocean.
Dosh – a diamond-shaped Goan sweet made during Christmas (Konkani).
Jambo – hello (Swahili)
Kanji – water drained from rice (Konhani)
Kanzu – a white or cream-coloured robe worn by men in Uganda, referred to as a tunic in English.
Kurtas – Indian-style shirts
Ladin – Litany (Konkani)
Mestre de sale – Master of Ceremonies
Moji mai – my mother (Konkani)
Neuris - deep-fried Goan sweet made during Christmas
Padkhars – Labourer that cuts down coconuts (Konkani)
Pai – father (Konkani)
Renderes - Makers of coconut feni (Konkani)
Salaam – Good Bye (Hindi)
Sana – steamed rice cakes (Konkani)
Sol – card game
Sorpotel – pork dish made during special occasions (Konkani).
Sudras - the fourth and lowest of the traditional social classes of India.
Toddy – Sap from the coconut
Truque – card game (Konkani)

ABOUT THE AUTHOR

Greg Dias was born in Uganda and immigrated to Canada at the age of 19. He was educated at McGill University where he graduated with a Bachelor's in Chemical Engineering. While working for Union Carbide he completed his MBA part time at McGill and later on took a course in creative writing.

He is the founder of three charitable organizations, The Global Aid Committee, Help U Grow Charity for Uganda and the Youth Empowerment Support (YES) Group.

Greg embarked on a journey of writing his father's memoir during his creative writing course and completed his manuscript several years later.

To follow Greg, and learn more about his charitable works and other authoring efforts, please visit his site: To learn more about the author, visit Greg's site: https://gregdiasauthor.wordpress.com.

Printed in the USA
CPSIA information can be obtained
at www.ICGtesting.com
JSHW080440280923
49137JS00003B/20

9 781739 06790